The View from Building 20

Current Studies in Linguistics
Samuel Jay Keyser, general editor

The View from Building 20
Essays in Linguistics
in Honor of Sylvain
Bromberger

edited by
Kenneth Hale and
Samuel Jay Keyser

The MIT Press
Cambridge, Massachusetts
London, England

This book was set in Times Roman by Asco Trade Typesetting Ltd., Hong Kong, and was printed and bound in the United States of America.

Library of Congress Cataloging-in-Publication Data

The View from building 20: essays in linguistics in honor of Sylvain
  Bromberger / edited by Kenneth Hale and Samuel Jay Keyser.
      p.   cm.—(Current studies in linguistics; 24)
    Includes bibliographical references.
    Contents: A minimalist program for linguistic theory / Noam Chomsky—
On argument structure and the lexical expression of syntactic relations /
Kenneth Hale and Samuel Jay Keyser—Distributed morphology and the pieces
of inflection / Morris Halle and Alec Marantz—Integrity of prosodic
constituents and the domain of syllabification rules in Spanish and Catalan /
James W. Harris—Interrogatives / James Higginbotham—Triggering
science-forming capacity through linguistic inquiry / Maya Honda and Wayne
O'Neil—Evidence for metrical constituency / Michael Kenstowicz.
    ISBN 0-262-08223-3.—ISBN 0-262-58124-8 (pbk.)
    1. Linguistics. I. Hale, Kenneth L. (Kenneth Locke), 1934–   . II. Keyser,
Samuel Jay, 1935–   . III. Bromberger, Sylvain. IV. Title: View from building
twenty. V. Title: Essays in linguistics in honor of Sylvain Bromberger.
VI. Series: Current studies in linguistics series; 24.
P26.B768V54   1993
410—dc20   92-38255
                                                                      CIP

Contents

Contributors

Noam Chomsky   Department of Linguistics and Philosophy, Massachusetts Institute of Technology

Kenneth Hale   Department of Linguistics and Philosophy, Massachusetts Institute of Technology

Morris Halle   Department of Linguistics and Philosophy, Massachusetts Institute of Technology

James W. Harris   Department of Linguistics and Philosophy, Massachusetts Institute of Technology

James Higginbotham   Department of Linguistics and Philosophy, Massachusetts Institute of Technology

Maya Honda   Department of Human Development, Wheelock College

Samuel Jay Keyser   Department of Linguistics and Philosophy, Massachusetts Institute of Technology

Alec Marantz   Department of Linguistics and Philosophy, Massachusetts Institute of Technology

Wayne O'Neil   Department of Linguistics and Philosophy, Massachusetts Institute of Technology

Michael Kenstowicz   Department of Linguistics and Philosophy, Massachusetts Institute of Technology

Preface

This volume is dedicated to Sylvain Bromberger.

The contributors to the volume have been colleagues of Sylvain's for anywhere from four to forty years. Whatever the time, his example to each of us of unwavering honesty in the face of difficult theoretical problems in linguistics and neighboring problems in philosophy has been not only a model but a signal example of the truth of the maxim that understanding in science depends as much on character as it does on insight.

In 1992 Sylvain published a collection of essays that gather together a lifetime of inquiry into scientific progress. The collection is entitled *On What We Know We Don't Know*. In that volume Sylvain explores a question that has concerned him throughout his scholarly life, namely, how we "come to know that there are things in the world that we don't know." Indeed, his exploration of our "ability to formulate and to entertain questions whose answers we know we do not know" led to a convergence of his philosophical life with that of his linguistic colleagues. Sylvain's work is devoted to understanding the character of scientific progress, beginning with the recognition that it is more than "additions to a stock of truths and highly confirmed propositions." He has devoted his life to shedding light on the nature of that "more than."

In his collection, the article entitled "Science and the Forms of Ignorance" begins with the characteristically modest sentence, "I am a very ignorant person and have long assiduously deplored this fact." Those of us who have had the privilege of working with Sylvain might easily reply, "We should all be so ignorant." Most of the contributors to this volume, its editors especially, can easily recall any number of occasions when Sylvain's "ignorant" questioning of a first draft has led to veils falling from their own eyes and, consequently, to immeasurably improved subsequent drafts.

Sylvain's contribution to our lives extends beyond intellectual collegiality. One of the editors of this volume, Jay Keyser, became a colleague of Sylvain's when Keyser was appointed head of a newly formed MIT department that combined both Linguistics and Philosophy into a single unit. This took place officially in the summer of 1977. Keyser held this position for seven years and for most of that period Sylvain served as chair of the Philosophy Section. The truth, however, is that while he was overt chair of Philosophy he was the conscience of the entire department. Throughout that formative period Keyser was faced with a host of difficult problems, most of them human in nature, and Sylvain's behind-the-scenes advice and support made the difference between a successful community of scholars working together and a failed experiment.

During those years Keyser would often tell Sylvain in the darker moments, "I am the only sane person I know," to which Sylvain would reply, "If you think that, you're crazy." As it happens, Keyser and Sylvain share the same birthday, July 7, and on their birthday each has been accustomed to taking the other to lunch. At one of those lunches Keyser said, "Sylvain, after all these years I've decided that you're right. I am crazy," to which Sylvain replied, "If you think that, you're acquiring an impressive degree of sanity."

The second editor, Ken Hale, had the wonderful luck of sharing office space with Sylvain during the academic year 1967–1968, his first year at MIT. This was very fortunate for Hale, as Sylvain was able not only to help him understand the semantics of an extremely tricky modal in Papago, but also to give him an enormous body of knowledge about how to survive in this new and strange environment. It was a big disappointment to Hale when he realized that Sylvain would be going back to Building 14 after that year. But ten years later, when Sylvain returned to Building 20 to chair the Philosophy Section of the newly formed Department of Linguistics and Philosophy, his mentoring relationship with Hale resumed in full. For Hale, this book is a long overdue payment on his debt of gratitude.

No tribute to Sylvain can be complete without its encompassing Nancy, his spouse of over forty years. If Sylvain has been the conscience of his colleagues, Nancy has been the conscience of the conscience. One of the editors, Keyser again, has had the privilege of working with her for well over a decade on *Linguistic Inquiry*. She has been the journal's proofreader for that period and quite simply put, there is no one better in the field. The present volume is as much an acknowledgment of the role she has played in Sylvain's life as it is of the role he has played in ours.

Sylvain dedicated his collection of essays to Aristides de Sousa Mendes, and we believe that Sylvain would be pleased to have the latter's name mentioned in connection with this tribute. In the closing paragraph of his introduction to the collection Sylvain writes:

Aristides de Sousa Mendes, to whom I dedicate this book, was Portuguese consul in Bordeaux in June 1940. As Hitler's troops were about to occupy the city, he issued visas to hundreds of Jewish refugees, defying edicts from the Salazar government which expressly forbade issuing visas to Jews. After being removed from Bordeaux by Salazar agents, he managed to get more visas issued to a crowd of frightened refugees huddled in the rain in front of the Portuguese consulate in Bayonne. My parents, my two brothers, and I were in that crowd. Back in Portugal, Aristides de Sousa Mendes was harshly punished and, as a consequence, died in poverty. His valor in saving hundreds of lives through his defiance of vicious orders was eventually acknowledged and officially commemorated by the Portuguese government in 1986 after a long campaign by his children. That is how I became aware of what he had done for me. I never saw him, he never saw me. May this dedication help, even if only in a small way, to perpetuate the memory of his name and of his saintly deeds.

We include this quotation here for two reasons. First, Sylvain would undoubtedly be pleased at this further opportunity to perpetuate the name of Aristides de Sousa Mendes. Second, and more importantly to us, for those of you who are reading this volume but who have never had the privilege of being Sylvain Bromberger's colleague, we can think of no better way to extend to you some sense of the kind of colleague he has been for us and the kind of human being he is.

When we conceived of this collection, we asked each author to write something especially for it. All of us responded with articles that, in retrospect, we believe to be among the more important examples of our recent work. We believe it is appropriate to call attention to this because, at the risk of appearing to be self-serving, it provides a real measure of the esteem in which we hold Sylvain Bromberger.

The View from Building 20

Chapter 1

A Minimalist Program for
Linguistic Theory

Noam Chomsky

1 Some General Considerations

Language and its use have been studied from varied points of view. One approach, assumed here, takes language to be part of the natural world. The human brain provides an array of capacities that enter into the use and understanding of language (the *language faculty*); these seem to be in good part specialized for that function and a common human endowment over a very wide range of circumstances and conditions. One component of the language faculty is a generative procedure (an *I-language*, henceforth language) that generates *structural descriptions* (SDs), each a complex of properties, including those commonly called "semantic" and "phonetic." These SDs are the *expressions* of the language. The theory of a particular language is its *grammar*. The theory of languages and the expressions they generate is *Universal Grammar* (UG); UG is a theory of the initial state S_0 of the relevant component of the language faculty. We can distinguish the language from a conceptual system and a system of pragmatic competence. Evidence has been accumulating that these interacting systems can be selectively impaired and developmentally dissociated (Curtiss 1981, Yamada 1990, Smith and Tsimpli 1991), and their properties are quite different.

A standard assumption is that UG specifies certain *linguistic levels*, each a symbolic system, often called a "representational system." Each linguistic level provides the means for presenting certain systematic information about linguistic expressions. Each linguistic expression (SD) is a sequence of representations, one at each linguistic level. In variants of the Extended Standard Theory (EST), each SD is a sequence $(\delta, \sigma, \pi, \lambda)$, representations at the D-Structure, S-Structure, Phonetic Form (PF), and Logical Form (LF) levels, respectively.

Some basic properties of language are unusual among biological systems, notably the property of discrete infinity. A working hypothesis in generative grammar has been that languages are based on simple principles that interact to form often intricate structures, and that the language faculty is nonredundant, in that particular phenomena are not "overdetermined" by principles of language. These too are unexpected features of complex biological systems, more like what one expects to find (for unexplained reasons) in the study of the inorganic world. The approach has, nevertheless, proven to be a successful one, suggesting that the hypotheses are more than just an artifact reflecting a mode of inquiry.

Another recurrent theme has been the role of "principles of economy" in determining the computations and the SDs they generate. Such considerations have arisen in various forms and guises as theoretical perspectives have changed. There is, I think, good reason to believe that they are fundamental to the design of language, if properly understood.[1]

The language is embedded in performance systems that enable its expressions to be used for articulating, interpreting, referring, inquiring, reflecting, and other actions. We can think of the SD as a complex of instructions for these performance systems, providing information relevant to their functions. While there is no clear sense to the idea that language is "designed for use" or "well adapted to its functions," we do expect to find connections between the properties of the language and the manner of its use.

The performance systems appear to fall into two general types: articulatory-perceptual and conceptual-intentional. If so, a linguistic expression contains instructions for each of these systems. Two of the linguistic levels, then, are the *interface levels* A-P and C-I, providing the instructions for the articulatory-perceptual and conceptual-intentional systems, respectively. Each language determines a set of pairs drawn from the A-P and C-I levels. The level A-P has generally been taken to be PF; the status and character of C-I have been more controversial.

Another standard assumption is that a language consists of two components: a lexicon and a computational system. The lexicon specifies the items that enter into the computational system, with their idiosyncratic properties. The computational system uses these elements to generate derivations and SDs. The derivation of a particular linguistic expression, then, involves a choice of items from the lexicon and a computation that constructs the pair of interface representations.

So far, we are within the domain of virtual conceptual necessity, at least if the general outlook is adopted.[2] UG must determine the class of possible languages. It must specify the properties of SDs and of the symbolic representations that enter into them. In particular, it must specify the interface levels (A-P, C-I), the elements that constitute these levels, and the computations by which they are constructed. A particularly simple design for language would take the (conceptually necessary) interface levels to be the only levels. That assumption will be part of the "minimalist" program I would like to explore here.

In early work in generative grammar, it was assumed that the interface C-I is the level of T-markers, effectively a composite of all levels of syntactic representation. In descendants of EST approaches, C-I is generally taken to be LF. On this assumption, each language will determine a set of pairs (π, λ) (π drawn from PF and λ from LF) as its formal representations of sound and meaning, insofar as these are determined by the language itself. Parts of the computational system are relevant only to π, not λ: the *PF component*.[3] Other parts are relevant only to λ, not π: the *LF component*. The parts of the computational system that are relevant to both are the *overt syntax*—a term that is a bit misleading, in that these parts may involve empty categories assigned no phonetic shape. The nature of these systems is an empirical matter; one should not be misled by unintended connotations of such terms as "logical form" and "represent" adopted from technical usage in different kinds of inquiry.

The standard idealized model of language acquisition takes the initial state S_0 to be a function mapping experience (primary linguistic data, PLD) to a language. UG is concerned with the invariant principles of S_0 and the range of permissible variation. Variation must be determined by what is "visible" to the child acquiring language, that is, by the PLD. It is not surprising, then, to find a degree of variation in the PF component, and in aspects of the lexicon: Saussurean arbitrariness (association of concepts with phonological matrices), properties of grammatical formatives (inflection, etc.), and readily detectable properties that hold of lexical items generally (e.g., the head parameter). Variation in the overt syntax or LF component would be more problematic, since evidence could only be quite indirect. A narrow conjecture is that there is no such variation: beyond PF options and lexical arbitrariness (which I henceforth ignore), variation is limited to nonsubstantive parts of the lexicon and general properties of lexical items. If so, there is only one computational system and one lexicon, apart from this limited kind of variety. Let us tentatively adopt that assumption—extreme, perhaps, but it seems not implausible—as another element of the minimalist program.[4]

Early generative grammar approached these questions in a different way, along lines suggested by long tradition: various levels are identified, with their particular properties and interrelations; UG provides a format for permissible rule systems; any instantiation of this format constitutes a specific language. Each language is a rich and intricate system of rules that are, typically, construction-particular and language-particular: the rules forming verb phrases or passives or relative clauses in English, for example, are specific to *these* constructions in *this* language. Similarities across constructions and languages derive from properties of the format for rule systems.

The more recent principles-and-parameters approach, assumed here, breaks radically with this tradition, taking steps toward the minimalist design just sketched. UG provides a fixed system of principles and a finite array of finitely valued parameters. The language-particular rules reduce to choice of values for these parameters. The notion of grammatical construction is eliminated, and with it, construction-particular rules. Constructions such as verb phrase, relative clause, and passive remain only as taxonomic artifacts, collections of phenomena explained through the interaction of the principles of UG, with the values of parameters fixed.

With regard to the computational system, then, we assume that S_0 is constituted of invariant principles with options restricted to functional elements and general properties of the lexicon. A selection Σ among these options determines a language. A language, in turn, determines an infinite set of linguistic expressions (SDs), each a pair (π, λ) drawn from the interface levels (PF, LF), respectively. Language acquisition involves fixing Σ; the grammar of the language states Σ, nothing more (lexical arbitrariness and PF component aside). If there is a parsing system that is invariant and unlearned (as often assumed), then it maps (Σ, π) into a structured percept, in some cases associated with an SD.[5] Conditions on representations—those of binding theory, Case theory, θ-theory, and so on—hold only at the interface, and are motivated by properties of the interface, perhaps properly understood as modes of interpretation by performance systems. The linguistic expressions are the optimal realizations of the interface conditions, where "optimality" is determined by the economy conditions of UG. Let us take these assumptions too to be part of the minimalist program.

In early work, economy considerations entered as part of the evaluation metric, which, it was assumed, selected a particular instantiation of the permitted format for rule systems, given PLD. As inquiry has progressed, the presumed role of an evaluation metric has declined, and within the principles-and-parameters approach, it is generally assumed to be completely dispensable: the principles are sufficiently restrictive so that PLD suffice in the normal case to set the parameter values that determine a language.[6]

Nevertheless, it seems that economy principles of the kind explored in early work play a significant role in accounting for properties of language. With a proper formulation of such principles, it may be possible to move toward the minimalist design: a theory of language that takes a linguistic expression to be nothing other than a formal object that satisfies the interface conditions in the optimal way. A still further step would be to show that the basic principles of language are formulated in terms of notions drawn from the domain of (virtual) conceptual necessity.

Invariant principles determine what counts as a possible derivation and a possible derived object (linguistic expression, SD). Given a language, these principles determine a specific set of derivations and generated SDs, each a pair (π, λ). Let us say that a derivation D *converges* if it yields a legitimate SD and *crashes* if it does not; D *converges at PF* if π is legitimate and *crashes at PF* if it is not; D *converges at LF if* λ is legitimate and *crashes at LF* if it is not. In an EST framework, with SD $= (\delta, \sigma, \pi, \lambda)$ (δ a D-Structure representation, σ an S-Structure representation), there are other possibilities: δ or σ, or relations among $(\delta, \sigma, \pi, \lambda)$, might be defective. Within the minimalist program, all possibilities are excluded apart from the status of π and λ. A still sharper version would exclude the possibility that π and λ are each legitimate but cannot be paired for UG reasons. Let us adopt this narrower condition as well. Thus, we assume that a derivation converges if it converges at PF and at LF; convergence is determined by independent inspection of the interface levels—not an empirically innocuous assumption.[7]

The principles outlined are simple and restrictive, so that the empirical burden is considerable; and fairly intricate argument may be necessary to support it—exactly the desired outcome, for whatever ultimately proves to be the right approach.

These topics have been studied and elaborated over the past several years, with results suggesting that the minimalist conception outlined may not be far from the mark. I had hoped to present an exposition in this paper, but that plan proved too ambitious. I will therefore keep to an informal sketch, only indicating some of the problems that must be dealt with.[8]

2   Fundamental Relations: X-Bar Theory

The computational system takes representations of a given form and modifies them. Accordingly, UG must provide means to present an array of items from the lexicon in a form accessible to the computational system. We may take this form to be some version of X-bar theory. The concepts of X-bar theory are therefore fundamental. In a minimalist theory, the crucial properties and relations will be stated in the simple and elementary terms of X-bar theory.

An X-bar structure is composed of projections of heads selected from the lexicon. Basic relations, then, will involve the head as one term. Furthermore, the basic relations are typically "local." In structures of the form (1), two local relations are present: the *Spec(ifier)-head* relation of ZP to X, and the *head-complement* relation of X to YP (order irrelevant; the usual conventions apply).

(1)

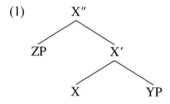

The head-complement relation is not only "more local" but also more fundamental—typically, associated with thematic (θ-) relations. The Spec-head relation, I will suggest below, falls into an "elsewhere" category. Putting aside adjunction for the moment, the narrowest plausible hypothesis is that X-bar structures are restricted to the form in (1); only local relations are considered (hence no relation between X and a phrase included within YP or ZP); and head-complement is the core local relation. Another admissible local relation is *head-head*, for example, the relation of a verb to (the head of) its Noun Phrase complement (selection). Another is *chain link*, to which we will return. The version of a minimalist program explored here requires that we keep to relations of these kinds, dispensing with such notions as government by a head (head government). But head government plays a critical role in all modules of grammar; hence, all of these must be reformulated, if this program is to be pursued.

Take Case theory. It is standardly assumed that the Spec-head relation enters into structural Case for the subject position, while the object position is assigned Case under government by V, including constructions in which the object Case-marked by a verb is not its complement (exceptional Case marking).[9] The narrower approach we are considering requires that all these modes of structural Case assignment be recast in unified X-bar-theoretic terms, presumably under the Spec-head relation. As discussed in Chomsky 1991a, an elaboration of Pollock's (1989) theory of inflection provides a natural mechanism, where we take the basic structure of the clause to be (2).

(2)

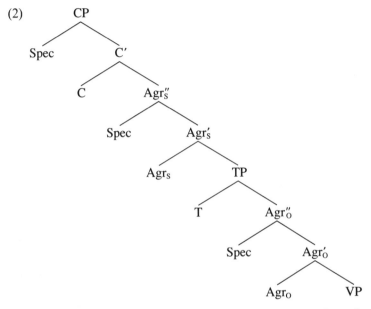

Omitted here are a possible Specifier of TP ([Spec, TP]) and a phrase headed by the functional element *negation*, or perhaps more broadly, a category that includes an affirmation marker and others as well (Pollock 1989, Laka 1990). Agr_S and Agr_O are informal mnemonics to distinguish the two functional roles of Agr. Agr is a collection of ϕ-features (gender, number, person); these are common to the systems of subject and object agreement, though Agr_S and Agr_O may of course be different selections, just as two verbs or NPs in (2) may differ.[10]

We now regard both agreement and structural Case as manifestations of the Spec-head relation (NP, Agr). But Case properties depend on characteristics of T and the V head of VP. We therefore assume that T raises to Agr_S, forming (3a), and V raises to Agr_O, forming (3b); the complex includes the ϕ-features of Agr and the Case feature provided by T, V.[11]

(3) a. $[_{Agr}$ T Agr]
    b. $[_{Agr}$ V Agr]

The basic assumption is that there is a symmetry between the subject and the object inflectional systems. In both positions the relation of NP to V is mediated by Agr, a collection of ϕ-features; in both positions agreement is determined by the ϕ-features of the Agr head of the Agr complex, and Case by an element that adjoins to Agr (T or V). An NP in the [Spec, head] relation to this Agr complex bears the associated Case and agreement features. The Spec-head and head-head relations are therefore the core configurations for inflectional morphology.

Exceptional Case marking by V is now interpreted as raising of NP to the Spec position of the Agr-phrase dominating V. It is raising to [Spec, Agr$_O$], the analogue of familiar raising to [Spec, Agr$_S$]. If the VP-internal subject hypothesis is correct (as I henceforth assume), the question arises why the object (direct, or in the complement) raises to [Spec, Agr$_O$] and the subject to [Spec, Agr$_S$], yielding unexpected crossing rather than the usual nested paths. We will return to this phenomenon below, finding that it follows on plausible assumptions of some generality, and in this sense appears to be a fairly "deep" property of language. If parameters are morphologically restricted in the manner sketched earlier, there should be no language variation in this regard.

The same hypothesis extends naturally to predicate adjectives, with the underlying structure shown in (4) (Agr$_A$ again a mnemonic for a collection of ϕ-features, in this case associated with an adjective).

(4)

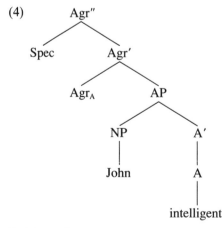

Raising of NP to Spec and A to Agr$_A$ creates the structure for NP-adjective agreement internal to the predicate phrase. The resulting structure is a plausible candidate for the small clause complement of *consider*, *be*, and so on. In the former construction (complement of *consider*), NP raises further to [Spec, Agr_O] at LF to receive accusative Case; in the latter (complement of *be*), NP raises overtly to receive nominative Case and verb agreement, yielding the overt form *John is intelligent* with *John* entering into three relations: (i) a Case relation with [T Agr_S] (hence ultimately the verbal complex [[T Agr_S] V]), (ii) an agreement relation with Agr_S (hence the verbal complex), and (iii) an agreement relation with Agr of (4) (hence the adjectival complex). In both constructions, the NP subject is outside of a full AP in the small clause construction, as required, and the structure is of a type that appears regularly.[12]

An NP, then, may enter into two kinds of structural relations with a predicate (verb, adjective): agreement, involving features shared by NP and predicate; or Case, manifested on the NP alone. Subject of verb or adjective, and object of verb, enter into these relations (but not object of adjective if that is an instance of inherent, not structural, Case). Both relations involve Agr: Agr alone, for agreement relations; the element T or V alone (raising to Agr), for Case relations.

The structure of CP in (2) is largely forced by other properties of UG, assuming the minimalist program with Agr abstracted as a common property of adjectival agreement and the subject-object inflectional systems, a reasonable assumption, given that agreement appears without Case (as in NP-AP agreement) and Case appears without agreement (as in transitive expletives, with the expletive presumably in the [Spec, Agr_S] position and the subject in [Spec, Tense], receiving Case; see note 11). Any appropriate version of the Case Filter will require two occurrences of Agr if two NPs in VP require structural Case; conditions on Move α require the arrangement given in (2) if structural Case is construed as outlined. Suppose that VP contains only one NP. Then one of the two Agr elements will be "active" (the other being inert or perhaps missing). Which one? Two options are possible: Agr_S or Agr_O. If the choice is Agr_S, then the single NP will have the properties of the subject of a transitive clause; if the choice is Agr_O, then it will have the properties of the object of a transitive clause (nominative-accusative and ergative-absolutive languages, respectively). These are the only two possibilities, mixtures apart. The distinction between the two language types reduces to a trivial question of morphology, as we expect.

Note that from this point of view, the terms *nominative, absolutive*, and so on, have no substantive meaning apart from what is determined by the choice of "active" versus "inert" Agr; there is no real question as to how these terms correspond across language types.

The "active" element (Agr_S in nominative-accusative languages and Agr_O in ergative-absolutive languages) typically assigns a less-marked Case to its Spec, which is also higher on the extractibility hierarchy, among other properties. It is natural to expect less-marked Case to be compensated (again, as a tendency) by more-marked agreement (richer overt agreement with nominative and absolutive than with accusative and ergative). The c-command condition on anaphora leads us to expect nominative and ergative binding in transitive constructions.[13]

Similar considerations apply to licensing of pro. Assuming Rizzi's theory (1982, 1986), pro is licensed in a Spec-head relation to "strong" Agr_S, or when governed by certain verbs V*. To recast these proposals in a unitary X-bar-theoretic form: pro is licensed only in the Spec-head relation to $[_{Agr} \alpha\, Agr]$, where α is [+tense] or V, Agr strong or V = V*. Licensing of pro thus falls under Case theory in a broad sense. Similar considerations extend rather naturally to PRO.[14]

Suppose that other properties of head government also have a natural expression in terms of the more fundamental notions of X-bar theory. Suppose further that antecedent government is a property of chains, expressible in terms of c-command and barriers. Then the concept of government would be dispensable, with principles of language restricted to something closer to conceptual necessity: local X-bar-theoretic relations to the head of a projection and the chain link relation.

Let us look more closely at the local X-bar-theoretic notions, taking these to be fundamental. Assume binary branching only, thus structures limited to (1). Turning to adjunction, on the assumptions of Chomsky 1986a, there is no adjunction to complement, adjunction (at least, in overt syntax) has a kind of "structure-preserving" character, and a segment-category distinction holds.[15] Thus, the structures to be considered are of the form shown in (5), where XP, ZP, and X each have a higher and lower segment, indicated by subscripting (H and X heads).

Let us now consider the notions that enter into a minimalist program. The basic elements of a representation are chains. We consider first the case of one-membered chains, construing notions abstractly with an eye to the general case. The structure (5) can only have arisen by raising of H to adjoin to X (we put aside questions about the possible origins of UP, WP). Therefore, H heads a chain $CH = (H, \ldots, t)$, and only this chain, not H in isolation, enters into head-α relations. The categories that we

(5)

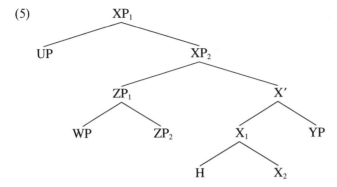

establish are defined for H as well as X, but while they enter into head-α relations for X, they do not do so for H (only for the chain CH), an important matter.

Assume all notions to be irreflexive unless otherwise indicated. Assume the standard notion of domination for the pair (σ, β), σ a segment. We say that the category α *dominates* β if every segment of α dominates β. The category α *contains* β if some segment of α dominates β. Thus, the two-segment category XP dominates ZP, WP, X', and whatever they dominate; XP contains UP and whatever UP and XP dominate; ZP contains WP but does not dominate it. The two-segment category X contains H but does not dominate it.

For a head α, take Max(α) to be the least full-category maximal projection dominating α. Thus, in (5) Max(H) = Max(X) = $[XP_1, XP_2]$, the two-segment category XP.

Take the *domain* of a head α to be the set of nodes contained in Max(α) that are distinct from and do not contain α. Thus, the domain of X in (5) is $\{UP, ZP, WP, YP, H\}$ and whatever these categories dominate; the domain of H is the same, minus H.

As noted, the fundamental X-bar-theoretic relation is head-complement, typically with an associated θ-relation determined by properties of the head. Define the *complement domain* of α as the subset of the domain reflexively dominated by the complement of the construction: YP in (5). The complement domain of X (and H) is therefore YP and whatever it dominates.

The remainder of the domain of α we will call the *residue* of α. Thus, in (5) the residue of X is its domain minus YP and what it dominates. The residue is a heterogeneous set, including the Spec position and anything adjoined (adjunction being allowed to the maximal projection, its Spec, or its head; UP, WP, and H, respectively, in (5)).

The operative relations have a local character. We are therefore interested not in the sets just defined, but rather in *minimal* subsets of them that include just categories locally related to the heads. For any set S of categories, let us take Min(S) (minimal S) to be the smallest subset K of S such that for any $\gamma \in$ S, some $\beta \in$ K reflexively dominates γ. In the cases that interest us, S is a function of a head α (e.g., S = domain of α). We keep to this case, that is, to Min(S(α)), for some head α. Thus, in (5) the minimal domain of X is {UP, ZP, WP, YP, H}; its minimal complement domain is YP; and its minimal residue is {UP, ZP, WP, H}. The minimal domain of H is {UP, ZP, WP, YP}; its minimal complement domain is YP; and its minimal residue is {UP, ZP, WP}.

Let us call the minimal complement domain of α its *internal domain*, and the minimal residue of α its *checking domain*. The terminology is intended to indicate that elements of the internal domain are typically internal arguments of α, while the the checking domain is typically involved in checking inflectional features. Recall that the checking domain is heterogeneous: it is the "elsewhere" set. The minimal domain also has an important role, to which we will turn directly.

A technical point should be clarified. The internal and checking domains of α must be uniquely defined for α; specifically, if α (or one of its elements, if it is a nontrivial chain) is moved, we do not want the internal and checking domains to be "redefined" in the newly formed construction, or we will have an element with multiple subdomains—for example, ambiguous specification of internal arguments. We must therefore understand the notion Min(S(α)) *derivationally*, not *representationally*: it is defined for α as part of the process of introducing α into the derivation. If α is a trivial (one-membered) chain, then Min(S(α)) is defined when α is lexically inserted; if α is a nontrivial chain $(\beta_1, \ldots, \beta_n)$, then Min(S($\alpha$)) is defined when α is formed by raising β_1. In (5) the head H has no minimal, internal, or checking domain, because it is raised from some other position to form the chain CH = (H, ..., t) and has already been assigned these subdomains in the position now occupied by t; such subdomains are, however, defined for the newly formed chain CH, in a manner to which we will turn directly. Similarly, if the complex [H X] is later raised to form the chain CH' = ([H X], t'), Min(S(α)) will be defined as part of the operation for α = CH', but not for α = X, H, or CH.

Returning to (5), suppose X is a verb. Then YP, the sole element of the internal domain of X, is typically an internal argument of X. Suppose X is Agr and H a verb raised to Agr forming the chain CH = (H, t). Then the specifier ZP (and possibly the adjoined elements UP, WP) of the checking domain of X and CH will have agreement features by virtue of their local relation to X, and Case features by virtue of their local relation to CH. H does not have a checking domain, but CH does.[16]

We have so far considered only one-membered chains. We must extend the notions defined to a nontrivial chain CH with $n > 1$ (α_1 a zero-level category), as in (6).

(6) $CH = (\alpha_1, \ldots, \alpha_n)$

Let us keep to the case of $n = 2$, the normal case for lexical heads though not necessarily the only one.[17]

The issue arises, for example, if we adopt an analysis of multi-argument verbs along the lines suggested by Larson (1988), for example, taking the underlying structure of (7) to be (8).

(7) John put the book on the shelf

(8)

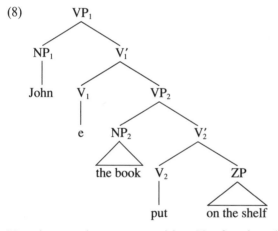

V_2 raises to the empty position V_1, forming the chain (put, t) (subsequently, NP_1 raises (overtly) to [Spec, Agr$_S$] and NP_2 (covertly) to [Spec, Agr$_O$]).

The result we want is that the minimal domain of the chain (put, t) is $\{NP_1, NP_2, ZP\}$ (the three arguments), while the internal domain is $\{NP_2, ZP\}$ (the internal arguments). The intended sense is given by the natural generalization of the definitions already suggested. Let us define the domain of CH in (6) to be the set of nodes contained in $Max(\alpha_1)$ and not containing any α_i. The complement domain of CH is the subset of the domain of CH reflexively dominated by the complement of α_1. Residue and $Min(S(\alpha))$ are defined as before, now for $\alpha = CH$. The concepts defined earlier are the special cases where CH is one-membered.

Suppose, for example, that $CH = (put, t)$, after raising of *put* to V_1 in (8), leaving t in the position V_2. Then the domain of CH is the set of nodes contained in VP_1 ($= Max(V_1)$) and not containing either *put* or t (namely, the set $\{NP_1, NP_2, ZP\}$ and whatever they dominate); the minimal domain is $\{NP_1, NP_2, ZP\}$. The internal domain of the chain CH is $\{NP_2, ZP\}$ (the two internal arguments), and the checking domain of CH is NP_1, the typical position of the external argument in this version of the VP-internal subject hypothesis (basically Larson's).

Suppose that instead of replacing *e, put* had adjoined to some nonnull element X, yielding the complex category $[_X put\ X]$, as in adjunction of H to X in (5). The domain, internal domain, and checking domain of the chain would be exactly the same. There is no minimal domain, internal domain, or checking domain for *put* itself after raising; only for the chain $CH = (put, t)$. It is in terms of these minimal sets that the local head-α relations are defined, the head now being the nontrivial chain CH.

In (8), then, the relevant domains are as intended after V-raising to V_1. Note that VP_2 is not in the internal domain of CH ($= (put, t)$) because it dominates t ($= \alpha_n$ of (6)).

The same notions extend to an analysis of lexical structure along the lines proposed by Hale and Keyser (1993). In this case an analogue of (8) would be the underlying structure for *John shelved the book*, with V_2 being a "light verb" and ZP an abstract version of *on the shelf* ($= [P\ shelf]$). Here *shelf* raises to P, the amalgam raises to V_2, and the element so formed raises to V_1 in the manner of *put* in (7).[18]

So far we have made no use of the notion "minimal domain." But this too has a natural interpretation, when we turn to Empty Category Principle (ECP) phenomena. I will have to put aside a careful development here, but it is intuitively clear how certain basic aspects will enter. Take the phenomena of Superiority (as in (9a)) and of Relativized Minimality in the sense of Rizzi (1990) (as in (9b)).

(9) a. i.   Whom$_1$ did John persuade t_1 [to visit whom$_2$]
     ii. *Whom$_2$ did John persuade whom$_1$ [to visit t_2]
   b. Superraising, the head Movement Constraint (HMC), [Spec, CP] islands (including *wh*-islands)

Looking at these phenomena in terms of economy considerations, it is clear that in all the "bad" cases, some element has failed to make "the shortest move." In (9aii) movement of *whom$_2$* to [Spec, CP] is longer in a natural sense (definable in terms of c-command) than movement of *whom$_1$* to this position. In all the cases of (9b) the moved element has "skipped" a position it could have reached by a shorter move, had that position not been filled. Spelling out these notions to account for the range of relevant cases is not a trivial matter. But it does seem possible in a way that accords reasonably well with the minimalist program. Let us simply assume, for present purposes, that this task can be carried out, and that phenomena of the kind illustrated are accounted for in this way in terms of economy considerations.[19]

There appears to be a conflict between two natural notions of economy: shortest move versus fewest steps in a derivation. If a derivation keeps to shortest moves, it will have more steps; if it reduces the number of steps, it will have longer moves. The paradox is resolved if we take the basic transformational operation to be not Move α but *Form Chain*, an operation that applies, say, to the structure (10a) to form (10b) in a single step, yielding the chain CH of (10c).

(10) a. e seems [e to be likely [John to win]]
      b. John seems [t' to be likely [t to win]]
      c. CH = $(John, t', t)$

Similarly, in other cases of successive-cyclic movement. There is, then, no conflict between reducing derivations to the shortest number of steps and keeping links minimal ("Shortest Movement" Condition). There are independent reasons to suppose that this is the correct approach: note, for example, that successive-cyclic *wh*-movement of arguments does not treat the intermediate steps as adjunct movement, as it should if it were a succession of applications of Move α. Successive-cyclic movement raises a variety of interesting problems, but I will again put them aside, keeping to the simpler case.

A number of questions arise in the case of such constructions as (8), considered now in the more abstract form (11).

(11)

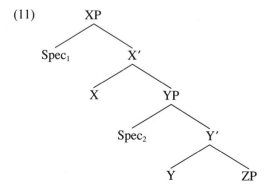

In the particular instance (8), $\text{Spec}_1 = \text{NP}_1$ (*John*), $X = $ null V_1, $\text{Spec}_2 = \text{NP}_2$ (*the book*), $Y = V_2$ (*put*) with ZP its complement (*on the shelf*). Another instance would be object-raising to [Spec, Agr] ($\text{Agr} = \text{Agr}_O$), as in (12).

(12)

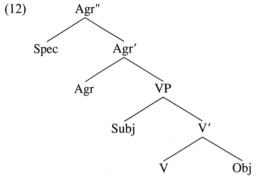

Here Subj is the VP-internal subject (or its trace), and Obj the object. The configuration and operations are exactly those of (8), except that in (12) V *adjoins* to Agr (as in the case of H of (5)), whereas in (8) it *substituted for* the empty position V_1. On our assumptions, Obj must raise to the Spec position for Case checking, crossing Subj or its trace. (12) is therefore a violation of Relativized Minimality, in effect, a case of superraising, a violation of the "Shortest Movement" Condition.

Another instance of (11) is incorporation in the sense of Baker (1988). For example, V-incorporation to a causative verb has a structure like (12), but with an embedded clause S instead of the object Obj, as in (13).

(13)

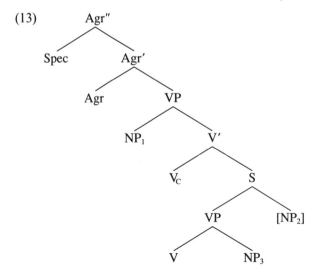

In an example of Baker's, modeled on Chicheŵa, we take NP_1 = *the baboons*, V_c = *make*, NP_2 = *the lizards*, V = *hit*, and NP_3 = *the children*; the resulting sentence is *The baboons made-hit the children* [*to the lizards*], meaning "The baboons made the lizards hit the children." Incorporation of V to the causative V_c yields the chain (V, t), with V adjoined to V_c. The complex head $[V\,V_c]$ then raises to Agr, forming the new chain $([V\,V_c], t')$, with $[V\,V_c]$ adjoining to Agr to yield $\alpha = [Agr[V\,V_c]\,Agr]$. The resulting structure is (14).[20]

(14)

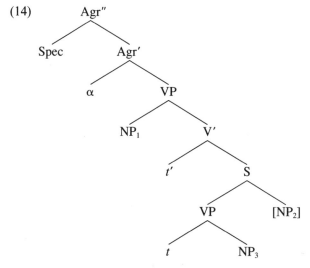

Here NP_3 is treated as the object of the verbal complex, assigned accusative Case (with optional object agreement). In our terms, that means that NP_3 raises to $[Spec, \alpha]$, crossing NP_1, the matrix subject or its trace (another option is that the complex verb is passivized and NP_3 is raised to $[Spec, Agr_S]$).

In the last example the minimal domain of the chain $([V\,V_c], t')$ is $\{Spec, NP_1, S\}$. The example is therefore analogous to (8), in which V-raising formed an enlarged minimal domain for the chain. It is natural to suppose that (12) has the same property: V first raises to Agr, yielding the chain (V, t) with the minimal domain $\{Spec, Subj, Obj\}$. The cases just described are now formally alike and should be susceptible to the same analysis. The last two cases appear to violate the "Shortest Movement" Condition.

Let us sharpen the notion of "shortest movement" as follows:

(15) If α, β are in the same minimal domain, they are equidistant from γ.

In particular, two targets of movement are equidistant if they are in the same minimal domain.

In the abstract case (11), if Y adjoins to X, forming the chain (Y, t) with the minimal domain $\{Spec_1, Spec_2, ZP\}$, then $Spec_1$ and $Spec_2$ are equidistant from ZP (or anything it contains), so that raising of (or from) ZP can cross $Spec_2$ to $Spec_1$. Turning to the problematic instances of (11), in (12) Obj can raise to Spec, crossing Subj or its trace without violating the economy condition; and in the incorporation example (14) NP_3 can raise to Spec, crossing NP_1.

This analysis predicts that object raising as in (12) should be possible only if V has raised to Agr. In particular, overt object raising will be possible only with overt V-raising. That prediction is apparently confirmed for the Germanic languages (Vikner 1990). The issue does not arise in the LF analogue, since we assume that invariably, V raises to Agr_O covertly, if not overtly, therefore "freeing" the raising of object to [Spec, Agr_O] for Case checking.

Baker explains such structures as (13)–(14) in terms of his Government Transparency Corollary (GTC), which extends the government domain of V_1 to that of V_2 if V_2 adjoins to V_1. The analysis just sketched is an approximate analogue, on the assumption that Case and agreement are assigned not by head government but in the [Spec, head] relation. Note that the GTC is not strictly speaking a corollary; rather, it is an independent principle, though Baker gives a plausibility argument internal to a specific theory of government. A possibility that might be investigated is that the GTC falls generally under the independently motivated condition (15), on the minimalist assumptions being explored here.

Recall that on these assumptions, we faced the problem of explaining why we find crossing rather than nesting in the Case theory, with VP-internal subject raising to [Spec, Agr_S] and object raising to [Spec, Agr_O], crossing the trace of the VP-internal subject. The principle (15) entails that this is a permissible derivation, as in (12) with V-raising to Agr_O. It remains to show that the desired derivation is not only permissible but obligatory: it is the only possible derivation. That is straightforward. Suppose that in (12) the VP-internal subject in [Spec, VP] raises to [Spec, Agr_O], either overtly or covertly, yielding (16), t_{Subj} the trace of the raised subject Subj.

Suppose further that V raises to Agr_O, either overtly or covertly, forming the chain (V, t_V) with the minimal domain $\{Subj, t_{Subj}, Obj\}$. Now Subj and its trace are equidistant from Obj, so that Obj can raise to the [Spec,

(16)

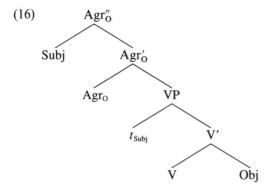

Agr_O] position. But this position is occupied by Subj, blocking that option. Therefore, to receive Case, Obj must move directly to some higher position, crossing [Spec, Agr_O]: either to [Spec, T] or to [Spec, Agr_S]. But that is impossible, even after the element [V, Agr_O] raises to higher inflectional positions. Raising of [V, Agr_O] will form a new chain with trace in the Agr_O position of (16) and a new minimal domain M. But t_{Subj} is not a member of M. Accordingly, Obj cannot cross t_{Subj} to reach a position in M (apart from the position [Spec, Agr_O] already filled by the subject). Hence, raising of the VP-internal subject to the [Spec, Agr_O] position blocks any kind of Case assignment to the object; the object is "frozen in place."[21]

It follows that crossing and not nesting is the only permissible option in any language. The paradox of Case theory is therefore resolved, on natural assumptions that generalize to a number of other cases.

3 Beyond the Interface Levels: D-Structure

Recall the (virtual) conceptual necessities within this general approach. UG determines possible symbolic representations and derivations. A language consists of a lexicon and a computational system. The computational system draws from the lexicon to form derivations, presenting items from the lexicon in the format of X-bar theory. Each derivation determines a linguistic expression, an SD, which contains a pair (π, λ) meeting the interface conditions. Ideally, that would be the end of the story: each linguistic expression is an optimal realization of interface conditions expressed in elementary terms (chain link, local X-bar-theoretic relations), a pair (π, λ) satisfying these conditions and generated in the most economical way. Any additional structure or assumptions require empirical justification.

The EST framework adds additional structure; for concreteness, take *Lectures on Government and Binding* (*LGB*; Chomsky 1981). One crucial assumption has to do with the way in which the computational system presents lexical items for further computation. The assumption is that this is done by an operation, call it Satisfy, which selects an array of items from the lexicon and presents it in a format satisfying the conditions of X-bar Theory. Satisfy is an "all-at-once" operation: all items that function at LF are drawn from the lexicon before computation proceeds[22] and are presented in the X-bar format.

We thus postulate an additional level, D-Structure, beyond the two external interface levels PF and LF. D-Structure is the *internal* interface between the lexicon and the computational system, formed by Satisfy. Certain principles of UG are then held to apply to D-Structure, specifically, the Projection Principle and the θ-Criterion. The computational procedure maps D-Structure to another level, S-Structure, and then "branches" to PF and LF, independently. UG principles of the various modules of grammar (binding theory, Case theory, the pro module, etc.) apply at the level of S-Structure (perhaps elsewhere as well, in some cases).

The empirical justification for this approach, with its departures from conceptual necessity, is substantial. Nevertheless, we may ask whether the evidence will bear the weight, or whether it is possible to move toward a minimalist program.

Note that the operation Satisfy and the assumptions that underlie it are not unproblematic. We have described Satisfy as an operation that selects an *array*, not a *set*; different arrangements of lexical items will yield different expressions. Exactly what an array is would have to be clarified. Furthermore, this picture requires conditions to ensure that D-Structure has basic properties of LF. At LF the conditions are trivial. If they are not met, the expression receives some deviant interpretation at the interface; there is nothing more to say. The Projection Principle and the θ-Criterion have no independent significance at LF.[23] But at D-Structure the two principles are needed to make the picture coherent; if the picture is abandoned, they will lose their primary role. These principles are therefore dubious on conceptual grounds, though it remains to account for their empirical consequences, such as the constraint against substitution into a θ-position. If the empirical consequences can be explained in some other way and D-Structure eliminated, then the Projection Principle and the θ-Criterion can be dispensed with.

What is more, postulation of D-Structure raises empirical problems, as noticed at once when EST was reformulated in the more restrictive principles-and-parameters framework. One problem, discussed in *LGB*, is posed by complex adjectival constructions such as (17a) with the S-Structure representation (17b) (*t* the trace of the empty operator O).

(17) a. John is easy to please
     b. John is easy [$_{CP}$ O [$_{IP}$ PRO to please *t*]]

The evidence for the S-Structure representation (17b) is compelling, but *John* occupies a non θ-position and hence cannot appear at D-Structure. Satisfy is therefore violated. In *LGB* it is proposed that Satisfy be weakened: in non θ-positions a lexical item, such as *John*, can be inserted in the course of the derivation and assigned its θ-role only at LF (and irrelevantly, S-Structure). That is consistent with the principles, though not with their spirit, one might argue.

We need not tarry on that matter, however, because the technical device does not help. As noted by Howard Lasnik, the *LGB* solution fails, because an NP of arbitrary complexity may occur in place of *John* (for example, an NP incorporating a structure such as (17a) internally). Within anything like the *LGB* framework, then, we are driven to a version of generalized transformations, as in the very earliest work in generative grammar. The problem was recognized at once, but left as an unresolved paradox. More recent work has brought forth other cases of expressions interpretable at LF but not in their D-Structure positions (Reinhart 1991), along with other reasons to suspect that there are generalized transformations, or devices like them (Kroch and Joshi 1985, Kroch 1989, Lebeaux 1988, Epstein 1991). If so, the special assumptions underlying the postulation of D-Structure lose credibility. Since these assumptions lacked independent conceptual support, we are led to dispense with the level of D-Structure and the "all-at-once" property of Satisfy, relying in its place on a theory of generalized transformations for lexical access—though the empirical consequences of the D-Structure conditions remain to be faced.[24]

A theory of the preferred sort is readily constructed and turns out to have many desirable properties. Let us replace the EST assumptions of *LGB* and related work by an approach along the following lines. The computational system selects an item X from the lexicon and projects it to an X-bar structure of one of the forms in (18), where $X = X^0 = [_X X]$.

(18) a. X
     b. [$_{X'}$ X]
     c. [$_{X''}$[$_{X'}$ X]]

This will be the sole residue of the Projection Principle.

We now adopt (more or less) the assumptions of *LSLT*, with a single generalized transformation GT that takes a phrase marker K^1 and inserts it in a designated empty position $\emptyset$ in a phrase marker K, forming the new phrase marker K*, which satisfies X-bar theory. Computation proceeds in parallel, selecting from the lexicon freely at any point. At each point in the derivation, then, we have a structure Σ, which we may think of as a set of phrase markers. At any point, we may apply the operation Spell-Out, which switches to the PF component. If Σ is not a single phrase marker, the derivation crashes at PF, since PF rules cannot apply to a set of phrase markers and no legitimate PF representation π is generated. If Σ is a single phrase marker, the PF rules apply to it, yielding π, which either is legitimate (so the derivation converges at PF) or not (the derivation again crashes at PF).

After Spell-Out, the computational process continues, with the sole constraint that it has no further access to the lexicon (we must ensure, for example, that *John left* does not mean "They wondered whether John left before finishing his work"). The PF and LF outputs must satisfy the (external) interface conditions. D-Structure disappears, along with the problems it raised.

GT is a substitution operation. It targets K and substitutes K^1 for $\emptyset$ in K. But $\emptyset$ is not drawn from the lexicon; therefore, it must have been inserted by GT itself. GT, then, targets K, adds $\emptyset$, and substitutes K^1 for $\emptyset$, forming K*, which must satisfy X-bar theory. Note that this is a description of the inner workings of a single operation, GT. It is on a par with some particular algorithm for Move α, or for the operation of modus ponens in a proof. Thus, it is invisible to the eye that scans only the derivation itself, detecting only its successive steps. We never see $\emptyset$; it is subliminal, like the "first half" of the raising of an NP to subject position.

Alongside the binary substitution operation GT, which maps (K, K^1) to K*, we also have the singulary substitution operation Move α, which maps K to K*. Suppose that this operation works just as GT does: it targets K, adds $\emptyset$, and substitutes α for $\emptyset$, where α in this case is a phrase marker within the targeted phrase marker K itself. We assume further that the operation leaves behind a trace t of α and forms the chain (α, t). Again, $\emptyset$ is invisible when we scan the derivation; it is part of the inner workings of an operation carrying the derivation forward one step.

Suppose we restrict substitution operations still further, requiring that $\emptyset$ be *external* to the targeted phrase marker K. Thus, GT and Move α extend K to K*, which includes K as a proper part.[25] For example, we can target K = V′, add $\emptyset$ to form $[_\beta \emptyset \text{ V}']$, and then either raise α from within

V' to replace $\emptyset$ or insert another phrase marker K^1 for $\emptyset$. In either case, the result must satisfy X-bar theory, which means that the element replacing $\emptyset$ must be a maximal projection YP, the specifier of the new phrase marker $V'' = \beta$.

The requirement that substitution operations always extend their target has a number of consequences. First, it yields a version of the strict cycle, one that is motivated by the most elementary empirical considerations: without it, we would lose the effects of those cases of the ECP that fall under Relativized Minimality (see (9b)). Thus, suppose that in the course of a derivation we have reached the stage (19).

(19) a. $[_{I'}$ seems $[_{I'}$ is certain [John to be here]]]
  b. $[_{C'}$ C $[_{VP}$ fix the car]]
  c. $[_{C'}$ C [John wondered $[_{C'}$ C $[_{IP}$ Mary fixed what how]]]]

Violating no "Shortest Movement" Condition, we can raise *John* directly to the matrix Spec in (19a) in a single step, later inserting *it* from the lexicon to form *John seems it is certain* t *to be here* (superraising); we can raise *fix* to adjoin to C in (19b) later inserting *can* from the lexicon to form *Fix John can* t *the car?* (violating the HMC); and we can raise *how* to the matrix [Spec, CP] position in (19c), later raising *what* to the embedded [Spec, CP] position to form *How did John wonder what Mary fixed* t_{how}? (violating the *Wh*-Island Constraint).[26]

The "extension" version of the strict cycle is therefore not only straightforward, but justified empirically without subtle empirical argument.

A second consequence of the extension condition is that given a structure of the form $[_{X'}$ X YP], we cannot insert ZP into X' (yielding, e.g., $[_{X'}$ X YP ZP]), where ZP is drawn from within YP (raising) or inserted from outside by GT. Similarly, given $[_{X'}$ X], we cannot insert ZP to form $[_{X'}$ X ZP]. There can be no raising to a complement position. We therefore derive one major consequence of the Projection Principle and θ-Criterion at D-Structure, thus lending support to the belief that these notions are indeed superfluous. More generally, as noted by Akira Watanabe, the binarity of GT comes close to entailing that X-bar structures are restricted to binary branching (Kayne's "unambiguous paths"), though a bit more work is required.

The operations just discussed are substitution transformations, but we must consider adjunction as well. We thus continue to allow the X-bar structure (5) as well as (1), specifically (20).[27]

(20) a. $[_X$ Y X]
  b. $[_{XP}$ YP XP]

In (20a) a zero-level category Y is adjoined to the zero-level category X, and in (20b) a maximal projection YP is adjoined to the maximal projection XP. GT and Move α must form structures satisfying X-bar theory, now including (20). Note that the very strong empirical motivation for the strict cycle just given does not apply in these cases. Let us assume, then, that adjunction need not extend its target. For concreteness, let us assume that the extension requirement holds only for substitution in overt syntax, the only case required by the trivial argument for the cycle.[28]

4   Beyond the Interface Levels: S-Structure

Suppose that D-Structure is eliminable along these lines. What about S-Structure, another level that has only theory-internal motivation? The basic issue is whether there are S-Structure conditions. If not, we can dispense with the concept of S-Structure, allowing Spell-Out to apply freely in the manner indicated earlier. Plainly this would be the optimal conclusion.

As shown in (21), there are two kinds of evidence for S-Structure conditions.

(21) a. Languages differ with respect to where Spell-Out applies in the
         course of the derivation to LF. (Are *wh*-phrases moved or in
         situ? Is the language French-style with overt verb raising or
         English-style with LF verb raising?)
     b. In just about every module of grammar, there is extensive
         evidence that the conditions apply at S-Structure.

To show that S-Structure is nevertheless superfluous, we must show that the evidence of both kinds, though substantial, is not compelling.

In the case of evidence of type (21a), we must show that the position of Spell-Out in the derivation is determined by either PF or LF properties, these being the only levels, on minimalist assumptions. Furthermore, parametric differences must be reduced to morphological properties if the minimalist program is framed in the terms so far assumed. There are strong reasons to suspect that LF conditions are not relevant. We expect languages to be very similar at the LF level, differing only as a reflex of properties detectable at PF; the reasons basically reduce to considerations of learnability. Thus, we expect that at the LF level there will be no relevant difference between languages with phrases overtly raised or in situ (e.g., *wh*-phrases or verbs). Hence, we are led to seek morphological properties that are reflected at PF. Let us keep the conclusion in mind, returning to it later.

With regard to evidence of type (21b), an argument against S-Structure conditions could be of varying strength, as shown in (22).

(22) a. The condition in question *can* apply at LF alone.
   b. Furthermore, the condition sometimes *must* apply at LF.
   c. Furthermore, the condition must *not* apply at S-Structure.

Even (22a), the weakest of the three, suffices: LF has independent motivation, but S-Structure does not. Argument (22b) is stronger on the assumption that, optimally, conditions are unitary: they apply at a single level, hence at LF if possible. Argument (22c) would be decisive.

To sample the problems that arise, consider binding theory. There are familiar arguments showing that the binding theory conditions must apply at S-Structure, not LF. Thus, consider (23).

(23) a. You said he liked [the pictures that John took]
   b. [How many pictures that John took] did you say he liked t
   c. Who [t said he liked [$_\alpha$ how many pictures that John took]]

In (23a) *he* c-commands *John* and cannot take *John* as antecedent; in (23b) there is no c-command relation and *John* can be the antecedent of *he*. In (23c) *John* again cannot be the antecedent of *he*. Since the binding properties of (23c) are those of (23a), not (23b), we conclude that *he* c-commands *John* at the level of representation at which Condition C applies. But if LF movement adjoins α to *who* in (23c), Condition C must apply at S-Structure.

The argument is not conclusive, however. We might reject the last assumption: that LF movement adjoins α of (23c) to *who*, forming (24), t' the trace of the LF-moved phrase.

(24) [[How many pictures that John took] who] [t said he liked t']

We might assume that the only permissible option is extraction of *how many* from the full NP α, yielding an LF form along the lines of (25), t' the trace of *how many*.[29]

(25) [[How many] who] [t said he liked [[t' pictures] that John took]]

The answer, then, could be the pair (*Bill, 7*), meaning that Bill said he liked 7 pictures that John took. But in (25) *he* c-commands *John*, so that Condition C applies as in (23a). We are therefore not compelled to assume that Condition C applies at S-Structure; we can keep to the preferable option that conditions involving interpretation apply only at the interface levels. This is an argument of the type (22a), weak but sufficient. We will return to the possibility of stronger arguments of the types (22b) and (22c).

The overt analogue of (25) requires "pied-piping" of the entire NP [*how many pictures that John took*], but it is not clear that the same is true in the LF component. We might, in fact, proceed further. The LF rule that associates the in-situ *wh*-phrase with the *wh*-phrase in [Spec, CP] need not be construed as an instance of Move α. We might think of it as the syntactic basis for absorption in the sense of Higginbotham and May (1981), an operation that associates two *wh*-phrases to form a generalized quantifier.[30] If so, then the LF rule need satisfy none of the conditions on movement.

There has long been evidence that conditions on movement do not hold for multiple questions. Nevertheless, the approach just proposed appeared to be blocked by the properties of Chinese- and Japanese-type languages, with *wh*- in situ throughout but observing at least some of the conditions on movement (Huang 1982). Watanabe (1991) has argued, however, that even in these languages there is overt *wh*-movement—in this case movement of an empty operator, yielding the effects of the movement constraints. If Watanabe is correct, we could assume that a *wh*-operator always raises overtly, that Move α is subject to the same conditions everywhere in the derivation to PF and LF, and that the LF operation that applies in multiple questions in English and direct questions in Japanese is free of these conditions. What remains is the question why overt movement of the operator is always required, a question of the category (21a). We will return to that.

Let us recall again the minimalist assumptions that I am conjecturing can be upheld: all conditions are interface conditions; and a linguistic expression is the optimal realization of such interface conditions. Let us consider these notions more closely.

Consider a representation π at PF. PF is a representation in universal phonetics, with no indication of syntactic elements or relations among them (X-bar structure, binding, government, etc.). To be interpreted by the performance systems A-P, π must be constituted entirely of *legitimate PF objects*, that is, elements that have a uniform, language-independent interpretation at the interface. In that case, we will say that σ satisfies the condition of *Full Interpretation* (FI). If π fails FI, it does not provide appropriate instructions to the performance systems. We take FI to be the convergence condition: if π satisfies FI, the derivation D that formed it converges at PF; otherwise, it crashes at PF. For example, if π contains a stressed consonant or a [+high, +low] vowel, then D crashes; similarly, if π contains some morphological element that "survives" to PF, lacking any interpretation at the interface. If D converges at PF, its output π receives an articulatory-perceptual interpretation, perhaps as gibberish.

All of this is straightforward—indeed, hardly more than an expression of what is tacitly assumed. We expect exactly the same to be true at LF.

To make ideas concrete, we must spell out explicitly what are the legitimate objects at PF and LF. At PF, this is the standard problem of universal phonetics. At LF, we assume each legitimate object to be a chain $CH = (\alpha_1, \ldots, \alpha_n)$: at least (perhaps at most) with CH a head, an argument, a modifier, or an operator-variable construction. We now say that the representation λ satisfies FI at LF if it consists entirely of legitimate objects; a derivation forming λ converges at LF if λ satisfies FI, and otherwise crashes. A convergent derivation may produce utter gibberish, exactly as at PF. Linguistic expressions may be "deviant" along all sorts of incommensurable dimensions, and we have no notion of "well-formed sentence" (see note 7). Expressions have the interpretations assigned to them by the performance systems in which the language is embedded: period.

To develop these notions properly, we must proceed to characterize notions with the basic properties of A- and Ā-position. These notions were well defined in the *LGB* framework, but in terms of assumptions that are no longer held, in particular, the assumption that θ-marking is restricted to sisterhood, with multiple-branching constructions. With these assumptions abandoned, the notions are used only in an intuitive sense. To replace them, let us consider more closely the morphological properties of lexical items, which play a major role in the minimalist program we are sketching.

Consider the verbal system of (2). The main verb typically "picks up" the features of Tense and Agr (in fact, both Agr_S and Agr_O in the general case), adjoining to an inflectional element I to form [V I]. There are two ways to interpret the process, for a lexical element α. One is to take α to be a bare, uninflected form; PF rules are then designed to interpret the abstract complex [α I] as a single inflected phonological word. The other approach is to take α to have inflectional features in the lexicon as an intrinsic property (in the spirit of lexicalist phonology); these features are then checked against the inflectional element I in the complex [α I].[31] If the features of α and I match, I disappears and α enters the PF component under Spell-Out; if they conflict, I remains and the derivation crashes at

PF. The PF rules, then, are simple rewriting rules of the usual type, not more elaborate rules applying to complexes [α I].

I have been tacitly assuming the second option. Let us now make that choice explicit. Note that we need no longer adopt the Emonds-Pollock assumption that in English-type languages I lowers to V. V will have the inflectional features before Spell-Out in any event, and the checking procedure may take place anywhere, in particular, after LF movement. French-type and English-type languages now look alike at LF, whereas lowering of I in the latter would have produced adjunction structures quite unlike those of the raising languages.

There are various ways to make a checking theory precise, and to capture generalizations that hold across morphology and syntax. Suppose, for example, that Baker's Mirror Principle is strictly accurate. Then we may take a lexical element—say, the verb V—to be a sequence $V = (\alpha, \text{Infl}_1, \ldots, \text{Infl}_n)$, where α is the morphological complex $[\text{R-Infl}_1\text{-}\ldots\text{-Infl}_n]$, R a root and Infl_i an inflectional feature.[32] The PF rules only "see" α. When V is adjoined to a functional category F (say, Agr_O), the feature Infl_1 is removed from V if it matches F; and so on. If any Infl_i remains at LF, the derivation crashes at LF. The PF form α always satisfies the Mirror Principle in a derivation that converges at LF. Other technologies can readily be devised. In this case, however, it is not clear that such mechanisms are in order; the most persuasive evidence for the Mirror Principle lies outside the domain of inflectional morphology, which may be subject to different principles. Suppose, say, that richer morphology tends to be more "visible," that is, closer to the word boundary; if so, and if the speculations of the paragraph ending with note 13 are on the right track, we would expect nominative or absolutive agreement (depending on language type) to be more peripheral in the verbal morphology.

The functional elements Tense and Agr therefore incorporate features of the verb. Let us call these features *V-features*: the function of the V-features of an inflectional element I is to check the morphological properties of the verb selected from the lexicon. More generally, let us call such features of a lexical item L *L-features*. Keeping to the X-bar-theoretic notions, we say that a position is *L-related* if it is in a local relation to an L-feature, that is, in the internal domain or checking domain of a head with an L-feature. Furthermore, the checking domain can be subdivided into two categories: nonadjoined (Spec) and adjoined. Let us call these positions *narrowly* and *broadly* L-related, respectively. A structural position that is narrowly L-related has the basic properties of A-positions; one that is not L-related has the basic properties of $\overline{A}$-positions, in particular, [Spec, C], not L-related if C does not contain a V-feature. The status of broadly L-related (adjoined) positions has been debated, particularly in the theory of scrambling.[33] For our limited purposes, we may leave the matter open.

Note that we crucially assume, as is plausible, that V-raising to C is actually I-raising, with V incorporated within I, and is motivated by properties of the (C, I) system, not morphological checking of V. C has other properties that distinguish it from the V-features.

The same considerations extend to nouns (assuming the D head of DP to have N-features) and adjectives. Putting this aside, we can continue to speak informally of A- and $\overline{A}$-positions, understood in terms of L-relatedness as a first approximation only, with further refinement still necessary. We can proceed, then, to define the legitimate LF objects CH = $(\alpha_1, \ldots, \alpha_n)$ in something like the familiar way: heads, with α_i an X^0; arguments, with α_i in an A-position; adjuncts, with α_i in an $\overline{A}$-position; and operator-variable constructions, to which we will briefly return.[34] This approach seems relatively unproblematic. Let us assume so, and proceed.

The morphological features of Tense and Agr have two functions: they check properties of the verb that raises to them, and they check properties of the NP (DP) that raises to their Spec position; thus, they ensure that DP and V are properly paired. Generalizing the checking theory, let us assume that, like verbs, nouns are drawn from the lexicon with all of their morphological features, including Case and ϕ-features, and that these too must be checked in the appropriate position:[35] in this case, [Spec, Agr] (which may include T or V). This checking too can take place at any stage of a derivation to LF.

A standard argument for S-Structure conditions in the Case module is that Case features appear at PF but must be "visible" at LF; hence, Case must be present by the time the derivation reaches S-Structure. But that argument collapses under a checking theory. We may proceed, then, with the assumption that the Case Filter is an interface condition—in fact, the condition that all morphological features must be checked somewhere, for convergence. There are many interesting and subtle problems to be addressed; reluctantly, I will put them aside here, merely asserting without argument that a proper understanding of economy of derivation goes a long way (maybe all the way) toward resolving them.[36]

Next consider subject-verb agreement, as in *John hits Bill.* The ϕ-features appear in three positions in the course of the derivation: internal to *John*, internal to *hits*, and in Agr$_S$. The verb *hits* raises ultimately to Agr$_S$ and the NP *John* to [Spec, Agr$_S$], each checking its morphological features. If the lexical items were properly chosen, the derivation converges. But at PF and LF the ϕ-features appear only twice, not three times: in the NP and verb that agree. Agr plays only a mediating role: when it has performed its function, it disappears. Since this function is dual, V-related and NP-related, Agr must in fact have two kinds of features: V-features that check V adjoined to Agr, and NP-features that check NP in [Spec, Agr]. The same is true of T, which checks the tense of the verb and the Case of the subject. The V-features of an inflectional element disappear when they check V, the NP-features when they check NP (or N, or DP; see note 35). All this is automatic, and within the minimalist program.

Let us now return to the first type of S-Structure condition (21a), the position of Spell-Out: after V-raising in French-type languages, before V-raising in English-type languages (we have now dispensed with lowering). As we have seen, the minimalist program permits only one solution to the problem: PF conditions reflecting morphological properties must force V-raising in French but not in English. What can these conditions be?

Recall the underlying intuition of Pollock's approach, which we are basically assuming: French-type languages have "strong" Agr, which forces overt raising, and English-type languages have "weak" Agr, which blocks it. Let us adopt that idea, rephrasing it in our terms: the V-features of Agr are strong in French, weak in English. Recall that when the V-features have done their work, checking adjoined V, they disappear. If V does not raise to Agr overtly, the V-features survive to PF. Let us now make the natural assumption that "strong" features are visible at PF and "weak" features invisible at PF. These features are not legitimate objects at PF; they are not proper components of phonetic matrices. Therefore, if a strong feature remains after Spell-out, the derivation crashes.[37] In French overt raising is a prerequisite for convergence; in English it is not.

Two major questions remain: Why is overt raising barred in English? Why do the English auxiliaries *have* and *be* raise overtly, as do verbs in French?

The first question is answered by a natural economy condition: LF movement is "cheaper" than overt movement (call the principle *Procrastinate*). The intuitive idea is that LF operations are a kind of "wired-in" reflex, operating mechanically beyond any directly observable effects. They are less costly than overt operations. The system tries to reach PF "as fast as possible," minimizing overt syntax. In English-type languages, overt raising is not forced for convergence; therefore, it is barred by economy principles.

To deal with the second question, consider again the intuition that underlies Pollock's account: raising of the auxiliaries reflects their semantic vacuity; they are placeholders for certain constructions, at most "very light" verbs. Adopting the intuition (but not the accompanying technology), let us assume that such elements, lacking semantically relevant features, are not visible to LF rules. If they have not raised overtly, they will not be able to raise by LF rules and the derivation will crash.[38]

Now consider the difference between SVO (or SOV) languages like English (Japanese) and VSO languages like Irish. On our assumptions, V has raised overtly to I (Agr_S) in Irish, while S and O raise in the LF component to [Spec, Agr_S] and [Spec, Agr_O], respectively.[39] We have only one way to express these differences: in terms of the strength of the inflectional features. One possibility is that the NP-feature of Tense is strong in English and weak in Irish. Hence, NP must raise to [Spec, [Agr T]] in English prior to Spell-Out or the derivation will not converge. The Procrastinate principle bars such raising in Irish. The Extended Projection Principle, which requires that [Spec, IP] be realized (perhaps by an empty category), reduces to a morphological property of Tense: strong or weak NP-features. Note that the NP-feature of Agr is weak in English; if it were strong, English would exhibit overt object shift. We are still keeping to the minimal assumption that Agr_S and Agr_O are collections of features, with no relevant subject-object distinction, hence no difference in strength of features. Note also that a language might allow both weak and strong inflection, hence weak and strong NP-features: Arabic is a suggestive case, with SVO versus VSO correlating with the richness of visible verb inflection.

Along these lines, we can eliminate S-Structure conditions on raising and lowering in favor of morphological properties of lexical items, in accord with the minimalist program. Note that a certain typology of languages is predicted; whether correctly or not remains to be determined.

If Watanabe's (1991) theory of *wh*-movement is correct, there is no parametric variation with regard to *wh*- in situ: language differences (say, English-Japanese) reduce to morphology, in this case, the internal morphology of the *wh*-phrases. Still, the question arises why raising of the *wh*-operator is ever overt, contrary to Procrastinate. The basic economy-of-derivation assumption is that operations are driven by necessity: they are "last resort," applied if they must be, not otherwise (Chomsky 1986b,

1991a). Our assumption is that operations are driven by morphological necessity: certain features must be checked in the checking domain of a head, or the derivation will crash. Therefore, raising of an operator to [Spec, CP] must be driven by such a requirement. The natural assumption is that C may have an operator feature (which we can take to be the Q- or *wh*-feature standardly assumed in C in such cases), and that this feature is a morphological property of such operators as *wh-*. For appropriate C, the operators raise for feature checking to the checking domain of C: [Spec, CP], or adjunction to specifier (absorption), thereby satisfying their scopal properties.[40] Topicalization and focus could be treated the same way. If the operator feature of C is strong, the movement must be overt. Raising of I to C may automatically make the relevant feature of C strong (the V2 phenomenon). If Watanabe is correct, the *wh*-operator feature is universally strong.

5   Extensions of the Minimalist Program

Let us now look more closely at the economy principles. These apply to both representations and derivations. With regard to the former, we may take the economy principle to be nothing other than FI: every symbol must receive an "external" interpretation by language-independent rules. There is no need for the Projection Principle or θ-Criterion at LF. A convergent derivation might violate them, but in that case it would receive a defective interpretation.

The question of economy of derivations is more subtle. We have already noted two cases: Procrastinate, which is straightforward, and the "Last Resort" principle, which is more intricate. According to that principle, a step in a derivation is legitimate only if it is necessary for convergence—had the step not been taken, the derivation would not have converged. NP-raising, for example, is driven by the Case Filter (now assumed to apply only at LF): if the Case feature of NP has already been checked, NP may not raise. For example, (26a) is fully interpretable, but (26b) is not.

(26) a. There is [$_\alpha$ a strange man] in the garden
     b. There seems to [$_\alpha$ a strange man] [that it is raining outside]

In (26a) α is not in a proper position for Case checking; therefore, it must raise at LF, adjoining to the LF affix *there* and leaving the trace *t*. The phrase α is now in the checking domain of the matrix inflection. The matrix subject at LF is [α-*there*], an LF word with all features checked but interpretable only in the position of the trace *t* of the chain (α, t), its head being "invisible" word-internally. In contrast, in (26b) α has its Case properties satisfied internal to the PP, so it is not permitted to raise, and we are left with freestanding *there*. This is a legitimate object, a one-membered A-chain with all its morphological properties checked. Hence, the derivation converges. But there is no coherent interpretation, because freestanding *there* receives no semantic interpretation (and in fact is unable to receive a θ-role even in a θ-position). The derivation thus converges, as semigibberish.

The notion of Last Resort operation is in part formulable in terms of economy: a shorter derivation is preferred to a longer one, and if the derivation D converges without application of some operation, then that application is disallowed. In (26b) adjunction of α to *there* would yield an intelligible interpretation (something like "There is a strange man to whom it seems that it is raining outside"). But adjunction is not permitted: the derivation converges with an unintelligible interpretation. Derivations are driven by the narrow mechanical requirement of feature checking only, not by a "search for intelligibility" or the like.

Note that raising of α in (26b) is blocked by the fact that *its own requirements* are satisfied without raising, even though such raising would arguably overcome inadequacies of the LF affix *there*. More generally, Move α applies to an element α only if morphological properties of α itself are not otherwise satisfied. The operation cannot apply to α to enable some different element β to satisfy *its* properties. Last Resort, then, is always "self-serving": benefiting other elements is not allowed. Alongside Procrastinate, then, we have a principle of *Greed*: self-serving Last Resort.

Consider the expression (27), analogous to (26b) but without *there*-insertion from the lexicon.

(27) Seems to [$_\alpha$ a strange man] [that it is raining outside]

Here the matrix T has an NP-feature (Case feature) to discharge, but α cannot raise (overtly or covertly) to overcome that defect. The derivation cannot converge, unlike (26b), which converges but without a proper interpretation. The self-serving property of Last Resort cannot be overridden even to ensure convergence.

Considerations of economy of derivation tend to have a "global" character, inducing high-order computational complexity. Computational complexity may or may not be an empirical defect; it is a question of whether the cases are correctly characterized (e.g., with complexity properly relating to parsing difficulty, often considerable or extreme, as is well known). Nevertheless, it makes sense to expect language design to limit such problems. The self-serving property of Last Resort has the effect of restricting the class of derivations that have to be considered in determining optimality, and might be shown on closer analysis to contribute to this end.[41]

Formulating economy conditions in terms of the principles of Procrastinate and Greed, we derive a fairly narrow and determinate notion of *most economical convergent derivation* that blocks all others. Precise formulation of these ideas is a rather delicate matter, with a broad range of empirical consequences.

We have also assumed a notion of "shortest link," expressible in terms of the operation Form Chain. We thus assume that, given two convergent derivations D_1 and D_2, both minimal and containing the same number of steps, D_1 blocks D_2 if its links are shorter. Pursuing this intuitive idea, which must be considerably sharpened, we can incorporate aspects of Subjacency and the ECP, as briefly indicated.

Recall that for a derivation to converge, its LF output must be constituted of legitimate objects: tentatively, heads, arguments, modifiers, and operator-variable constructions. A problem arises in the case of pied-piped constructions such as (28).

(28) (Guess) [[$_{wh\text{-}}$ in which house] John lived t]

The chain $(wh\text{-}, t)$ is not an operator-variable construction. The appropriate LF form for interpretation requires "reconstruction," as in (29).

(29) a. [which x, x a house] John lived [in x]
     b. [which x] John lived [in [x house]]

Assume that (29a) and (29b) are alternative options. There are various ways in which these options can be interpreted. For concreteness, let us select a particularly simple one.[42]

Suppose that in (29a) x is understood as a DP variable: regarded substitutionally, it can be replaced by a DP (the answer can be *The old one*); regarded objectually, it ranges over houses, as determined by the restricted operator. In (29b) x is a D variable: regarded substitutionally, it can be replaced by a D (the answer can be *That (house)*); regarded objectually, it ranges over entities.

Reconstruction is a curious operation, particularly when it is held to follow LF movement, thus restoring what has been covertly moved, as often proposed (e.g., for (23c)). If possible, the process should be eliminated. An approach that has occasionally been suggested is the "copy theory" of movement: the trace left behind is a copy of the moved element, deleted by a principle of the PF component in the case of overt movement. But at LF the copy remains, providing the materials for "reconstruction." Let us consider this possibility, surely to be preferred if it is tenable.

The PF deletion operation is, very likely, a subcase of a broader principle that applies in ellipsis and other constructions. Consider such expressions as (30a–b).

(30) a. John said that he was looking for a cat, and so did Bill
     b. John said that he was looking for a cat, and so did Bill [$_E$ say that he was looking for a cat]

The first conjunct is several-ways ambiguous. Suppose we resolve the ambiguities in one of the possible ways, say, by taking the pronoun to refer to Tom and interpreting *a cat* nonspecifically, so that John said that Tom's quest would be satisfied by any cat. In the elliptical case (30a), a parallelism requirement of some kind (call it PR) requires that the second conjunct must be interpreted the same way—in this case, with *he* referring to *Tom* and *a cat* understood nonspecifically (Lakoff 1970, Lasnik 1972, Sag 1976, Ristad 1990). The same is true in the full sentence (30b), a nondeviant linguistic expression with a distinctive low-falling intonation for E; it too must be assigned its properties by the theory of grammar. PR surely applies at LF. Since it must apply to (30b), the simplest assumption would be that only (30b) reaches LF, (30a) being derived from (30b) by an operation of the PF component deleting copies. There would be no need, then, for special mechanisms to account for the parallelism properties of (30a). Interesting questions arise when this path is followed, but it seems promising. If so, the trace deletion operation may well be an obligatory variant of a more general operation applying in the PF component.

Assuming this approach, (28) is a notational abbreviation for (31).

(31) [$_{wh-}$ in which house] John lived [$_{wh-}$ in which house]

The LF component converts the phrase *wh-* to either (32a) or (32b) by an operation akin to QR.

(32) a. [which house] [$_{wh-}$ in t]
     b. [which] [$_{wh-}$ in [t house]]

We may give these the intuitive interpretations of (33a–b).

(33) a. [which x, x a house] [in x]
     b. [which x] [in [x house]]

For convergence at LF, we must have an operator-variable structure. Accordingly, in the operator position [Spec, CP], everything but the operator phrase must delete; therefore, the phrase *wh-* of (32) deletes. In the trace position, the copy of what remains in the operator position deletes, leaving just the phrase *wh-* (an LF analogue to the PF rule just described). In the present case (perhaps generally), these choices need not be specified; other options will crash. We thus derive LF forms interpreted as (29a) or (29b), depending on which option we have selected. The LF forms now consist of legitimate objects, and the derivations converge.

Along the same lines, we will interpret *Which book did John read* either as "[which x, x a book] [John read x]" (answer: *War and Peace*) or "[which x] [John read [x book]]" (answer: *That (book)*).

The assumptions are straightforward and minimalist in spirit. They carry us only partway toward an analysis of reconstruction and interpretation; there are complex and obscure phenomena, many scarcely understood. Insofar as these assumptions are tenable and properly generalizable, we can eliminate reconstruction as a separate process, keeping the term only as part of informal descriptive apparatus for a certain range of phenomena.

Extending observations of Van Riemsdijk and Williams (1981), Freidin (1986) points out that such constructions as (34a–b) behave quite differently under reconstruction.[43]

(34) a. Which claim [that John was asleep] was he willing to discuss
       b. Which claim [that John made] was he willing to discuss

In (34a) reconstruction takes place: the pronoun does not take *John* as antecedent. In contrast, in (34b) reconstruction is not obligatory and the anaphoric connection is an option. While there are many complications, to a first approximation the contrast seems to reduce to a difference between complement and adjunct, the bracketed clause of (34a) and (34b), respectively. Lebeaux (1988) proposed an analysis of this distinction in terms of generalized transformations. In case (34a) the complement must appear at the level of D-Structure; in case (34b) the adjunct could be adjoined by a generalized transformation in the course of derivation, in fact, after whatever processes are responsible for the reconstruction effect.[44]

The approach is appealing, if problematic. For one thing, there is the question of the propriety of resorting to generalized transformations. For another, the same reasoning forces reconstruction in the case of A-movement. Thus, (35) is analogous to (34a); the complement is present before raising and should therefore force a Condition C violation.

(35) The claim that John was asleep seems to him [$_{IP}$ t to be correct]

Under the present interpretation, the trace t is spelled out as identical to the matrix subject. While it deletes at PF, it remains at LF, yielding the unwanted reconstruction effect. Condition C of the binding theory requires that the pronoun *him* cannot take its antecedent within the embedded IP (compare *I seem to him [to like John], with *him* anaphoric to *John*). But *him* can take *John* as antecedent in (35), contrary to the prediction.

The proposal now under investigation overcomes these objections. We have moved to a full-blown theory of generalized transformations, so there is no problem here. The extension property for substitution entails that complements can only be introduced cyclically, hence before *wh*-extraction, while adjuncts can be introduced noncyclically, hence adjoined to the *wh*-phrase after raising to [Spec, CP]. Lebeaux's analysis of (34) therefore could be carried over. As for (35), if "reconstruction" is essentially a reflex of the formation of operator-variable constructions, it will hold only for $\overline{\text{A}}$-chains, not for A-chains. That conclusion seems plausible over a considerable range, and yields the right results in this case.

Let us return now to the problem of binding-theoretic conditions at S-Structure. We found a weak but sufficient argument (of type (22a)) to reject the conclusion that Condition C applies at S-Structure. What about Condition A?

Consider constructions such as those in (36).[45]

(36) a. i. John wondered [which picture of himself] [Bill saw t]
          ii. The students asked [what attitudes about each other]
               [the teachers had noticed t]
      b. i. John wondered [who [t saw [which picture of himself]]]
          ii. The students asked [who [t had noticed [what attitudes
               about each other]]]

The sentences of (36a) are ambiguous, with the anaphor taking either the matrix or embedded subject as antecedent; but those of (36b) are unambiguous, with the trace of *who* as the only antecedent for *himself*, *each other*. If (36b) were formed by LF raising of the in-situ *wh*-phrase, we would have to conclude that Condition A applies at S-Structure, prior to this operation. But we have already seen that the assumption is unwarranted; we have, again, a weak but sufficient argument against allowing binding theory to apply at S-Structure. A closer look shows that we can do still better.

Under the copying theory, the actual forms of (36a) are (37a–b).

(37) a. John wondered [$_{wh\text{-}}$ which picture of himself] [Bill saw
      [$_{wh\text{-}}$ which picture of himself]]

   b. The students asked [$_{wh\text{-}}$ what attitudes about each other]
      [the teachers had noticed [$_{wh\text{-}}$ what attitudes about each other]]

The LF principles map (37a) to either (38a) or (38b), depending on which option is selected for analysis of the phrase *wh-*.

(38) a. John wondered [[which picture of himself] [$_{wh\text{-}}$ *t*]] [Bill saw
      [[which picture of himself] [$_{wh\text{-}}$ *t*]]]

   b. John wondered [which [$_{wh\text{-}}$ *t* picture of himself]] [Bill saw
      [which [$_{wh\text{-}}$ *t* picture of himself]]]

We then interpret (38a) as (39a) and (38b) as (39b), as before.

(39) a. John wondered [which *x*, *x* a picture of himself] [Bill saw *x*]

   b. John wondered [which *x*] [Bill saw [*x* picture of himself]]

Depending on which option we have selected, *himself* will be anaphoric to *John* or to *Bill*.[46]

The same analysis applies to (37b), yielding the two options of (40) corresponding to (39).

(40) a. The students asked [what *x*, *x* attitudes about each other]
      [the teachers had noticed *x*]

   b. The students asked [what *x*] [the teachers had noticed
      [*x* attitudes about each other]]

In (40a) the antecedent of *each other* is *the students*; in (40b) it is *the teachers*.

Suppose that we change the examples of (36a) to (41a–b), replacing *saw* by *took* and *had noticed* by *had*.

(41) a. John wondered [which picture of himself] [Bill took *t*]

   b. The students asked [what attitudes about each other]
      [the teachers had]

Consider (41a). As before, *himself* can take either *John* or *Bill* as antecedent. There is a further ambiguity: the phrase *take . . . picture* can be interpreted either idiomatically (in the sense of "photograph") or literally ("pick up and walk away with"). But the interpretive options correlate with the choice of antecedent for *himself*: if the antecedent is *John*, the idiomatic interpretation is barred; if the antecedent is *Bill*, it is permitted. If *Bill* is replaced by *Mary*, the idiomatic interpretation is excluded.

The pattern is similar for (41b), except that there is no literal-idiomatic ambiguity. The only interpretation is that the students asked what attitudes each of the teachers had about the other teacher(s). If *the teachers* is replaced by *Jones*, there is no interpretation.

Why should the interpretations distribute in this manner?

First consider (41a). The principles already discussed yield the two LF options in (42a–b).

(42) a. John wondered [which x, x a picture of himself] [Bill took x]
       b. John wondered [which x] [Bill took [x picture of himself]]

If we select the option (42a), then *himself* takes *John* as antecedent by Condition A at LF; if we select the option (42b), then *himself* takes *Bill* as antecedent by the same principle. If we replace *Bill* with *Mary*, then (42a) is forced. Having abandoned D-Structure, we must assume that idiom interpretation takes place at LF, as is natural in any event. But we have no operations of LF reconstruction. Thus, *take . . . picture* can be interpreted as "photograph" only if the phrase is present as a unit at LF—that is, in (42b), not (42a). It follows that in (42a) we have only the non-idiomatic interpretation of *take*; in (42b) we have either. In short, only the option (42b) permits the idiomatic interpretation, also blocking *John* as antecedent of the reflexive and barring replacement of *Bill* by *Mary*.

The same analysis holds for (41b). The two LF options are (43a–b).

(43) a. The students asked [what x, x attitudes about each other]
         [the teachers had x]
       b. The students asked [what x] [the teachers had [x attitudes
         about each other]]

Only (43b) yields an interpretation, with *have . . . attitudes* given its unitary sense.

The conclusions follow on the crucial assumption that Condition A *not* apply at S-Structure, prior to the LF rules that form (42).[47] If Condition A were to apply at S-Structure, *John* could be taken as antecedent of *himself* in (41a) and the later LF processes would be free to choose either the idiomatic or the literal interpretation, however the reconstruction phenomena are handled; and *the students* could be taken as antecedent of *each other* in (41b), with reconstruction providing the interpretation of *have . . . attitudes*. Thus, we have the strongest kind of argument against an S-Structure condition (type (22c)): Condition A *cannot* apply at S-Structure.

Note also that we derive a strong argument for LF representation. The facts are straightforwardly explained in terms of a level of representation with two properties: (i) phrases with a unitary interpretation such as the idiom *take...picture* or *have...attitudes* appear as units; (ii) binding theory applies. In standard EST approaches, LF is the only candidate. The argument is still clearer in this minimalist theory, lacking D-Structure and (we are now arguing) S-Structure.

Combining these observations with the Freidin-Lebeaux examples, we seem to face a problem, in fact a near-contradiction. In (44a) either option is allowed: *himself* may take either *John* or *Bill* as antecedent. In contrast, in (44b) reconstruction appears to be forced, barring *Tom* as antecedent of *he* (by Condition C) and *Bill* as antecedent of *him* (by Condition B).

(44) a. John wondered [which picture of himself] [Bill saw *t*]
    b. i.   John wondered [which picture of Tom] [he liked *t*]
      ii. John wondered [which picture of him] [Bill took *t*]
      iii. John wondered [what attitude about him] [Bill had *t*]

The Freidin-Lebeaux theory requires reconstruction in all these cases, the *of*-phrase being a complement of *picture*. But the facts seem to point to a conception that distinguishes Condition A of the binding theory, which does not force reconstruction, from Conditions B and C, which do. Why should this be?

In our terms, the trace *t* in (44) is a copy of the *wh*-phrase at the point where the derivation branches to the PF and LF components. Suppose we now adopt an LF movement approach to anaphora, assuming that the anaphor or part of it raises by an operation similar to cliticization—call it *cliticization*$_{LF}$. This approach at least has the property we want: it distinguishes Condition A from Conditions B and C. Note that cliticization$_{LF}$ is a case of Move α; though applying in the LF component, it necessarily precedes the "reconstruction" operations that provide the interpretations for the LF output. Applying cliticization$_{LF}$ to (44a), we derive either (45a) or (45b), depending on whether the rule applies to the operator phrase or its trace TR.[48]

(45) a. John self-wondered [which picture of t_{self}] [NP saw [$_{TR}$ which picture of himself]]
    b. John wondered [which picture of himself] [NP self-saw [$_{TR}$ which picture of t_{self}]]

We then turn to the LF rules interpreting the *wh*-phrase, which yield the two options (46a–b) (α = either t_{self} or *himself*).

(46) a. [[which picture of α] t]
    b. [which] [t picture of α]

Suppose that we have selected the option (45a). Then we cannot select the interpretive option (46b) (with $\alpha = t_{self}$); that option requires deletion of [t *picture of* t_{self}] in the operator position, which would break the chain (*self*, t_{self}), leaving the reflexive element without a θ-role at LF. We must therefore select the interpretive option (46a), yielding a convergent derivation without reconstruction:

(47) John self-wondered [which x, x a picture of t_{self}] NP saw x

In short, if we take the antecedent of the reflexive to be *John*, then only the nonreconstructing option converges.

If we had *Tom* or *him* in place of *himself*, as in (44b), then these issues would not arise and either interpretive option would converge. We thus have a relevant difference between the two categories of (44). To account for the judgments, it is only necessary to add a preference principle for reconstruction: Do it when you can (i.e., try to minimize the restriction in the operator position). In (44b) the preference principle yields reconstruction, hence a binding theory violation (Conditions C and B). In (44a) we begin with two options with respect to application of cliticization$_{LF}$: either to the operator or to the trace position. If we choose the first option, selecting the matrix subject as antecedent, then the preference principle is inapplicable because only the nonpreferred case converges, and we derive the nonreconstruction option. If we choose the second option, selecting the embedded subject as antecedent, the issue of preference again does not arise. Hence, we have genuine options in the case of (44a), but a preference for reconstruction (hence the judgment that binding theory conditions are violated) in the case of (44b).[49]

Other constructions reinforce these conclusions, for example, (48).[50]

(48) a. i.   John wondered what stories about us we had heard
       ii'. *John wondered what stories about us we had told
       ii". John wondered what stories about us we expected Mary to tell
    b. i'.   John wondered what opinions about himself Mary had heard
       i".   *John wondered what opinions about himself Mary had

> ii′.   They wondered what opinions about each other Mary had heard
>
> ii″.   *They wondered what opinions about each other Mary had
>
> c. i.   John wondered how many pictures of us we expected Mary to take
>
>   ii.   *John wondered how many pictures of us we expected to take [idiomatic sense]

Note that we have further strengthened the argument for an LF level at which all conditions apply: the LF rules, including now anaphor raising, provide a crucial distinction with consequences for reconstruction.

The reconstruction process outlined applies only to operator-variable constructions. What about A-chains, which we may assume to be of the form $CH = (\alpha, t)$ at LF (α the phrase raised from its original position t, intermediate traces deleted or ignored)? Here t is a full copy of its antecedent, deleted in the PF component. The descriptive account must capture the fact that the head of the A-chain is assigned an interpretation in the position t. Thus, in *John was killed t*, *John* is assigned its θ-role in the position t, as complement of *kill*. The same should be true for such idioms as (49).

(49) Several pictures were taken t

Here *pictures* is interpreted in the position of t, optionally as part of the idiom *take...pictures*. Interesting questions arise in the case of such constructions as (50a–b).

(50) a. The students asked [which pictures of each other] [Mary took t]
>   b. The students asked [which pictures of each other] [t' *were taken* t by Mary]

In both cases the idiomatic interpretation requires that t be [x *pictures of each other*] after the operator-variable analysis ("reconstruction"). In (50a) that choice is blocked, while in (50b) it remains open. The examples reinforce the suggested analysis of $\overline{A}$-reconstruction, but it is now necessary to interpret the chain (t', t) in (50b) just as the chain (*several pictures*, t) is interpreted in (49). One possibility is that the trace t of the A-chain enters into the idiom interpretation (and, generally, into θ-marking), while the head of the chain functions in the usual way with regard to scope and other matters.

Suppose that instead of (44a) we have (51).

(50) The students wondered [$_{wh-}$ how angry at each other (themselves)] [John was t]

As in the case of (44a), anaphor raising in (51) should give the interpretation roughly as "The students each wondered [how angry at the other John was]" (similarly with reflexive). But these interpretations are impossible in the case of (51), which requires the reconstruction option, yielding gibberish. Huang (1990) observes that the result follows on the assumption that subjects are predicate-internal (VP-, AP-internal; see (4)), so that the trace of *John* remains in the subject position of the raised operator phrase *wh*-, blocking association of the anaphor with the matrix subject (anaphor raising, in the present account).

Though numerous problems remain unresolved, there seem to be good reasons to suppose that the binding theory conditions hold only at the LF interface. If so, we can move toward a very simple interpretive version of binding theory as in (52) that unites disjoint and distinct reference (D the relevant local domain), overcoming problems discussed particularly by Howard Lasnik.[51]

(52) A. If α is an anaphor, interpret it as coreferential with a c-commanding phrase in D.

B. If α is a pronominal, interpret it as disjoint from every c-commanding phrase in D.

C. If α is an r-expression, interpret it as disjoint from every c-commanding phrase.

Condition A may be dispensable if the approach based upon cliticization$_{LF}$ is correct and the effects of Condition A follow from the theory of movement (which is not obvious); and further discussion is necessary at many points. All indexing could then be abandoned, another welcome result.[52]

Here too we have, in effect, returned to some earlier ideas about binding theory, in this case those of Chomsky 1980a, an approach superseded largely on grounds of complexity (now overcome), but with empirical advantages over what appeared to be simpler alternatives (see note 51).

I stress again that what precedes is only the sketch of a minimalist program, identifying some of the problems and a few possible solutions, and omitting a wide range of topics, some of which have been explored, many not. The program has been pursued with some success. Several related and desirable conclusions seem within reach.

(53) a. A linguistic expression (SD) is a pair (π, λ) generated by an optimal derivation satisfying interface conditions.

b. The interface levels are the only levels of linguistic representation.

    c. All conditions express properties of the interface levels, reflecting interpretive requirements.

    d. UG provides a unique computational system, with derivations driven by morphological properties to which syntactic variation of languages is restricted.

    e. Economy can be given a fairly narrow interpretation in terms of FI, length of derivation, length of links, Procrastinate, and Greed.

Notes

I am indebted to Samuel Epstein, James Higginbotham, Howard Lasnik, and Alec Marantz for comments on an earlier draft of this paper, as well as to participants in courses, lectures, and discussions on these topics at MIT and elsewhere, too numerous to mention.

1. For early examination of these topics in the context of generative grammar, see Chomsky 1951, 1955 (henceforth *LSLT*). On a variety of consequences, see Collins 1992.

2. Not literal necessity, of course; I will avoid obvious qualifications here and below.

3. On its nature, see Bromberger and Halle 1991.

4. Note that while the intuition underlying proposals to restrict variation to elements of morphology is clear enough, it would be no trivial matter to make it explicit, given general problems in selecting among equivalent constructional systems. An effort to address this problem in any general way would seem premature. It is a historical oddity that linguistics, and "soft sciences" generally, are often subjected to methodological demands of a kind never taken seriously in the far more developed natural sciences. Strictures concerning Quinean indeterminacy and formalization are a case in point. See Chomsky 1990, 1992a, Ludlow 1991. Among the many questions ignored here is the fixing of lexical concepts; see Jackendoff 1990 for valuable discussion. For my own views on some general aspects of the issues, see Chomsky 1992a,b.

5. Contrary to common belief, assumptions concerning the reality and nature of I-language (competence) are much better-grounded than those concerning parsing. For some comment, see Chomsky 1992a.

6. Markedness of parameters, if real, could be seen as a last residue of the evaluation metric.

7. See Marantz 1984, Baker 1988, on what Baker calls "the Principle of PF Interpretation," which appears to be inconsistent with this assumption. One might be tempted to interpret the class of expressions of the language L for which there is a convergent derivation as "the well-formed (grammatical) expressions of L." But this seems pointless. The class so defined has no significance. The concepts "well-formed" and "grammatical" remain without characterization or known empirical justification; they played virtually no role in early work on generative

grammar except in informal exposition, or since. See Chomsky 1955, 1965; and on various misunderstandings, Chomsky 1980b, 1986b.

8. Much additional detail has been presented in class lectures at MIT, particularly in Fall 1991. I hope to return to a fuller exposition elsewhere. As a starting point, I assume here a version of linguistic theory along the lines outlined in Chomsky and Lasnik 1991.

9. In Chomsky 1981 and other work, structural Case is unified under government, understood as m-command to include the Spec-head relation (a move that was not without problems); in the framework considered here, m-command plays no role.

10. I will use *NP* informally to refer to either NP or DP, where the distinction is playing no role. *IP* and *I* will be used for the complement of C and its head where details are irrelevant.

11. I overlook here the possibility of NP-raising to [Spec, T] for Case assignment, then to [Spec, Agr$_S$] for agreement. This may well be a real option. For development of this possibility, see Bures 1992, Bobaljik and Carnie 1992, Jonas 1992.

12. Raising of A to Agr$_A$ may be overt or in the LF component. If the latter, it may be the trace of the raised NP that is marked for agreement, with further raising driven by the morphological requirement of Case marking (the Case Filter); I put aside specifics of implementation. The same considerations extend to an analysis of participial agreement along the lines of Kayne 1989; see Chomsky 1991a, Branigan 1992.

13. For development of an approach along such lines, see Bobaljik 1992a,b. For a different analysis sharing some assumptions about the [Spec, head] role, see Murasugi 1991, 1992. This approach to the two language types adapts the earliest proposal about these matters within generative grammar (De Rijk 1972) to a system with inflection separated from verb. See Levin and Massam 1985 for a similar conception.

14. See Chomsky and Lasnik 1991.

15. I put aside throughout the possibility of moving X′ or adjoining to it, and the question of adjunction to elements other than complement that assign or receive interpretive roles at the interface.

16. This is only the simplest case. In the general case V will raise to Agr$_O$, forming the chain CH$_V$ = (V, t). The complex [V Agr$_O$] raises ultimately to adjoin to Agr$_S$. Neither V nor CH$_V$ has a new checking domain assigned in this position. But V is in the checking domain of Agr$_S$ and therefore shares relevant features with it, and the subject in [Spec, Agr$_S$] is in the checking domain of Agr$_S$, hence agrees indirectly with V.

17. To mention one possibility, V-raising to Agr$_O$ yields a two-membered chain, but subsequent raising of the [V Agr$_O$] complex might pass through the trace of T by successive-cyclic movement, finally adjoining to Agr$_S$. The issues raised in note 11 are relevant at this point. I will put these matters aside.

18. Hale and Keyser make a distinction between (i) operations of lexical conceptual structure that form such lexical items as *shelve* and (ii) syntactic operations that raise *put* to V$_1$ in (8), attributing somewhat different properties to (i) and (ii).

These distinctions do not seem to me necessary for their purposes, for reasons that I will again put aside.

19. Note that the ECP will now reduce to descriptive taxonomy, of no theoretical significance. If so, there will be no meaningful questions about conjunctive or disjunctive ECP, the ECP as an LF or PF phenomenon (or both), and so on. Note that no aspect of the ECP can apply at the PF interface itself, since there we have only a phonetic matrix, with no relevant structure indicated. The proposal that the ECP breaks down into a PF and an LF property (as in Aoun et al. 1987) therefore must take the former to apply either at S-Structure or at a new level of "shallow structure" between S-Structure and PF.

20. Note that the two chains in (14) are ([V V_c], t') and (V, t). But in the latter, V is far removed from its trace because of the operation raising [V V_c]. Each step of the derivation satisfies the HMC, though the final output violates it (since the head t' intervenes between V and its trace). Such considerations tend to favor a derivational approach to chain formation over a representational one. See Chomsky 1991a, Chomsky and Lasnik 1991. Recall also that the crucial concept of minimal subdomain could only be interpreted in terms of a derivational approach.

21. Recall that even if Obj is replaced by an element that does not require structural Case, Subj must still raise to [Spec, Agr_S] in a nominative-accusative language (with "active" Agr_S).

22. This formulation allows later insertion of functional items that are vacuous for LF interpretation, for example, the *do* of *do*-support or the *of* of *of*-insertion.

23. This is not to say that θ-theory is dispensable at LF, for example, the principles of θ-discharge discussed in Higginbotham 1985. It is simply that the θ-Criterion and Projection Principle play no role.

24. I know of only one argument against generalized transformations, based on restrictiveness (Chomsky 1965): only a proper subclass of the I-languages (there called "grammars") allowed by the *LSLT* theory appear to exist, and only these are permitted if we eliminate generalized transformations and T-markers in favor of a recursive base satisfying the cycle. Elimination of generalized transformations in favor of cyclic base generation is therefore justified in terms of explanatory adequacy. But the questions under discussion then do not arise in the far more restrictive current theories.

25. A modification is necessary for the case of successive-cyclic movement, interpreted in terms of the operation Form Chain. I put this aside here.

26. Depending on other assumptions, some violations might be blocked by various "conspiracies." Let us assume, nevertheless, that overt substitution operations satisfy the extension (strict cycle) condition generally, largely on grounds of conceptual simplicity.

27. In case (19b) we assumed that V adjoins to (possibly empty) C, the head of CP, but it was the substitution operation inserting *can* that violated the cycle to yield the HMC violation. It has often been argued that LF adjunction may violate the "structure-preserving" requirement of (20), for example, allowing XP incorporation to X^0 or quantifier adjunction to XP. Either conclusion is consistent with the present considerations. See also note 15.

28. On noncyclic adjunction, see Branigan 1992 and section 5 below.

29. See Hornstein and Weinberg 1990 for development of this proposal on somewhat different assumptions and grounds.

30. The technical implementation could be developed in many ways. For now, let us think of it as a rule of interpretation for the paired *wh*-phrases.

31. Technically, α raises to the lowest I to form $[_I \, \alpha \, I]$; then the complex raises to the next higher inflectional element; and so on. Recall that after multiple adjunction, α will still be in the checking domain of the "highest" I.

32. More fully, $Infl_i$ is a collection of inflectional features checked by the relevant functional element.

33. The issue was raised by Webelhuth (1989) and has become a lively research topic. See Mahajan 1990 and much ongoing work. Note that if I adjoins to C, forming $[_C \, I \, C]$, [Spec, C] is in the checking domain of the chain (I, t). Hence, [Spec, C] is L-related (to I), and non-L-related (to C). A sharpening of notions is therefore required to determine the status of C after I-to-C raising. If C has L-features, [Spec, C] is L-related and would thus have the properties of an A-position, not an $\overline{A}$-position. Questions arise here related to proposals of Rizzi (1990) on agreement features in C, and his more recent work extending these notions; these would take us too far afield here.

34. Heads are not narrowly L-related, hence not in A-positions, a fact that bears on ECP issues. See Chomsky and Lasnik 1991: sec. 4.1.

35. I continue to put aside the question whether Case should be regarded as a property of N or D, and the DP-NP distinction generally.

36. See Chomsky and Lasnik 1991: sec. 4.3 for some discussion.

37. Alternatively, weak features are deleted in the PF component so that PF rules can apply to the phonological matrix that remains; strong features are not deleted so that PF rules do not apply, causing the derivation to crash at PF.

38. Note that this is a reformulation of proposals by Emmon Bach and others in the framework of the Standard Theory and Generative Semantics: that these auxiliaries are inserted in the course of derivation, not appearing in the semantically relevant underlying structures. See Tremblay 1991 for an exploration of similar intuitions.

39. This leaves open the possibility that in VSO languages subject raises overtly to [Spec, TP] while T (including the adjoined verb) raises to Agr_S; for evidence that that is correct, see the references of note 11.

40. Raising would take place only to [Spec, CP], if absorption does not involve adjunction to a *wh*-phrase in [Spec, CP]. See note 30. I assume here that CP is not an adjunction target.

41. See Chomsky 1991a,b. The self-serving property may also bear on whether LF operations are costless, or simply less costly.

42. There are a number of descriptive inadequacies in this overly simplified version. Perhaps the most important is that some of the notions used here (e.g., objectual quantification) have no clear interpretation in the case of natural lan-

guage, contrary to common practice. Furthermore, we have no real framework within which to evaluate "theories of interpretation"; in particular, considerations of explanatory adequacy and restrictiveness are hard to introduce, on the standard (and plausible) assumption that the LF component allows no options. The primary task, then, is to derive an adequate descriptive account, no simple matter; comparison of alternatives lacks any clear basis. Another problem is that linking to performance theory is far more obscure than in the case of the PF component. Much of what is taken for granted in the literature on these topics seems to me highly problematic, if tenable at all. See Chomsky 1981, 1992a,b for some comment.

43. The topicalization analogues are perhaps more natural: *the claim that John is asleep (that John made),* ... The point is the same, assuming an operator-variable analysis of topicalization.

44. In Lebeaux's theory, the effect is determined at D-Structure, prior to raising; I will abstract away from various modes of implementing the general ideas reviewed here. For discussion bearing on these issues, see Speas 1990, Epstein 1991. Freidin (1992) proposes that the difference has to do with the difference between LF representation of a predicate (the relative clause) and a complement; as he notes, that approach provides an argument for limiting binding theory to LF (see (22)).

45. In all but the simplest examples of anaphora, it is unclear whether distinctions are to be understood as tendencies (varying in strength for different speakers) or sharp distinctions obscured by performance factors. For exposition, I assume the latter here. Judgments are therefore idealized, as always; whether correctly or not, only further understanding will tell.

46. Recall that LF *wh*-raising has been eliminated in favor of the absorption operation, so that in (36b) the anaphor cannot take the matrix subject as antecedent after LF raising.

47. I ignore the possibility that Condition A applies irrelevantly at S-Structure, the result being acceptable only if there is no clash with the LF application.

48. I put aside here interesting questions that have been investigated by Pierre Pica and others about how the morphology and the raising interact.

49. Another relevant case is (i),

(i) (Guess) which picture of which man he saw t

a Condition C violation if *he* is taken to be bound by *which man* (Higginbotham 1980). As Higginbotham notes, the conclusion is much sharper than in (44b). One possibility is that independently of the present considerations, absorption is blocked from within [Spec, CP], forcing reconstruction to (iia), hence (iib),

(ii) a. which x, he saw [x picture of which man]
    b. which x, y, he saw x picture of [$_{NP}$ y man]

a Condition C violation if *he* is taken to be anaphoric to NP (i.e., within the scope of *which man*). The same reasoning would imply a contrast between (iiia) and (iiib),

(iii) a.   Who would have guessed that proud of John, Bill never was
    b. *who would have guessed that proud of which man, Bill never was

(with absorption blocked, and no binding theory issue). That seems correct; other cases raise various questions.

50. Cases (48ai), (48aii) correspond to the familiar pairs *John* (*heard, told*) *stories about him,* with antecedence possible only in the case of *heard,* presumably reflecting the fact that one tells one's own stories but can hear the stories told by others; something similar holds of the cases in (48b).

51. See the essays collected in Lasnik 1989; also Chomsky and Lasnik 1991.

52. A theoretical apparatus that takes indices seriously as entities, allowing them to figure in operations (percolation, matching, etc.), is questionable on more general grounds. Indices are basically the expression of a relationship, not entities in their own right. They should be replaceable without loss by a structural account of the relation they annotate.

References

Aoun, J., N. Hornstein, D. Lightfoot, and A. Weinberg. 1987. Two types of locality. *Linguistic Inquiry* 18:537–77.

Baker, M. 1988. *Incorporation: A theory of grammatical function changing.* Chicago: University of Chicago Press.

Bobaljik, J. 1992a. Nominally absolutive is not absolutely nominative. In *Proceedings of the 11th West Coast Conference on Formal Linguistics.* CSLI, Stanford University, Stanford, Calif.

Bobaljik, J. 1992b. Ergativity, economy, and the Extended Projection Principle. Ms., MIT.

Bobaljik, J., and A. Carnie. 1992. A minimalist approach to some problems of Irish word order. Ms., MIT. [To appear in the proceedings of the 12th Harvard Celtic Colloquium.]

Branigan, P. 1992. Subjects and complementizers. Doctoral dissertation, MIT.

Bromberger, S., and M. Halle. 1991. Why phonology is different. In *The Chomskyan turn,* ed. A. Kasher. Oxford: Blackwell.

Bures, T. 1992. Re-cycling expletive (and other) sentences. Ms., MIT.

Chomsky, N. 1951. The morphophonemics of Modern Hebrew. Master's thesis, University of Pennsylvania. [Revised 1951 version published by Garland, New York, 1979.]

Chomsky, N. 1955. The logical structure of linguistic theory. Ms., Harvard University. [Revised 1956 version published in part by Plenum, New York, 1975; University of Chicago Press, Chicago, 1985.]

Chomsky, N. 1965. *Aspects of the theory of syntax.* Cambridge, Mass.: MIT Press.

Chomsky, N. 1980a. On binding. *Linguistic Inquiry* 11:1–46.

Chomsky, N. 1980b. *Rules and representations.* New York: Columbia University Press.

Chomsky, N. 1981. *Lectures on government and binding*. Dordrecht: Foris.

Chomsky, N. 1986a. *Barriers*. Cambridge, Mass.: MIT Press.

Chomsky, N. 1986b. *Knowledge of language: Its nature, origin, and use*. New York: Praeger.

Chomsky, N. 1990. On formalization and formal linguistics. *Natural Language & Linguistic Theory* 8:143–47.

Chomsky, N. 1991a. Some notes on economy of derivation and representation. In *Principles and parameters in comparative grammar*, ed. R. Freidin. Cambridge, Mass.: MIT Press.

Chomsky, 1991b. Linguistics and cognitive science: Problems and mysteries. In *The Chomskyan turn*, ed. A. Kasher. Oxford: Blackwell.

Chomsky, N. 1992a. Language and interpretation: Philosophical reflections and empirical inquiry. In *Inference, explanation and other philosophical frustrations*, ed. J. Earman. Berkeley and Los Angeles: University of California Press.

Chomsky, N. 1992b. Explaining language use. Ms., MIT. [Forthcoming in *Philosophical Studies*.]

Chomsky, N., and H. Lasnik. 1991. Principles and parameters theory. To appear in *Syntax: An international handbook of contemporary research*, ed. J. Jacobs, A. von Stechow, W. Sternefeld, and T. Vennemann. Berlin: de Gruyter.

Collins, C. 1992. Economy of derivation and the Generalized Proper Binding Condition. Ms., MIT.

Curtiss, S. 1981. Dissociations between language and cognition. *Journal of Autism and Developmental Disorders* 11:15–30.

De Rijk, R. 1972. Studies in Basque syntax. Doctoral dissertation, MIT.

Epstein, S. D. 1991. *Traces and their antecedents*. Oxford: Oxford University Press.

Freidin, R. 1986. Fundamental issues in the theory of binding. In *Studies in the acquisition of anaphora*, ed. B. Lust. Dordrecht: Reidel.

Freidin, R. 1992. The principles and parameters framework of generative grammar. Ms., Princeton University. [To appear in *Encyclopedia of languages and linguistics*, ed. R. E. Asher. Edinburgh: Pergamon.]

Hale, K., and S. J. Keyser. 1993. On argument structure and the lexical expression of syntactic relations. In *The view from Building 20: Essays in linguistics in honor of Sylvain Bromberger*, ed. K. Hale and S. J. Keyser. Cambridge, Mass.: MIT Press. [This volume.]

Higginbotham, J. 1980. Pronouns and bound variables. *Linguistic Inquiry* 11:679–708.

Higginbotham, J. 1985. On semantics. *Linguistic Inquiry* 16:547–93.

Higginbotham, J., and R. May. 1981. Questions, quantifiers, and crossing. *The Linguistic Review* 1:41–80.

Hornstein, N., and A. Weinberg. 1990. The necessity of LF. *The Linguistic Review* 7: 129–67.

Huang, C.-T. J. 1982. Logical relations in Chinese and the theory of grammar. Doctoral dissertation, MIT.

Huang, C.-T. J. 1990. A note on reconstruction and VP movement. Ms., Cornell University.

Jackendoff, R. 1990. *Semantic structures.* Cambridge, Mass.: MIT Press.

Jonas, D. 1992. Transitive expletive constructions in Icelandic and Middle English. Ms., Harvard University.

Kayne, R. 1989. Facets of past participle agreement in Romance. In *Dialect variation in the theory of grammar,* ed. P. Benincà. Foris: Dordrecht.

Kroch, A. 1989. Asymmetries in long distance extraction in a tree adjoining grammar. In *Alternative conceptions of phrase structure,* ed. M. Baltin and A. Kroch. Chicago: University of Chicago Press.

Kroch, A., and A. Joshi. 1985. The linguistic relevance of tree adjoining grammar. Technical report MS-CIS-85-16, Department of Computer and Informational Sciences, University of Pennsylvania.

Laka, I. 1990. Negation in syntax: On the nature of functional categories and projections. Doctoral dissertation, MIT.

Lakoff, G. 1970. *Irregularity in syntax.* New York: Holt, Rinehart and Winston.

Larson, R. 1988. On the double object construction. *Linguistic Inquiry* 19: 335–91.

Lasnik, H. 1972. Analyses of negation in English. Doctoral dissertation, MIT.

Lasnik, H. 1989. *Essays on anaphora.* Dordrecht: Reidel.

Lebeaux, D. 1988. Language acquisition and the form of the grammar. Doctoral dissertation, University of Massachusetts, Amherst.

Levin, J., and D. Massam. 1985. Surface ergativity: Case/Theta relations reexamined. In *Proceedings of NELS 15.* GLSA, University of Massachusetts, Amherst.

Ludlow, P. 1991. Formal rigor and linguistic theory. Ms., SUNY, Stony Brook.

Mahajan, A. 1990. The A/A-bar distinction and movement theory. Doctoral dissertation, MIT.

Marantz, A. 1984. *On the nature of grammatical relations.* Cambridge, Mass.: MIT Press.

Murasugi, K. 1991. The role of transitivity in ergative and accusative languages: The cases of Inuktitut and Japanese. Paper presented at the Association of Canadian Universities for Northern Studies.

Murasugi, K. 1992. NP-movement and the ergative parameter. Doctoral dissertation, MIT.

Pollock, J.-Y. 1989. Verb movement, Universal Grammar, and the structure of IP. *Linguistic Inquiry* 20:365–424.

Reinhart, T. 1991. Elliptic conjunctions—nonquantificational LF. In *The Chomskyan turn*, ed. A. Kasher. Oxford: Blackwell.

Riemsdijk, H. van, and E. Williams. 1981. NP-Structure. *The Linguistic Review* 1:171–217.

Ristad, E. 1990. Computational structure of human language. Doctoral dissertation, MIT.

Rizzi, L. 1982. *Issues in Italian syntax*. Dordrecht: Foris.

Rizzi, L. 1986. Null objects in Italian and the theory of *pro*. *Linguistic Inquiry* 17:501–57.

Rizzi, L. 1990. *Relativized Minimality*. Cambridge, Mass.: MIT Press.

Sag, I. 1976. Deletion and Logical Form. Doctoral dissertation, MIT.

Smith, N., and I. M. Tsimpli. 1991. Linguistic modularity? A case study of a *"savant"* linguist. *Lingua* 84:315–51.

Speas, M. 1990. Generalized transformations and the D-Structure position of adjuncts. Ms., University of Massachusetts, Amherst.

Tremblay, M. 1991. Possession and datives. Doctoral dissertation, McGill University.

Vikner, S. 1990. Verb movement and the licensing of NP-positions in the Germanic languages. Doctoral dissertation, University of Geneva.

Watanabe, A. 1991. *Wh*-in-situ, Subjacency, and chain formation. Ms., MIT.

Webelhuth, G. 1989. Syntactic saturation phenomena and the modern Germanic languages. Doctoral dissertation, University of Massachusetts, Amherst.

Yamada, J. 1990. *Laura: A case for the modularity of language*. Cambridge, Mass.: MIT Press.

Chapter 2

On Argument Structure and
the Lexical Expression of
Syntactic Relations

Kenneth Hale and
Samuel Jay Keyser

1 Introduction

For a number of years we have been investigating the relation between lexical items, particularly verbs, and the syntactic structures into which they enter. This is one part of a general program that seeks to explore and understand the implications of the thesis that syntax is projected from the lexicon (see, among other works, Chomsky 1981).

During the course of our investigations, we have become persuaded that the proper representation of predicate argument structure is itself a syntax. That is to say, as a matter of strictly lexical representation, each lexical head projects its category to a phrasal level and determines within that projection an unambiguous system of structural relations holding between the head, its categorial projections, and its arguments (specifier, if present, and complement). We will refer to these projections sometimes as *lexical argument structures* and sometimes as *lexical relational structures* (LRSs), and we will use the now conventional tree diagrams to represent them in our discussions here. The diagrams will also make use of the conventional labels for the lexical categories V, N, P, A, and their phrasal projections V', VP, and so on, but these are to be understood in terms of a particular theory of lexical categories, to be introduced below.

We have been led to this syntactic view of lexical argument structure in large part through an investigation of denominal verbs of the type represented by *calve, lamb, shelve, bottle, saddle, hobble*, and the like. See Clark and Clark 1979 for an impressive array of denominal verb types, and see Talmy 1985 for a discussion of a wide range of lexicalization patterns, including so-called *conflation*, a term we sometimes use to refer to derivation of denominal verbs of the type under consideration here.

Assuming that these verbs are in fact derived from nouns, the process involved in their derivation is almost certainly *lexical*, in the widely accepted sense of that term (see Chomsky 1970). But, we argue, this is quite independent of the question of whether the process is *syntactic* in some equally accepted sense. Thus, for example, if established principles of syntax function to constrain denominal verb derivations, then the simplest assumption to make is that these derivations are in fact syntactic in nature.

The evidence we hint at in the foregoing paragraph only makes sense, of course, within a particular *theory* of denominal verb formation. We assume that verbs like *shelve* and *saddle* are formed by means of the "head movement" variant of Move α—more specifically, by means of the process known as *incorporation*, whose theoretical properties have been studied in detail by Baker (1988). If denominal verb formation takes place by means of incorporation, then it is to be expected that it would be subject to syntactic principles that govern the application of incorporation (e.g., those identified in Baker 1988 and in Baker and Hale 1990). This would be the "evidence" in favor of the syntactic theory (cf. Walinska de Hackbeil 1986, 1989, for a conception of denominal verb formation closely similar to ours).

The so-called unergative verbs (see Perlmutter 1978, Pullum 1988), all called simply *(true) intransitive* verbs (Burzio 1981), represent by far the simplest class of denominal verbs derived by incorporation. For English, these include, among many others, the verbs *laugh, sneeze, neigh, dance, calve*. As shown in (1), their initial lexical projection is simply that of a verb and a nominal complement.

(1)

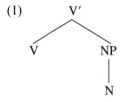

This structure is the same as that projected by verbs such as *make* (as in *make trouble, have* (as in *have puppies*), and *do* (as in *do a jig*). The difference is that the lexical structure representation of an unergative verb, like *laugh*, involves incorporation, into an abstract V, of the nominal head N of its NP complement. We assume, with Baker (1988) and others, that this process is as depicted in (2); that is, the head N of the NP governed by the V is moved and adjoined to the latter. The resulting "compound," of which only the N component is phonologically realized, corresponds to the denominal verb.[1]

(2)

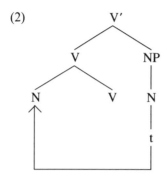

The derivation depicted in (2) conforms to the principles that constrain the syntactic process of incorporation. In particular, it conforms to the Head Movement Constraint in (3) (from Travis 1984; also see Baker 1988).

(3) *The Head Movement Constraint*

An X^0 may only move into the Y^0 that properly governs it.

To this extent at least, we are justified in our assumption that unergative verbs have an initial lexical structure of the simple transitive type. This position is strengthened by the observation that the unergatives of one language are matched in other languages either (i) by the simple transitive VP structure without incorporation (e.g., Basque *lo egin* (sleep do) 'sleep') or (ii) by the transitive VP modified by "visible" incorporation (e.g., Jemez *-záae-'a* (song-do) 'sing').

The relation between the simple transitive structure (1) and the incorporation structure (2) belongs to the class of phenomena sometimes known as *lexical alternations*, whose study has been so revealing in relation to the lexical representations of argument structure (see, for example, Levin 1991). If we are correct in our belief that derivations of the type represented by (2) involve a syntactic process, defined over syntactic objects, then this has clear implications in relation to the nature of argument structure. Argument structure is syntactic, necessarily, since it is to be identified with the syntactic structures projected by lexical heads.

A somewhat more complex class of denominal verbs is that represented by "location" verbs, like *shelve* (as in *shelve the books*), *corral* (as in *corral the horses*), *box* (as in *box the apples*), and "locatum" verbs, like *saddle* (as in *saddle the horse*), *hobble* (as in *hobble the mule*). We will assume that these also, like verbs of the simpler unergative type, are formed by incorporation.

We suppose that, abstractly speaking, the LRS representation of location verbs is identical to that of the English verb *put*, as used in such sentences as (4).

(4) She put her books on the shelf.

And we assign to *put* the structure set out in (5).

(5)

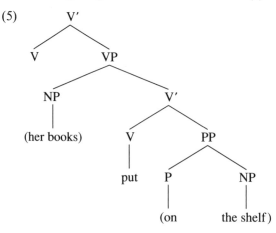

This is the structure that Larson (1988) assigns to verbs of the type represented by *put*, as well as to "double object" or "dative" verbs like *give*. For Larson, this is the D-Structure representation of these verbs. For us, this is their Lexical Argument Structure representation (which, of course, determines the D-Structure representation). In both cases the representations are fundamentally syntactic in the sense that they are structures over which fundamental syntactic relations and principles are defined.[2]

The complex structure (5) is the initial lexical representation of English *put*. The form that appears in the D-Structure representations of sentences containing this verb is derived by head movement, or incorporation, which, in this instance, moves the lower V up into the matrix "clause" and adjoins it to the matrix verb, as depicted in (6).

Like the noun incorporation process involved in (2), the verb incorporation of (6) is in conformity with the Head Movement Constraint, since the matrix verb properly governs the lower verb. Our reasons for assuming the structures (5) and (6) will be explicated in part later in this paper, but they are essentially the reasons found in Larson 1988, Hale 1989, and Hale and Keyser 1991.

It is a fundamental assumption of our account that English verbs like *shelve*, and other location verbs, are "denominal" precisely in the sense

(6)

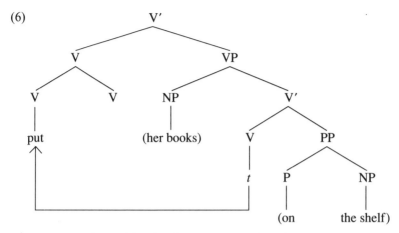

that they are derived by head movement. Their initial LRS representations share their essential relational structure with verbs like *put*, with the exception that the morphological "constant" (i.e., the phonologically overt morpheme ultimately realized in the matrix verb position) is not a verb but a noun, heading the complement of the PP in the LRS representation. This is shown in (7).

(7)

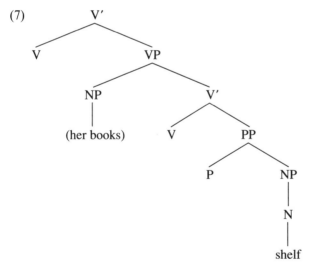

As shown in (8), the surface form of the verb is derived by three applications of head movement, the first of which incorporates the lower N (*shelf*) into the P that governs it. The compound so formed is then moved into the verb that governs it, there forming a compound that makes the final move to incorporate into the matrix verb.

(8)

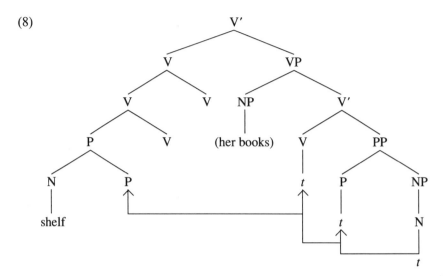

Each step in this derivation conforms to the Head Movement Constraint. At each point, incorporation involves movement into a head that properly governs the moving element.[3]

With the background afforded by these two examples—denominal unergative and location verbs—we can illustrate the central point of this introduction. By hypothesis, these two verb types involve incorporation in their derivations, and the process that effects the incorporation conforms to the Head Movement Constraint. It is appropriate to view this constraint as a special case of the Empty Category Principle (ECP) in (9) (see Chomsky 1981:273).

(9) *Empty Category Principle*

[e] (an empty category) must be properly governed.

For present purposes, we will simply assume Baker's (1988:51–68) argument that the Head Movement Constraint can be derived from the ECP, the trace of head movement being the relevant empty category [e] of (9). The ECP, then, is the effective principle constraining head movement. For reasons noted by Baker (1988:54ff.), *antecedent government* is the relevant government relation for head movement in relation to the ECP.

In the incorporation structures of interest here, an empty category will be properly governed if, among other things, it is antecedent-governed by the relevant incorporated head, for example, by the incorporated N in (2), repeated here as (10).

(10)

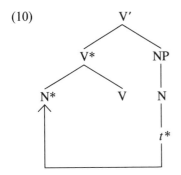

We assume that this condition is met here and in other cases we have examined. The c-command requirement is met under the assumption that the adjunction node (e.g., the upper V-node in (10)) immediately dominating the incorporated element does not count as the first branching node relevant in defining the c-command relation (see Baker 1988:54–55), a circumstance that will follow automatically if, as we will suppose, a zero-level adjunction node acquires the index (or indices, symbolized *) of the adjunct it dominates. In effect, the indexed adjunction node functions as the required antecedent, satisfying the government requirement of the ECP. And the locality requirement for government is met by virtue of the fact that no barrier intervenes between the antecedent and the trace.

Similarly, in more complex derivations (e.g., that of *shelve* depicted in (8), each instance of incorporation results in an antecedent-trace relation that satisfies the ECP. This follows, since each trace in a well-formed derivation is governed by a local c-commanding head that is coindexed with it, given our assumptions.

Let us imagine that the unergative and location verbs briefly examined here are in fact derived by incorporation, or head movement, in the manner indicated. Head movement is a process that is constrained by syntactic principles, and it is expected therefore to limit the range of theoretically possible incorporations. If this is empirically the case, then to that extent we are justified in our belief that these lexical processes are syntactic in nature. And, most important, since the lexical processes we are examining affect the argument structures of lexical items, we are justified in our belief that argument structures are themselves syntactic objects.

To put this another way, if denominal verb formation were not constrained by syntactic principles—if it were simply a process of category change, say—then the range of possible denominal verb types would be expected to include verbs of the sort exemplified in (11). But English simply does not have verbs of this type—transitive verbs that take an expletive subject and have meanings corresponding more or less to the parenthetic paraphrases given here.[4]

(11) a. *It cowed a calf.
          (cf. A cow had a calf. A cow calved.)
     b. *It mared a foal.
          (cf. A mare had a foal. A mare foaled.)
     c. *It dusted the horses blind.
          (cf. The dust made the horses blind. The dust blinded the horses.)
     d. *It machined the wine into bottles.
          (cf. A machine got the wine into bottles. A machine bottled the wine.)

This gap in the English verbal lexicon can be explained within the incorporation theory of denominal verb formation under the natural assumption that the hypothetical verbs of (11) are formed by incorporation of a subject, rather than of a complement. It is well known that a subject (i.e., a subject that originates as an external argument) cannot incorporate into the verb that heads its predicate (see Baker 1988, Mithun 1984). Presumably, incorporation from the subject position, external to VP, would violate the ECP. The question may in fact be academic. We will argue later that the subject of verbs of the type represented in (11) is external in the sense that it is not present at all in Lexical Relational Structure. Lexical incorporation would therefore be impossible. In any event, the incorporation theory of denominal verb formation, a theory determined by syntactic principles, accounts for the nonexistence of the verbs of (11), and of their counterparts in other languages.

English has many lexical items of the form [V ... P], where P is a prepositional particle, such as *take (the business) over, take (a stray cat) in, turn (the stove) on, plow (the corn) under.* Whatever the source and proper analysis of these items, there are no such [V ... P] items that correspond to the hypothetical verbs of the sentences in (12).

(12) a. *He shelved the books on.
          (cf. He put the books on a shelf. He shelved the books.)
     b. *He corralled the horses in.
          (cf. He put the horses in a corral. He corralled the horses.)
     c. *He bottled the wine in.
          (cf. He put the wine in bottles. He bottled the wine.)

Each of these hypothetical items, *shelve (books) on, corral (horses) in, bottle (wine) in*, is derived by incorporation of the noun that heads the complement of the preposition, as shown in (13). The trace of incorporation is thus "too far" from its antecedent and is therefore not properly governed, violating the ECP.

(13)

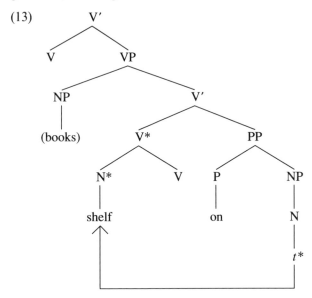

Although the trace is coindexed with the verb to which its antecedent is adjoined (as indicated by the asterisk notation), this verb does not govern the trace. The preposition is a "closer governor," defining PP as the minimal governing domain for the trace (see Chomsky 1986a). By Minimality, therefore, PP is a barrier to government from the more distant verb.

Minimality is also at issue in explaining why English lacks verbs of the hypothetical type in (14).

(14) a. *She churched her money.
        (cf. She gave a church her money.)
     b. *He bushed a trim.
        (cf. He gave a bush a trim.)
     c. *They housed a coat of paint.
        (cf. They gave a house a coat of paint.)

While *church, bush, house,* and many others exist as denominal verbs, they do not exist as denominal verbs having meanings comparable to those of the parenthetic sentences. While the verbs here may be impossible for a variety of reasons, there is a clear structural reason for their nonexistence, on the assumption that their LRS representations would correspond to that depicted in (15) for the hypothetical *house* of (14c).

(15)

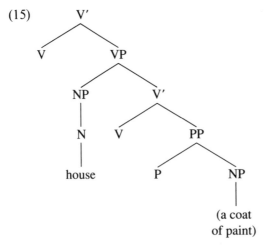

The abstract P here would be a nonovert variant of the category appearing overtly in the expression *provide a house with a coat of paint*. This
structure is in fact widely used in English—as (16) shows, it is the LRS
representation for the large class of locatum verbs, like *saddle, blindfold,
harness, shoe.*

(16)

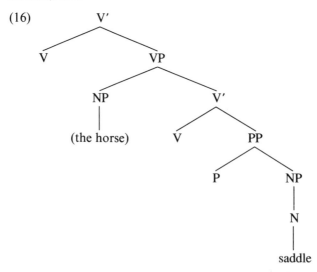

Thus, the verb *saddle* has a structure closely parallel to that of *provide* in
provide the horse with a saddle. Here, the overt noun *saddle* may incorpo-

rate in cyclic fashion into each governing head in complete accordance with the principles of syntax.

But this structure cannot legitimately give rise to verbs of the type represented in (14). These would require incorporation from the "internal subject" position, that is, from Spec(ifier) of VP [(Spec, VP)]. Such incorporation would violate the ECP. Since the inner VP contains a governor (the V that heads it), that VP counts as the immediate governing domain in relation to the NP in its Spec. By Minimality, therefore, the inner VP is a barrier to government from the higher V. Movement of N from Spec position in the inner VP thus violates the ECP (see Baker and Hale 1990).

The same reasoning might explain why English also lacks verbs like those in (17).[5]

(17) a. *She metaled flat.
          (cf. She flattened some metal.)
      b. *He speared straight.
          (cf. He straightened a spear.)
      c. *They screened clear.
          (cf. They cleared a screen.)

Again, these verbs exist, but not in the meanings indicated. Like the verbs of (14), those of (17) are ruled out by virtue of the ECP, on the view that their hypothetical lexical structures would correspond to that assigned to *screen* in (18).

(18)

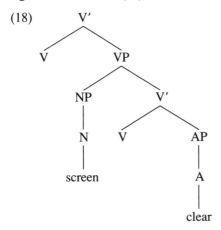

This is essentially the structure of the analytic expressions *make a screen clear, get a screen clear*, and it is the source, by hypothesis, of the well-formed incorporation structure *clear a screen*, formed by successive-cyclic incorporation of the adjective *clear* in conformity with the principles of syntax. But this structure cannot be used to derive the verb of (17c), since that would require incorporation from the Spec position of the inner VP, violating the minimality requirement of the ECP.

In this discussion, we have maintained that certain verbal lexical items of English are derived through the operation of the head movement variant of Move α, that is, by incorporation. We have maintained that this is so because certain gaps in the lexicon can, we think, be explained on the assumption that the formation of the lexical items in question is subject to principles known to be operative in syntax. If this is true, it follows that the structures over which lexical derivations are defined are true syntactic structures, over which syntactic relations are defined. The final step in developing our position in regard to lexical representation is one we must simply assert. But we assert it with the belief that it is well supported by the kinds of linguistic material we have been considering. It is this: the notion "argument structure" is to be identified with the notion "lexical relational structure." Thus, the representation of the argument structure of a verb is a syntactic representation of the usual sort.

This brings us to the main discussion of this paper, namely, a theory of argument structures and the proper characterization of limitations on them.

2   Argument Structure

We take the work we are doing here to be part of a general program of study implied by the Projection Principle (Chomsky 1981) and the notion that syntax is projected from the lexicon. An understanding of argument structure is central to this program. For us, argument structure is to be identified with the syntactic structures defined in Lexical Relational Structure (LRS), as characterized in section 1. In this section we will attempt to be more explicit about the principal features of this conception of argument structure. We begin with an aside, a discussion of the concept "thematic role" (also called θ-role or semantic role) and its relationship to the syntactic projections that we identify with argument structure.

A number of investigators have noted that thematic roles are assigned in a manner corresponding to a hierarchical organization within which certain arguments (associated with certain thematic roles) are "higher" than others (e.g., Bresnan and Kanerva 1989, Carrier-Duncan 1985, Grimshaw 1990, Larson 1988). While there is some disagreement about the exact hierarchical arrangement, particularly in the "middle" and "lower" ranges of the hierarchy, the results of careful and detailed investigations on a number of languages converge to a remarkable degree. The hierarchy of roles set out by Grimshaw (1990:8), depicted in (19), where the most deeply embedded role is the lowest in the hierarchy, exemplifies a system utilized in a fully worked-out theory of argument structure. Other published hierarchies differ from this one in the positioning of the theme role (above GOAL, typically).

(19) (AGENT (EXPERIENCER (GOAL/SOURCE/LOCATION (THEME))))

Among the observable correlates of the hierarchy, for example, is the association of thematic roles with the subject function in syntax (agent, otherwise experiencer, and so on). Moreover, assuming the correct hierarchy, the correlations are universal—that is, they conform to Baker's *Uniformity of Theta Assignment Hypothesis* (UTAH), according to which, for any two natural languages, or for any two items within a single language, the relation in (20) holds.

(20) Identical thematic relationships between items are represented by identical structural relationships between those items at the level of D-Structure.
(Baker 1988:46)

While we feel that the grammatical effects commonly attributed to the thematic hierarchy are genuine, we are not committed to the idea that the hierarchy itself has any status in the theory of grammar—as an autonomous linguistic system, that is. And we are sympathetic with the view (expressed by a number of scholars, often tacitly or indirectly) that questions the autonomous existence of thematic roles as well.

In what follows, we would like to address two questions these matters suggest to us.

(21) a. Why are there so few thematic roles?
     b. Why the UTAH?

The number of thematic roles suggested in the literature is rather small —the total does not exceed by much the number found in (19). Moreover, it seems correct that the inventory is so small. If so, why? Why aren't there twenty thematic roles, or a hundred? Surely, if thematic roles exist, there could in theory be any learnable number of them. And why are thematic

roles "assigned" according to a universal hierarchy and in conformity
with the UTAH? Why isn't the assignment random? Or, at least, why isn't
it as nearly random as would be allowed by limitations relating to learnability? This is the content of our questions, and we will be concerned to
suggest partial answers to them.

2.1   Categories and Projections

The linguistic elements that we believe to be fundamental in answering the
questions in (21) are nothing new. They are (i) the lexical categories, or
parts of speech, and (ii) the projection of syntactic structure (i.e., phrase
structure, or X-bar structure) from lexical items.

For our purposes, we will assume the traditional categories V, N, A,
P (see Chomsky 1970), and we will continue to employ this traditional
alphabetic notation for them.[6] Furthermore, we assume here that this
exhausts the inventory of major lexical categories. The fact that the inventory of categories is restricted in this way is relevant, we will claim, to
understanding why the inventory of "thematic roles" is also small. In
part, the answer to the first of the questions posed above will reduce to
another question—namely, assuming it to be (approximately) true, why
are the lexical categories just V, N, A, P? We do not pretend to have an
answer to this question, guessing simply that it has something to do with
how certain basic "notional" categories (e.g., event, instance or entity,
state, and relation) are expressed in linguistic form. But given this restricted inventory, we are interested in the possibility that there is a
relationship between that and the similarly impoverished inventory of
thematic roles.

Our understanding of the second of the two factors we have taken to be
directly relevant to our questions—projection of syntactic structure—
is due in some measure to Kayne's discussion of Unambiguous Paths
(Kayne 1984) and to Larson's related proposal, the Single Complement
Hypothesis, which requires that the head-complement relation be biunique (Larson 1988).

In particular, we suggest that the questions in (21) find their answer in
part in the fundamental nature of the syntactic projections that define
LRS representations (and therefore also the syntactic structures dominating lexical heads at D-Structure). Each lexical head X determines an
unambiguous projection of its category—to a phrasal level, XP—and an
unambiguous arrangement of its arguments, as specifier and complement,
as depicted in (22).

(22)

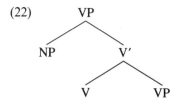

This structure is "unambiguous" in the sense we intend. Thus, for example, the sister relation holds unambiguously between V and VP and between NP and V'. Moreover, the relation is asymmetrical in each case, since just one member in the relation is a maximal projection. The c-command relation is likewise unambiguous, in the relevant sense: the "subject" or "specifier" (NP in this instance) asymmetrically c-commands the "internal argument" or "complement" (lower VP in this case).

(22) is unambiguous in part because branching is binary at all non-terminal nodes, and in part because it conforms to the X-bar theory of "types," according to which the levels in a given categorial projection (i.e., the lexical, intermediate, and phrasal levels) are distinct from one another (and are so indicated notationally in various ways, here as X, X', and XP). Our belief is that these aspects of the syntax of LRS representations are not *stipulated*, but follow directly from the notion *unambiguous projection*. That is to say, the theory of grammar does not include a stipulation to the effect that all branching must be binary, or that the projection of types (lexical, intermediate, and phrasal) must conform to the distinctness criterion. The theory of grammar requires merely that projections be unambiguous. And we suppose that it simply follows from this that the syntactic structures initially projected from the lexicon must have the (branching and type) properties we have identified.

We will speculate further that the unambiguous structure requirement will yield an additional limitation on the projection of categories to types: to wit, the requirement that "intermediate" types (X') be restricted to just one for any given projection. Thus, the structure depicted in (22) represents a full projection of the category V: it includes a specifier (NP), a complement (VP), as well as the lexical (X), intermediate (X'), and phrasal (XP) type-projections. The limitation on types follows, we wager, from the assumption that multiple "intermediate" types would be linguistically (though perhaps not notationally) indistinct. This is pure speculation at this point, but we will assume it in what follows.

Given Unambiguous Projection, and given the four lexical categories traditionally assumed (V, N, A, P), we can propose an answer to the questions posed in (21).

2.2 Thematic Relations and Thematic Role Assignment

Our basic answer to question (21a)—why there are so few thematic roles
—is that, in an important sense, there *are* no thematic roles. Instead, there
are just the relations determined by the categories and their projections,
and these are limited by the small inventory of lexical categories and by
Unambiguous Projection.

While we might assign a particular thematic label—say, "agent"—to
the NP in (22), its grammatical status is determined entirely by the rela-
tion(s) it bears in the relational structure projected by the lexical head V.
Specifically, the NP of (22) bears the "specifier" relation within a VP
whose head takes a complement that is also a projection of the category
V. It is not without reason that the term *agent* is associated with the
subjects of verbs—like *cut, break, drop, send, give, tighten, put, shelve,
saddle*—that share the LRS representation of (22). But we would like to
suggest that the thematic terminology typically applied in this case simply
reflects the *relational* status of the NP in the upper Spec position.

The use of the term *agent*, we imagine, is appropriate here simply because of the elementary semantic relations associated with (22) by virtue
of the elements that enter into the structure. Each of the lexical categories
is identified with a particular notional "type," and the relational structures they project define an associated system of semantic relations, an
"elementary meaning," so to speak. Thus, for example, the category V is
associated with the elementary notional type "event" (or perhaps, "dynamic event"), which we can symbolize e (see the usage in Higginbotham
1985, and in references cited there). The LRS representation depicted in
(22) contains a V heading the structure as a whole, and another (implicit
in the tree) heading the complement VP. The structural relation of complementation involves an asymmetrical c-command relation between the
two verbs: the matrix V asymmetrically c-commands the subordinate V
(head of the complement VP).

The structural relations of c-command and complementation are unambiguous in (22), as required. Since the lexical items involved there have
elementary notional content, it seems reasonable to suppose that, in addition to the structural relations associated with the projection, there are
elementary semantic relations associated with (22) as well. And further,
the semantic relations associated with (22) are unambiguous and fully
determined by the LRS projections of categories. The matrix V of (22)
governs another V, the head of its complement. Corresponding to this
syntactic relation, there is a similarly asymmetric (semantic) relation between two events, a relation we will take to be that of *implication*. Accord-

ingly, the matrix event "implicates" the subordinate event as in (23), a relation that makes perfect sense if the syntactic embedding corresponds to a "semantic" composite in which the subordinate event is a proper part of the event denoted by the structure projected by the main verb.

(23) $e_1 \rightarrow e_2$

Let us assume that (23) is the "semantic" relation associated uniformly with the complementation structure (24), in which a lexical V takes VP as its complement in LRS representations.

(24)
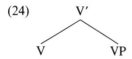

The syntactic structure (24) and the associated semantic relation (23) comprise the LRS expression of what is commonly called the *causal* relation (see Lombard 1985 for relevant discussion of relations among events and for an appropriate formal semantic representation of the causal relation). In this light, it is with some justification that the NP in (22) is typically associated with the thematic role term *agent*—inasmuch as it bears the specifier relation in the structure projected by the "causative" verb. This NP bears a syntactically unambiguous relation to the V′ of (22), and, by hypothesis, its semantic relation within the structure is likewise unambiguous and fully determined by the LRS. Suppose we symbolize this relation as > and devise a composite elementary "semantic" representation for the entirety of (22), as in (25).

(25) $n > (e_1 \rightarrow e_2)$

In (25) we express the notional type of the category N as *n*, representing the notional type of nouns, whatever that is in fact. We can choose to use the expression *agent of* to refer to the relation borne by *n* in (25), but this, like (25) itself, is entirely derivative under the assumptions we hold here.

Similar remarks are appropriate to the syntactic and semantic characterizations of the relations inherent in other LRS projections determined by lexical items. And a survey of plausible LRS representations suggests ready candidates for association with the standard thematic terminology. That the list of thematic role terms is not endless or even large follows, we claim, from the fact (if it is a fact) that the roles are derivative of lexical syntactic relations, and these are limited in the manner we have described.

Consider now the "inner VP" of (24). One possible system of projections dominated by that node is the structure we have associated with the English verb *put* (following Larson 1988; also see Hale and Keyser 1991, 1992), as in *She put the book on the shelf* (26).

(26)

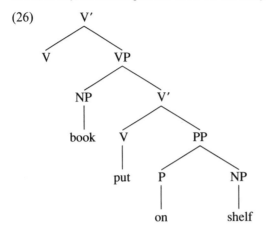

This LRS representation is shared by a vast number of English verbs, including a large number of denominal location and locatum verbs, putatively formed by incorporation of a nominal into an abstract P and thence successively into the abstract Vs (see above and Hale and Keyser, 1991, 1992).[7]

By hypothesis, the syntactic relation between the matrix V and the inner VP corresponds uniformly to the "causal" relation, by virtue of the syntactic relation itself and by virtue of the elementary notional type associated with the V category. The external argument of the matrix verb bears an unambiguous syntactic relation to it, and, by hypothesis, its elementary semantic connection to the structure is likewise unambiguous —following accepted usage, it is the "agent."

Now let us turn to the inner VP itself, depicted in (27).

(27)

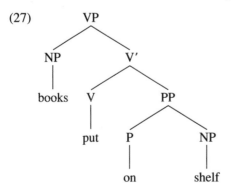

In this structure the head-complement relation involves the categories V and P, the latter subordinate to the former. We will continue to assume that the notional type of V is "(dynamic) event" e, and we will suggest that the notional type of P is "interrelation" (symbolized by r). The r-relation includes, but is not to be strictly identified with, relations commonly thought of as spatial or locational (see Kipka 1990 for detailed criticism of the "locationist" conception of adpositions). If these basic semantic notions combine to assign an elementary semantic value to the syntactic structure in which they appear, then they will do so unambiguously, since the syntax is itself unambiguous. We suppose that the semantics of the relation embodied in V' of (27) is that according to which a (dynamic) event "implicates" an interrelation, as expressed in (28), utilizing the elementary notation we have adopted.

(28) $e \rightarrow r$

The most salient "meaning" attached to this structure is "change." Thus, the elementary semantic expression embodied in (28) corresponds to the situation in which some entity, represented by the subject, comes to be involved in an interrelation with an entity corresponding to the NP object of the P.

An interrelation involves at least two entities, of course. Thus, the preposition *on*, for example, relates some entity (typically functioning as a place) and some other entity (typically a thing, substance, or the like), as in sentences like *A fly got in the soup* or *Mud got on the wall*. However, given Unambiguous Projection, the syntax of V' in (27) has just one expression (NP object of P) corresponding to an entity entering into the interrelation r established by P. Therefore, a "subject" ([Spec, VP]) is required in VP as an absolute necessity in the lexical syntactic projection of V here. We continue to use the symbol $>$ to represent the semantic relation that the subject bears in relation to the V' expression, but this is nothing more than a notational filler at this point—more will be said presently about the syntax and semantics of the subject relation in LRS representations.

The subject NP in (27) corresponds to an entity that completes the interrelation r. It is the subject of a "predicate of change" and therefore, as in the syntax, it is external to the semantic expression assigned to V', as in (29).

(29) $n > (e \rightarrow r)$

The subject of a change predicate is sometimes called a "theme" (Gruber 1965, Jackendoff 1972) or an "affected patient" (Anderson 1977, Pesetsky 1990). Again, however, these semantic roles, like the elementary semantic interpretations in general, are derivative of the lexical syntactic relations.

In an accepted view of thematic relations, the "theme" role, and the associated elementary semantic relation "change," extend to predicates of the type represented in (30).

(30) a. The oven browned the roast.
     b. The storm cleared the air.
     c. The cook thinned the gravy.
     d. This narrows our options.

We assume that verbs of this type, like the others we have examined here, are derived by head movement. In this case, however, the incorporating elements are adjectival. The LRS representation of the verb in (30c) is depicted in (31).

(31)

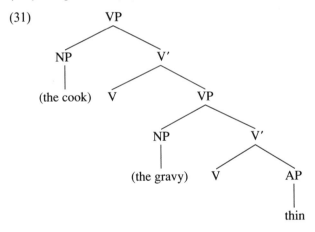

The upper V in (31) projects the LRS associated with the "causal" relation represented in (24). The lower V projects a structure that is parallel to the VP displayed in (27), but with the PP of the latter replaced by AP, the phrasal projection of the adjectival category A.

The lexical category A is associated with the notional type "state" (s), and the elementary semantic relation associated with the V' projection is presumably as shown in (32).

(32) $e \rightarrow s$

That is to say, an action or dynamic event "implicates" a state. Or to put it another way, a state is achieved as an integral, or defining, part of a dynamic event. This corresponds, we suggest, to the notion of a "change resulting in a state."

It is a fundamental semantic requirement of AP that it be attributed of something, for example, of an entity. Thus, just as in the case of PP complements, so also in the case of AP complements, a "subject" necessarily appears in [Spec, VP] (i.e., *the gravy* in (31)). And this subject is integrated into the associated semantic representation in the usual way, as shown in (33).

(33) $n > (e \rightarrow s)$

Again, the subject can be thought of as the "theme," inasmuch as it corresponds to an entity undergoing change.

We have examined three of the complement types available in LRS representations, namely, those projected by the categories V, P, and A. The fourth type, that projected by the category N, is exemplified by the unergative verbs of (34) and the simple transitives of (35).

(34) a. The child laughed.
   b. The colt sneezed.
   c. Petronella sang.
   d. The ewes lambed.

(35) a. We had a good laugh.
   b. She did her new song.
   c. The ewe had twins.
   d. This mare does a nice trot.

In both cases the abstract relational structures here involve a verbal head projecting a V′ structure containing an NP in complement position, as shown in (36).

(36)

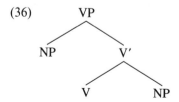

In the case of (35), of course, the complement NP is a categorial variable in the LRS representation of the various verbal lexical items; it is realized as an NP argument in s-syntax, through lexical insertion in the usual manner.[8] In the case of (34), on the other hand, the complement NP dominates a constant: the nominal source, through incorporation, of the denominal verb (see above and Hale and Keyser 1991).

If it is appropriate to assume that the elementary semantic structures are associated with syntactic structures in the unambiguous manner suggested so far, then the semantic structure associated with the V′ of (36) is as in (37).

(37) $e \rightarrow n$

Here, an action or dynamic event "implicates" an entity, assuming that to be the notional type (n) associated with the noun category. This corresponds to the notion that the implicating event is completed, or perfected, by virtue of the "creation," "production," or "realization" of the relevant entity.

If (36) is the correct relational structure for unergatives, and for the "simple transitive" (light verb, cognate object, and creation predicate constructions), then full expression of the associated semantic structure is as shown in (38), integrating the "subject" into the interpretation in the customary manner.

(38) $n > (e \rightarrow n)$

This correctly reflects the fact that the sentences of (34) and (35) clearly have subjects at S-Structure. In fact, all members of the category V that we have examined here project structures that, at some point or other, have subjects. It is nevertheless legitimate to ask whether the LRS representations of verbs necessarily express the specifier relation. We will turn to this question in the following subsection.

2.3 Categories and Specifiers

We have been considering a conception of lexical syntactic projections according to which any appropriate VP may "embed" as the complement of a verb. Structures (26) and (31) represent projections of just this type. And verbs projecting both these structures are energetically represented in the verbal vocabulary of English, for example.

But there are some gaps, and the theory of argument structure that we are considering must have an explanation for them. Consider the ill-formed usages in (39).

(39) a. *The clown laughed the child. (i.e., got the child to laugh)
     b. *The alfalfa sneezed the colt. (i.e., made the colt sneeze)
     c. *We'll sing Loretta this evening. (i.e., have Loretta sing)
     d. *Good feed calved the cows early. (i.e., got the cows to calve)

These sentences represent an extremely large and coherent class of impossible structures in English. In particular, unergative VPs cannot appear as

complements of V in LRS representations—that is, an unergative may
not appear in the lexical syntactic "causative" construction, as depicted in
(40).[9]

(40)

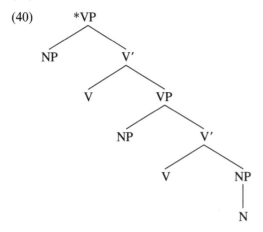

This structure, the putative source of the verbs in (39), satisfies all conditions we have considered to this point. So far no principle precludes it. But
the structure is consistently absent, as far as we can tell, from the English
vocabulary of denominal verbs. Why should this be?

The answer, we think, lies in the LRS representation of unergative
verbs. The verbs of (39) are a problem only under the assumption that
they have the relational structure (36)—in particular, that they have VP-
internal subjects. If we assume instead that unergatives do not have a
subject in l-syntax, then the problem disappears, since the structure depicted in (40) cannot exist and, therefore, the verbs of (39) cannot exist
either.

This is our answer. Unergatives have no subjects in their LRS representations. But for this to be a solution of any interest, it must be something
other than a stipulation to the effect that some verbs have a subject in
LRS and others do not. Which verbs are allowed not to have VP-internal
subjects in l-syntax? Which verbs must have a subject, as the inner VP of
shelve and *clear* surely must? If these questions have no answer, our suggested explanation for (39) is no more than an observation.

In the relational structures of the location and locatum verbs studied in
earlier sections (and in Hale and Keyser 1991) and, likewise, in the relational structures of change-of-state verbs of the type represented by (30),
the appearance of a subject in the inner VP is "forced," being required by
the complement within that inner VP. In essence, since the complement in
the inner VP is a predicate in the LRS representation of those verbs, "full

interpretation" (see below) of the inner VP requires that a subject appear, internal to the VP, so that predication can be realized locally, as required (see Williams 1980, Rothstein 1983), thereby correctly relating the complement of the inner VP to the subject of that VP.

We will assume that the Spec position of VP in the LRS representation of a lexical verb is filled only when that is forced by some principle. In the case of the change-of-state or location verbs just considered, we suggest that the appearance of a subject is forced by predication.

For verbs of the class now commonly termed "unergative," nothing forces the appearance of a subject. This follows, since the complement in the LRS representations of such verbs is not a predicate. We can assume, then, that the subject is in fact excluded from the LRS representations of unergatives.

In our attempt to answer the questions formulated in (21), we suggested that argument structures, or LRS projections, are constrained in their variety by (i) the relative paucity of lexical categories, and (ii) the unambiguous nature of lexical syntactic projections. If what we have suggested here for unergative verbs is correct, then we must consider an additional limit on the variety of possible argument structures—specifically, we must also determine what it is that forces the appearance, or absence, of a subject.

We believe that nothing new need be added to achieve the correct result. This result is in fact given by the general principle according to which linguistic structures must be "fully interpreted" (Chomsky 1986b). The principle of Full Interpretation will guarantee that verbs of change of location or state *have* a subject in the inner VP; absence of the subject would leave the complement of the inner VP uninterpreted (see Rothstein 1983, which we take to be the true origin of this idea). The same principle will also guarantee that unergative verbs *lack* a subject in their LRS representations; a subject, if present in an unergative LRS representation, would itself be uninterpreted for lack of a predicate in the complement position.[10] The D-Structure or S-Structure subject of an unergative verb is therefore a "true external argument," appearing in the Spec position of the functional projection IP (or, in the case of small clause constructions, in the adjoined position assumed by the subject).

Of course, these remarks on LRS internal subjects do not only apply to verbs that involve conflation; they also apply to "analytic" constructions in which the main verb appears with an overt complement. Thus, for example, various constructions employing the relatively abstract English verb *get* exhibit the predicted range of acceptability in the causative: *get drunk* and *get into the Peace Corps*, with complements that are inherently predicative, not only permit the intransitive form (e.g., *My friend got drunk, My friend got into the army*), but also appear freely in the causative form (*We got my friend drunk, We got my friend into the Peace Corps*). By contrast, expressions like *get the measles* and *get smallpox*, with nominal or verbal (hence nonpredicative) complements, cannot appear in the causative, as expected by hypothesis (e.g., **get my friend the measles, get my friend smallpox*, in the relevant sense, and **We got my friend leave early*). Alternative proposals exist that might explain this contrast, but we would like to suggest that a more straightforward lexical syntactic explanation also exists, accounting not only for these examples but also for the ill-formedness of **laugh my friend*, where a Case Theory account, for example, is not plausible (given *laugh my friend off the stage*, in which *laugh* apparently does assign Case; see Burzio 1981). Branigan (1992) suggests that *make John leave* involves a subjunctive, rather than the bare VP, as the complement of *make*. Hence the contrast with *get*, which cannot form **get John leave*. There is a serious question about the latter case, however, given the analysis suggested in section 4.2 for overt causative morphology. Specifically, why does the Case-marking capability of transitive *get* fail to "save" the structure in question?

Given these considerations, we can assume that the structures that express the relations among the arguments of a verb are characterized by the operation of two fundamental defining principles, (41a) and (41b).

(41) *Lexical Relational Structure (Argument Structure)*

    a. Unambiguous Projection

    b. Full Interpretation

To the extent that they are correct, these principles, in conjunction with the restricted set of lexical categories (V, N, A, P), determine the limits on the range of relations into which arguments can enter. This effectively answers question (21a), concerning the paucity of so-called thematic roles. The principles also define a precise class of relational structures. To that extent, they answer question (21b) as well, since the LRS representations embody biunique structural-semantic (i.e., structural-thematic) relationships for all lexical items.

2.4 The Specifier Position and the Depth of Embedding in Lexical Relational Structure Representations

If the Spec position for so-called unergative verbs, like those in (34), is excluded by virtue of Full Interpretation, then their expressed subjects must be "external," as we have said. The LRS representation of a verb like *laugh* cannot be (36). Rather, it must be something on the order of (42a) or (42b). For the sake of expository simplicity, we will assume the former, since it is not clear to us what a truly "empty" Spec position means in our framework (though it may well be necessary to posit such a position; Unambiguous Projection is satisfied in either case).

(42) a.   b.

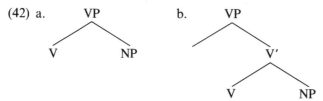

The precise sense in which the subject of an unergative verb is external can be left vague for the moment (see section 4.2 for discussion), but it will involve at least the assumption that the subject is not present in the LRS projection of the predicator, that is, the lexical VP. In English, at least, S-Structure subjects in general are in the Spec position of the functional category IP. Thus, omitting some irrelevant details, the S-Structure representation of (34a), *The child laughed*, is essentially as in (43).

(43)

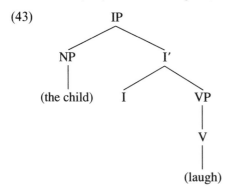

By hypothesis, the verb is the result of incorporation—specifically of the LRS object *laugh* into the abstract V that heads the lexical item as a whole. The expressed subject is external to VP.[11] If we adopt the accepted view according to which the VP in (43) is a predicate at D-Structure, we must also assume that it requires a subject at some s-syntactic level, by the Extended Projection Principle (Chomsky 1982, Rothstein 1983), presumably a corollary of the general principle of Full Interpretation. The required s-syntactic subject must at least appear in [Spec, IP] at S-Structure. Its D-Structure position is another question, and the VP-internal subject hypothesis, according to which the subject is dominated by the VP node in s-syntax, is not in conflict with our claim that the subjects of unergative verbs are external to VP in LRS representations.

If this reasoning is correct, then it must apply equally to the LRS representations of verbs associated with the "causal semantics" informally expressed in (25)—that is, to location verbs (like *put, shelve*), to locatum verbs (like *saddle, blindfold*), and to verbs of change of state (like *thin, lengthen, break*). This follows, since the inner VP, being "complete" and therefore not a predicate, cannot force the appearance of a subject in the matrix VP. Accordingly, the structure presented in (31), for the verb *to thin (as of gravy, paint)*, must be corrected to (44), omitting the matrix subject.

(44)

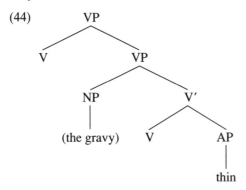

Thus, in a sentence employing this verb, like *The cook thinned the gravy*, the expressed subject (*the cook*) must be external to the lexical VP projection, as is the subject of an unergative verb. Further, as in the case of unergatives, predication in s-syntax is the means by which the expressed subject is interpreted. This subject occupies [Spec, IP] in the s-syntax of a tensed clause, as in the abbreviated D-Structure representation (45).

(45)

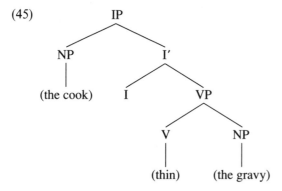

The verb of (45) is derived (in l-syntax) by successive incorporation of the adjective *thin* into the abstract verbs of (44), in conformity with the provisions of the head movement process.

Our analysis of unergative and causative verbs depends on the notion that a VP is not a predicate in l-syntax. We extend this to all VP projections: none is an l-syntactic predicate in the relevant sense, that is, a maximal projection forcing the appearance of a subject internal to LRS (see Hale and Keyser 1991 for fuller discussion of this). If this notion is correct, then we can explain—in part, at least—why there is a limit on recursion in LRS representations. Empirically, the LRS representation for a verb generally has at most one VP embedding. Thus, so far as we know, no verb corresponds to the hypothetical LRS representation (46), because that structure fails to satisfy the requirement of full interpretation. The most deeply embedded VP is not a predicate; so, by that hypothesis, the inner subject is not licensed.

(46)

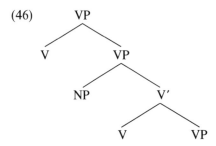

But if this structure is illicit because of a failure of predication, then what if the NP is simply omitted? This would give (47), also nonexistent, so far as we know.

(47)

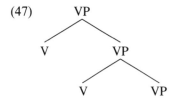

We assume that the same general principle precludes this structure as well. The "double causative structure" cannot be interpreted, since only one causative can be predicated of a subject in s-syntax. Again, this is a failure of predication (of the inner VP in this case) and hence a failure to achieve full interpretation. Thus, unrestricted recursion of the VP category— although similar in character to the s-syntactic recursion freely permitted, for example, by clausal complementation—is impossible in the syntax of LRS representations, precisely because of the full interpretation requirement. To be sure, full interpretation is a requirement of s-syntactic structures as well, but its effect there is different, due, among other things, to the properties of the various functional categories, which define a Spec position for external arguments.

2.5 External and Internal "Subjects"

If the s-syntactic subjects of transitives and unergatives are "external subjects," how are they in fact related to their verbs? In a sense, the answer is simple: they are related to their verbs through predication. Relative to the VP, they appear in an s-syntactic position appropriate for predication (see Williams 1980, Rothstein 1983, Rapoport 1987).

We will assume that this answer is correct. But of course there is a deeper question. Is this external subject a part of the argument structure of the verb that heads the VP predicated of it? Is the external subject an argument, in any sense, in the l-syntactic representation of the verb? Does it, so to speak, receive its thematic role from the verb?

We believe the answer to this question is negative. The external subject is not present in the LRS representation of the verbs under consideration here. At least, it is not present in the sense of this framework—for example, in the sense in which an object is present as a point in the LRS projection defined by the verb. It therefore cannot "receive its thematic role" from the verb, since the concept "thematic role," to the extent that it can be understood in the context of LRS representations, corresponds precisely to the notion "lexical relation," defined over the LRS projection. If the subject is absent from the LRS representation of a verb, then clearly it cannot "receive its thematic role" from the verb.

How, then, do we account for the fact that the external subjects of unergative and causative verbs, say, are understood as "agents" in relation to the events named by those verbs? How is the "agent role" assigned?

We assume that it is correct to say that the subjects in question are associated with a semantic role, typically the role termed "agent," and we will adhere to the traditional usage in saying that these subjects are "assigned the agent role." However, we assume that this assignment is "constructional," in the sense that it is effected in a syntactic configuration defined in s-syntax. This manner of assignment, we contend, is to be distinguished entirely from that associated with the semantic roles (theme, patient, goal, etc.) corresponding to the l-syntactic relations defined by LRS projections. The agent role is a function of s-syntactic predication.

Insofar as it concerns the agent role, this view is essentially that developed by Chomsky (1981) and Marantz (1984), according to which the subject receives its semantic role from VP, not from the V itself.

Not all subjects are "external" in this sense. And, accordingly, not all subjects are "agents." Verbs of the type represented by *thin (the gravy), tighten (the cinch), loosen (the girth)*—that is, members of the class of "ergative verbs" (Burzio 1981, Keyser and Roeper 1984)—have the property that they may project both transitive and intransitive s-syntactic verb phrases. In the latter case the internal NP undergoes movement to subject position—that is, to [Spec, I] in (48a–c).

(48) a. The gravy is thinning nicely.
     b. The cinch finally tightened.
     c. The girth loosened.

Here, the s-syntactic subject is "internal" in the sense that it is an argument internal to the LRS representation of the verbs. We maintain that it is exactly this internal subject that is to be identified with the "affected argument" of the Affectedness Condition, which has played an important role in lexical and syntactic studies since Anderson's work on passive nominals (Anderson 1977; and for relevant recent studies of the role of the affectedness property, see Jaeggli 1986 and Pesetsky 1990). If the affected argument is an internal subject in l-syntax, as we believe, the semantic notion "affected" is correlated with a structural position in the l-syntactic representations of verbs.

The verbs of (48) belong to the class of so-called ergative verbs, exhibiting an "uncompromised" transitivity alternation along the ergative pattern—that is, with object of transitive and subject of intransitive the stable argument in the alternation. But to this class of verbs must be added those that enter into the middle construction of English. These exhibit the same transitivity alternation, "compromised" by various well-known requirements that must be met for full acceptability (e.g., use of the generic, a modal, or an adverb like *easily*, as in (49)).

(49) a. Rye bread cuts easily.
     b. These bolts tighten easily.
     c. Limestone crushes easily.

Of course, all ergative verbs can be used in the middle construction; (49b) is a good example. Like the inchoative (i.e., the intransitive use of ergatives, as in (48)), the middle involves s-syntactic movement of an argument bearing the *internal* subject relation (in the case of the middle, this is an object in s-syntax). Transitive verbs that can undergo middle formation are just those whose s-syntactic object is an "affected argument"—that is, those whose s-syntactic object corresponds to an internal subject in LRS.

Under these assumptions, it is perhaps not sufficient to assume that the relevant portion of the S-Structure representation of the middle sentence (49b) is simply that depicted in (50), in which the derived subject heads a chain with the trace (of NP-movement) in s-syntactic object position.

(50)

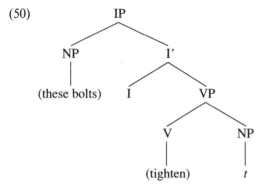

This assumption is insufficient, since the VP here is indistinguishable from that of expressions like *make trouble, have a baby, do a job*, whose l-syntactic and s-syntactic representations alike correspond to the simple transitive type [$_{VP}$ V NP] (i.e., the same as that projected by unergative verbs). The latter do not enter into the middle construction—predictably, by hypothesis, since they do not involve an "affected" argument in the relevant sense. By contrast, the l-syntactic counterpart of the VP of (49b) is that depicted in (51), in which the argument at issue (these bolts) is an internal subject.

(51)

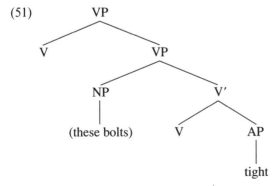

The middle construction of English appears to be restricted to verbs that have an internal subject in this sense. This implies that transitive verbs like *cut, break, crush* partake of the complex l-syntactic causative structures assumed here for the conflated denominal location/locatum verbs and for deadjectival verbs of the type represented in (49b). And if the English middle construction is formed in s-syntax, then the relevant aspects of these structures must be "visible" at that level.

Although we speculate that this account of the English verbs under discussion is essentially correct, there are a number of serious problems that must eventually be dealt with. Here we will deal with only one. It concerns an asymmetry in the transitivity alternations exhibited by ergative and location/locatum verbs, reflected by (among other things) an asymmetry within the class in the distribution of the middle and inchoative forms.

3   Transitives, Inchoatives, Middles, and Verbal Modifiers

The difference between inchoatives and middles is an old issue, and it is the focus of an extensive literature (e.g., Van Oosten 1977, Lakoff 1977, Keyser and Roeper 1984, Jaeggli 1984, Hale and Keyser 1986, 1987, 1988, Condoravdi 1989). Why is the acceptability of the middle conditional? Why does the middle, unlike the inchoative, require some modification— such as modal, aspectual, an adverb—to achieve acceptability? In the following discussion we will be concerned, not with this time-honored problem, but with a problem defined by our own system: the distribution, across verbs, of the inchoative and the middle constructions.

The problem is this. As shown in (52), ergative verbs, like *narrow, clear,* and *tighten,* all have an inchoative use in addition to their transitive and related middle uses.

(52) a. The screen cleared.
      b. I cleared the screen.
      c. This screen clears easily.

We have assumed that such verbs, in their transitive uses at least, all have the structure depicted in (51). Further, we have assumed that this structure is, in the relevant respects, the same as that associated with location and locatum verbs. However, these verbs lack the inchoative, as shown in (53).

(53) a. *The books shelved.
      b.   I shelved the books.
      c.   These books shelve easily.

Thus, although both the middle and the inchoative, by hypothesis, involve s-syntactic movement of an internal argument, the two processes are not coextensive: the inchoative is more restricted than the middle. Why is there this difference?

To this point we have assumed that both ergative verbs and location/ locatum verbs involve an inner VP of the form shown in (54).

(54)

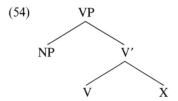

The head of XP belongs to a category that forces the appearance of a subject, hence the NP in [Spec, VP]—in other words, XP is either PP or AP. Since the two verb classes involve essentially the same structure, there is no obvious reason for the difference they exhibit in relation to the inchoative. It is possible, of course, that the assumption embodied in (54) is in error and that the two verb classes are structurally distinct, the structural difference accounting for the difference in behavior. In earlier work (Hale and Keyser 1991) we entertained this possibility and attempted to develop it. Here, however, we will consider an alternative proposal (adapted from Hale and Rapoport, in progress), and we will attribute the structure depicted in (54) to ergative verbs and location/locatum verbs alike.

The proposal we will consider here does not actually solve the problem we have identified. We suspect, however, that the solution lies in the direction indicated by the observations we will make. The observations in question have to do with semantic components of manner or means present in the lexical representations of verbs, and, whatever their relevance to the present problem, their grammatical properties are properly part of a full account of the verbal lexicon (see Levin and Rapoport 1988 for a promising proposal in this regard).

3.1 The Transitivity Alternation

In the following discussion we will momentarily turn away from the denominal verbs themselves to the more general phenomenon of transitivity alternations and observed asymmetries in their distribution.

Basically, we will be concerned with members of two large classes of verbs. The members of one class participate in the simple transitivity alternation shown in (55).

(55) a. The pigs got mud on the wall.
     b. Mud got on the wall.

In contrast, the members of the other class fail to occur in pairs of this type, as shown in (56), taking only the transitive form.

(56) a. We put mud on the wall.
     b. *Mud put on the wall.

In these uses, both *get* and *put*, like other members of the classes they represent, depict events in which some entity or material (in this instance, *mud*) undergoes a change of location, so that it "comes to be located" at a place corresponding to the nominal expression in the prepositional phrase (in this instance, *the wall*). In accepted parlance of semantic and thematic roles, the moving entity or material is called the *theme* (Gruber 1965, Jackendoff 1972); and in syntactic terms, it corresponds to the grammatical object in the transitive uses of *get* and *put*, and to the grammatical subject in the intransitive use of *get*.

The issue here, of course, is the transitivity asymmetry exhibited by these two verb classes. Continuing our earlier usage, we will refer to the transitive sentences of (55)–(56) as the *causative* alternant; the intransitive sentences represent the *inchoative* alternant. The question here is the same as the one formulated in relation to the denominal verbs of (52) and (53): Why does (55) admit an inchoative alternant, while (56) does not?

By assumption, the lexical argument structure of intransitive *get*, as in (55b), is as shown in (57).

(57)

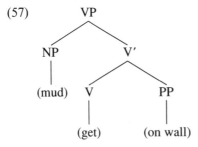

By contrast, the transitive use exemplified in (55a) involves a more complex structure. Whereas (55b) involves a simple and single event, that of a change in location (e.g., mud comes to be on the wall), the transitive (55a) depicts a complex situation consisting of two subevents: a cause and an effect. The lexical argument structure of transitive *get*, as used in (55a), is the correspondingly more complex (58); of course, the same structure is shared by English *put*.

(58)

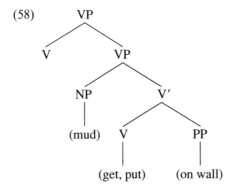

By Full Interpretation, the agent of causation (*The pigs* in (55a), *we* in (56a)) is necessarily an *external* argument. The VP complement of the matrix (causative) V in (58), being fully evaluated, is not a predicate and therefore cannot license the appearance of a subject NP in the Spec position of the LRS projection defined by the causative verb. From this it follows that "further causativization" of *get* is impossible in lexical structure (hence, **we got the pigs mud on the wall*, in the sense *We brought it about that the pigs got mud on the wall*).

Structures of the type represented by (58) are of course subject to incorporation, as depicted in (59).

(59)

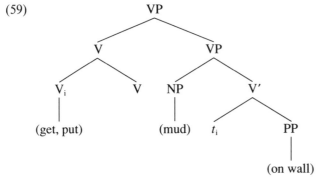

The structures given in (57)–(59) are l-syntactic representations. The D-Structure representation of a given sentence comprises a pair consisting of lexical structure and the system of functional categories that select designated lexical projections. D-Structure is itself subject to various well-known principles that, in some cases will force displacement, or movement, of phrases and/or heads.

The D-Structure representation of (55b) involves at least the lexical argument structure (57) and the functional category I, as shown in (60).

(60)

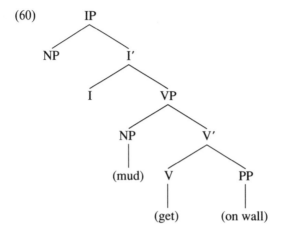

This will be modified in s-syntax, in accordance with principles of both Universal Grammar and English-specific grammar, deriving an S-Structure representation in which (i) the lexical "subject," originating in [Spec, VP], appears in [Spec, IP] (substituting for NP there), thereby satisfying the Case and agreement requirements associated with the subject, and (ii) the head of the functional category I is combined with the lexical head of the construction (i.e., with V) in accordance with principles of English morphology, among other things.

By hypothesis, the D-Structure representation of the transitive verb *put* and of the transitive alternant of *get*, as used in (55a), will take the form shown in (61).

(61)

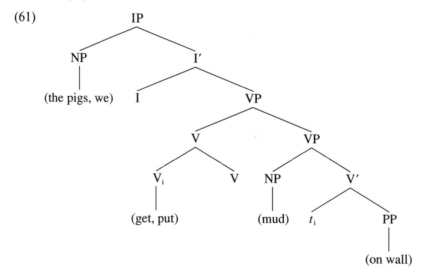

Here, of course, the external subject NP (e.g., *the pigs, we*) is truly an "external" argument, appearing in D-Structure in [Spec, IP] and getting its semantic role directly through the predication relation that holds between it and the verb phrase as a whole. The inner "subject" (e.g., *mud*) does not "raise" in this case, since it is assigned Case by the transitive verb that heads the projection bearing the predicate relation to the external subject. In this circumstance, therefore, the inner "subject" is the D-Structure "object" of the transitive verb.

Returning now to the original question—why English *get* may enter into both the transitive and intransitive constructions, whereas *put* may only be transitive—we begin to consider a possible answer.

3.2   Inchoatives and the Licensing of Means and Manner

To address this problem, it is necessary to move beyond this very restricted set of data to a larger group of transitive and intransitive verbs of "change of location," which share the selectional property that they take a PP complement, together with an NP corresponding to the semantic role "theme." Consider first the set of verbs in (62), having to do with the motion or transfer of liquids, or liquid-like matter.

(62) splash, drip, dribble, pour, squirt,...

As shown in (63)–(65), these verbs appear readily in both the inchoative (intransitive) and transitive forms.

(63) a. The pigs splashed mud on the wall.
      b. Mud splashed on the wall.

(64) a. We dripped honey on the cornbread.
      b. Honey dripped on the cornbread.

(65) a. They poured gas into the tank.
      b. Gas poured into the tank.

Now compare these verbs to the ones in (66).

(66) smear, daub, rub, wipe,...

Like *put*, these fail to appear in the inchoative.

(67) a. We smeared mud on the wall.
      b. *Mud smeared on the wall.

(68) a. They daubed pipeclay on their bodies.
      b. *Pipeclay daubed on their bodies.

(69) a.   He rubbed ochre on his chest.
     b.   *Ochre rubbed on his chest.

There is a sense in which the verbs of (62) and (66) are more "complex" than the simple verbs examined so far. They are more complex, not in their argument structure, which rather closely parallels those of the verbs *get* and *put* in the relevant uses, but in terms of the presence of an additional factor. Thus, for example, sentences (63a–b) do not speak simply of mud getting on the wall, but of mud getting on the wall in a particular way—namely, in the manner customarily referred to as "splashing." Similarly, sentence (67a) speaks of mud getting on the wall by a particular means or manner—that referred to as "smearing."

We wish to suggest that the difference in syntactic behavior between the two classes of verbs is related to this extra level of complexity, which we will refer to as the *manner component*, in the lexical representation of verbs. The difference between the "ergative" class (the class that has both transitive and intransitive members), like (62), and the transitive class, like (66), lies in the principles according to which the manner component is "licensed."

The manner component modifiers of the verbs of (62) are primarily "internal" in their orientation. In effect, they are adverbial modifications to the VP and in particular to the event depicted by the verb and its most prominent direct argument. Thus, "splashing" describes the configuration and motion of the liquid or liquid-like matter corresponding to the internal subject of the verb *splash*; "dripping" describes the configuration and motion of the liquid or viscous material corresponding to the internal subject of *drip*; and so on. That is to say, the manner component in these verbs is justified internally to the argument structure of the verb.

For present purposes, we will represent the manner component of a verb as a "tag" on the appropriate V node, leaving open the question of how it should properly be represented and of how it is introduced into the LRS representation. Further, we will assume that the internal "licensing" relation just discussed is represented by coindexing the manner component with the internal subject, as in (70), representing the verbs of (63a–b).

By hypothesis, a corresponding representation exists for each of the ergative verbs of this type. By contrast, transitive verbs of the type represented by (66) involve a manner component that relates, not internally to the lexical argument structure, but to the external argument, or "agent." Thus, for example, the manner component in the verb of (67a)—[smear] —receives no licensing index in the LRS representation (71).

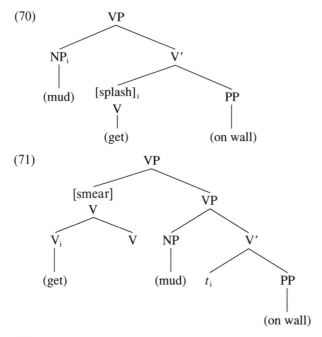

(70), (71)

Only at D-Structure is the manner component [smear] properly licensed, since it is only at D-Structure that the required external argument is "visible" to the manner tag associated with the verb.

Assuming that all of the transitive verbs of the type represented in (66) share this property of having an externally licensed manner component, then the ill-formedness of the inchoative, or intransitive, (b) variants of (67)–(69) can be explained. The intransitive variant is formed by moving the internal subject into [Spec, IP]. If this raising process applied to the verbs in question, the appearance of an external argument would be blocked. This would prevent licensing of the manner component of these verbs, violating Full Interpretation.

In light of this, is it possible to explain the ill-formedness of inchoatives formed from location verbs like *shelve*, as in (53a)? We believe that the solution to this problem is in fact to be found in the study of the means and manner modifier components. At this point, though, we can only suggest what the solution will be. Location verbs are verbs of "putting," suggesting that they share certain essential properties with *put*. They clearly share the basic relational structure; but it is possible that they share a manner, or means, component as well. Like the denominal location verbs, *put* fails to participate in the transitivity alternation; it has no inchoative form. If this is because its manner component requires external licensing, and if the denominal location verbs share this property, then the problem is solved. The inchoative is impossible for *put*, and for the denominal location verbs as well, because raising the object to [Spec, IP] blocks licensing of the externally oriented manner modifier. By contrast, English *get*, though structurally identical to *put* in l-syntax, is evidently devoid of all means or manner modification; and, as expected in view of the fact that no licensing is required, the inchoative is possible for *get* (as in (55b)).

If the inchoative blocks licensing of externally oriented manner modifiers, then why is the middle construction possible for denominal location verbs, as in (53c)? With respect to middle formation, these verbs do not differ from ergative verbs. If the middle involves extraction of an object, as is usually assumed, then how is the manner component of the verb of (53c) licensed?

Here again, we can only suggest the answer to this question. The middle is uniformly possible, we contend, for all (single-complement) transitive verbs that have an internal subject, whether or not the inchoative is also possible.[12] We suspect that the middle is formed from a transitive structure, rather than from the simple intransitive structure in which the internal subject is immediately dominated by the uppermost VP node. The latter is the structure associated with the inchoative. Thus, the verb of *The screen cleared* is the intransitive depicted in (72), whereas the verb of the middle construction, as in *These horses corral easily*, is the (causative) transitive construction depicted in (73).

(72)

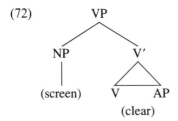

If this is true, then the presence of the upper, causative VP projection is relevant to the issue we are addressing. Imagine that the distinction between externally and internally oriented manner components has a structural basis. Suppose that, as a matter of lexical structure, internally oriented manner components are associated with the inner verb, and externally oriented manner components are associated with the upper, causative verb. Licensing of a manner component is nothing more than that: association with a particular verbal element in the LRS represen-

(73)

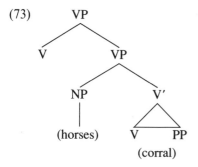

tation. The verbs of (66) cannot appear in the intransitive, inchoative form because their externally oriented manner modifiers are associated with the causative verb. They are *necessarily* transitive—and the (b) sentences of (67)–(69) are accordingly impossible. On the other hand, if the middle is formed from the transitive, that construction will not interfere with the licensing of externally oriented manner modifiers, since their required locus—the causative verb—is present in the transitive LRS representation.

4 Final Remarks and Remaining Questions

The purpose of this paper has been to explore the limits on (verbal) lexical items with respect to their argument structures and, if possible, to give an explanatory account of linguistically relevant limitations on lexical entries. Our intent has been to contribute to the effort to determine what is and what is not a possible lexical argument structure. We have made use of denominal verb formation as a probe into the inner organization of lexical argument structure, concluding that argument structure can be properly viewed as a *syntax* and, accordingly, subject to the laws of syntax, as known generally. In particular, it is subject to the principles determining the grammatical uses of head movement or incorporation (Baker 1988). A full attempt to account for argument structure must, we have argued, assume that the syntactic projection of lexical categories and arguments conforms to the principles of Unambiguous Projection (Kayne 1984) and Full Interpretation (Chomsky 1986b). We suspect, and have intended to show, that this is essentially all that is needed to give a full account of the notion "argument structure." If so, then there are no linguistic mechanisms that are specific to argument structure. For example, there is no process of "thematic role assignment," apart from predication; and there are no "thematic roles," apart from the lexical relations expressed in unambiguous, fully interpreted projections of the elementary lexical categories.

Clearly, however, this research program has a long way to go before it can be claimed with any surety to have demonstrated that argument structure is in fact a properly constrained syntax defined by elementary, independently established principles and elements. Only a small fraction of the total range of verb types, of English or any other language, has been submitted to analysis along the lines suggested here. This fact is immediately evident, for example, from even the most cursory examination of Levin's excellent annotated corpus of English verbs and argument structures (Levin 1991). Here we have discussed essentially only two verb classes: unergatives and a class whose members are characterized by the appearance of an internal predication and therefore an internal subject (the steadfastly transitive location and locatum verbs, and the alternating deadjectival causative/inchoative verbs).

We will not attempt now to extend the range of coverage, leaving that for later stages in our research program. But we will briefly address two of the many questions that have arisen in exploring the proposal set out here, beginning with the issue of what is lexical and what is syntactic, in the traditional sense (i.e., s-syntactic, in the usage temporarily adopted here). In closing, we will briefly summarize our position in relation to the theory of lexical argument structures.

4.1   Lexical versus Syntactic

We have proposed that argument structure is a syntax, but we have also separated it from s-syntax, referring to it as a collection of Lexical Relational Structure (LRS) representations. This is probably an onerous distinction, as many of our colleagues have pointed out in discussions with us, and it is important to determine whether it is anything more than a temporary terminological convenience. Although we suspect that the latter is the case, and although we will "chip away" at the distinction in future work, we must nevertheless assume that there is *something* lexical about the entries for verbs like *shelve*, or any verbal entry, in fact.

What is it that is lexical about the entry corresponding to *shelve*? Clearly, it is a lexical fact that *shelve* exists as a simple transitive verb in English, with a "meaning" embodying the same system of elemental relations as *put*. And if our analysis of it is correct, it is derived by incorporation of a noun in the manner suggested in preceding sections. This latter circumstance is also a lexical fact, since not all nouns can incorporate in this manner.

In thinking about this, we have taken a conservative view and assumed that this array of facts compels us to suppose that the lexical entry for *shelve* includes at least the full the syntactic structure depicted in (74).

(74)

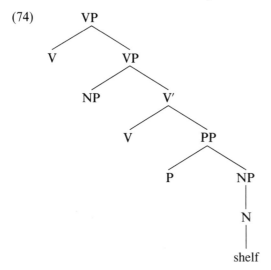

The entry will, of course, be inserted into an s-syntactic structure as a phrasal category, and its insertion will be grammatical if the point of insertion sanctions a verb phrase. The entry itself contains an empty phrasal position (symbolized *NP* here, but in fact, most likely neutral for category). This identifies a structural position in which an NP (or more accurately, a DP) will be sanctioned at D-Structure, other things being equal.

We believe that the conservative position would have the lexical entry stipulate all of this, plus the special property of *shelve*, shared with a few other location verbs, that its final consonant is voiced in the verbal form. This position is reasonable in one respect, since it assigns idiosyncratic properties to the lexicon, honoring an established and long-standing tradition that the lexicon is the "repository of irregularities." But it is unreasonable in another respect. The structural representations proposed here are identical to those defined in syntax generally, and they are subject to principles of grammar that determine well-formed syntactic structures in general. In short, the conservative position is moderately in conflict with the general thesis of this paper, that argument structure is a syntax of the conventional sort. We cannot resolve this contradiction here, though we expect that its resolution will not be specific to denominal verbs, or any other particular class of verbs, but will rather be part of a general theory of argument structure that takes into account the relational structures inherent in individual lexical entries. In reality, all verbs are to some extent phrasal idioms, that is, syntactic structures that must be learned as the conventional "names" for various dynamic events. That is our view of the matter, in any event, and it seems to be forced on us by the very framework we are considering. Moreover, it is not without empirical support, at least at the observational level. In many languages a large percentage of verbal lexical items are *overtly* phrasal (e.g., Igbo, Nwachukwu 1987); in others a healthy inventory of "light verb" constructions represents the class of overtly phrasal lexical entries (e.g., Japanese, Grimshaw and Mester 1988; English, Kearns 1988); and in still others (e.g., the Tanoan languages, including Jemez, Tewa, and the Tiwa languages), the verbal lexicon contains an extraordinary number of entries whose morphological make-up is overtly the result of incorporation. To be sure, many languages boast a large inventory of simple monomorphemic verbs. But our guess is that most, probably all, superficially monomorphemic verbs are lexically phrasal, possessing a structure that is syntactic, satisfying the requirements of Unambiguous Projection and Full Interpretation.

The above remarks are concerned with the notion "lexical" as it pertains to the *lexical entries* we assume for verbal lexical items. Our conservative position holds that the lexical entry of an item consists in the syntactic structure that expresses the full system of lexical grammatical relations inherent in the item. Thus, all of (74) is included in the lexical entry for *shelve*. But here, as elsewhere, the syntactic structure itself is determined by *general* syntactic principles that define unambiguous projections of category and argument structure. Whereas a particular entry, on the conservative view, must list the argument structure representation in full, the structure in which the lexical relations (specifier, complement, head, etc.) are expressed is purely syntactic in every sense of the word. This is not a "contradiction" that concerns us very much at this point.

But there is more to the issue than this, of course. We claim that the observed surface form of a verb like *shelve* is due to incorporation, an instance of the head movement variant of Move α. This is a purely syntactic process, constrained by grammatical principles that function generally to define well-formed syntactic structures. But, given our conservative view of lexical entries, it is legitimate to ask whether incorporation—say, in the formation of denominal verbs—is lexical or syntactic.

The notion that syntactic processes might apply in the lexicon is a familiar one (see Keyser and Roeper 1984, 1992), and it is coherent where lexical and syntactic structures are rigidly distinct. But in the system we are examining here, the two domains are not necessarily rigidly distinct,

even under the conservative view of lexical entries just outlined, which seeks simply to place the lexicon-syntax "boundary" where it belongs by defining the notion "lexical entry."

This is not to say that it is impossible to imagine what it might mean, in our framework, for Move α to "apply in the lexicon." Suppose it means that the process applies within lexical items "prior to lexical insertion." And imagine further that the derivation of a lexical item (i.e., the chain structure defined by incorporation in the lexicon) is invisible in what we have been referring to as s-syntax. It would then be a simple empirical matter to decide whether there are, in this sense, syntactic processes that "apply in the lexicon." But, so far as we can tell, the results are negative, or at least inconclusive, in this regard.

For example, if the structure to which lexical incorporation applies were invisible to s-syntax, in the sense of the preceding paragraph, there would, contrary to fact, be no syntactic distinction between simple transitive verbs like *make (trouble), have (puppies), dance (a jig)* and, say, the ergative verbs, like *break, clear, thicken.* Any conceivable algorithm for "masking" the derivation and underlying structure of the latter class of verbs renders them effectively indistinguishable from the former. Both would involve just a verb and a single argument; but their syntactic properties are utterly different, as is well known. Simple transitives fail to participate in the middle and inchoative constructions, whereas the "ergatives" do so freely. This difference in syntactic behavior relates, of course, to the difference in structural position (complement versus specifier) occupied by the relevant internal NP argument in the distinct LRS representations assumed for the two classes, a difference that is "visible" in the full derivations of lexical items, but not, presumably, in some "trimmed" version devoid of traces.

Observations of this type will, we believe, lead to the conclusion that it is wrong to insist too firmly upon the distinction implied by our use of such terms as Lexical Relational Structure, an expression we will continue to employ for expository convenience. The "structures" implicated in that usage are simply syntactic structures, expressing such normal syntactic structural relations as "head," "specifier," and "complement." And they are present in the syntactic representations over which normal syntactic processes and principles are defined. The qualification "lexical" refers to the property that the argument structures of verbs are "listed" in the lexicon, perhaps in the manner suggested by the conservative view of lexical entries.

There is a sense in which incorporation of the type we have been considering here is in fact "restricted to the lexicon." It is restricted to the domains defined by lexical items, that is, to LRS representations. But this apparent restriction reflects an accidental circumstance, having to do with the fact that incorporation effecting denominal and deadjectival verb formation involves strictly local movement from lexical head to lexical head. In contrast to movement processes in what we have we have termed s-syntax, no functional categories are involved in the verb formation processes at issue here, since no functional projections are present at points internal to the domains defined by lexical entries. Thus, there are real differences among movement processes that can, with some justice, be associated with a distinction between lexical and nonlexical phenomena, in some accepted sense. Denominal verb formation is in some sense lexical, whereas the passive, say, is nonlexical ("syntactic" in the traditional sense). But these differences are in reality ones of structural and categorial domain. The two types share the property that they are syntactic and are defined over syntactic structures.

We should mention here that, on the assumption that the passive (or NP-movement in general, perhaps) involves crucial reference to functional categories (e.g., to I and Case), Larson's appealing and conceptually productive analysis of the double object construction (Larson 1988) is incompatible with the view that LRS representations exclude functional projections. Although Larson's analysis does not itself directly obtrude this problem, since he does not necessarily share our assumptions, our own framework simply cannot make use of an "internal passive" to derive the double object construction—NP-movement cannot be motivated, and there can be no "place" for the agent in LRS representations (but see Hale and Keyser 1991:chap. 1, in which the passive analysis is briefly assumed).

Our position is that the double object construction is not an "internal passive" of the sort proposed by Larson. Rather, it involves a nonovert preposition expressing "central coincidence" (Hale 1986), corresponding to the overt *with* in its "possessive" use. This is the same as the nonovert preposition appearing in the LRS representations of locatum verbs like *saddle*, and it contrasts with the *to* of "terminal coincidence" that appears in the overtly prepositional partner in the dative alternation. On this view, *saddle the horse, give John a saddle,* and *provide John with a saddle* all have the same LRS representation involving the preposition of central coincidence (see (15), (16), and associated text), whereas *give a saddle to John* involves the preposition of terminal coincidence. By hypothesis, therefore, the dative alternation involves a lexical parameter: namely, the choice of the central or the terminal preposition at the head of the internal PP predicate (see Hoffman 1991 for a related conception of certain Bantu applied constructions).

4.2   The External Subject Relation

The idea that the passive may not apply, internal to an LRS representation, to introduce an NP argument into the Spec position is perhaps akin to the general fact that the Spec position may not be occupied unless the appearance of an NP there is "motivated" in some manner, whether by predication (as in section 2.3) or by circumstances having to do with Case and agreement, irrelevant in LRS, by hypothesis. But this raises again the question of what permits the appearance of subjects—at D-Structure, at least—with unergative and transitive verbs, and with passives, for that matter.

The matter is not simple, by any means, but it appears that the presence of an NP in [Spec, VP] can be motivated, and therefore required, by factors having to do with the *matrix syntactic environment* in which a lexical item appears, regardless of properties internal to its LRS representation. For example, the causative of an unergative verb is perfectly well formed in many languages that have *overt* causative morphology, as exemplified by the Papago (Tohono O'odham) verbs in (75), in which the matrix causative verb is realized overtly by the suffix *-cud*.

(75) a. bisck-cud   'cause to sneeze'
      b. 'a'as-cud   'cause to laugh'
      c. wihos-cud   'cause to vomit'
      d. 'i'ihog-cud   'cause to cough'

Here, we might suppose, some grammatical property of the suffixal causative verb—for example, its "transitivity," including the ability to assign accusative Case—licenses the NP in the Spec position of the unergative verb. This NP will correspond to the semantic "agent" in the event named by the unergative predicate; that is, it will bear the same semantic relation to the unergative predicate that its s-syntactic subject bears in the intransitive construction. But in the causative, this "agent" —the *causee*, as it is sometimes called—is realized by an NP argument having the properties of a grammatical object in relation to the derived causative verb. The latter, in its general syntactic behavior, is simply a transitive verb. In (76a), for example, the NP *(g)* *'a'al* 'children' is the grammatical subject of the intransitive verb *bisck* (perfective *bisc*) 'sneeze', requiring third person agreement in the auxiliary (the element appearing in second, or Wackernagel's, position) in accordance with the general principles of subject agreement in the language. In the causative construction (76b), the same NP appears as the grammatical object, requiring object agreement in the verb word; the subject function in this transitive form is assumed by the NP corresponding to the "agent of causation," and it is this argument (represented here by the first person singular pronominal *'a:ñ(i)*) that determines subject agreement in the auxiliary.

(76) a. 'A'al   'at   bisc.
        children 3:PERF sneeze:PERF
        'The children sneezed.'
    b. 'A:ñ 'ant   g   'a'al   ha-bisck-c.
        I   1sg:PERF ART children 3PL-sneeze-CAUSE:PERF
        'I made the children sneeze.'

In both sentences the nominal expression *(g) 'a'al* 'children' represents the semantic role commonly called "agent" in relation to the verb *bisck* 'sneeze'—that is to say, the children are the sneezers in the events depicted in both (76a) and (76b). In the framework we are examining here, however, the "agent" of an unergative is not, strictly speaking, an argument of the verb. The "agent" enters into no relation in the syntactic representations of the argument structures of lexical items headed by unergative verbs. It is an external argument, related to the unergative verb indirectly through predication, the same being true of the "agent" of transitive verbs as well.

If at some point in the derivation of (76b) the NP *(g) 'a'al* 'child' is in fact in the Spec position of the verb *bisck* 'sneeze', then it must be permitted there by virtue of some feature of its environment—some property that sanctions, in fact forces, an NP to appear there. Presumably, the feature in question is some property of the affixal causative verb *-cud* 'cause', as suggested above. And the derived verb does indeed have the property of transitivity and therefore requires an argument to which it can assign accusative Case (realized overtly in object agreement). We will assume for present purposes that this is the circumstance that forces the appearance of an NP in the Spec position of the embedded unergative verb *bisck* in the Papago causative *bisckcud* 'cause to sneeze'.[13] The relevant structure is roughly as in (77), abbreviating the derivation of the unergative verb itself.

(77)

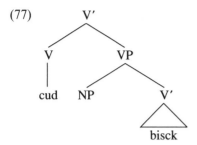

If the NP in (77) is permitted to appear there by virtue of features associated with the matrix causative, what factors are responsible in sanctioning the subject of (76a)? Here again, we assume that it is properties of the local matrix environment that are responsible for the appearance of a grammatical subject—that is, for the effect commonly referred to as the Extended Projection Principle (Chomsky 1982). We will adopt the traditional view that the relevant properties—nominative Case and associated subject agreement—are lodged in the functional category I (termed the "auxiliary" in most of the literature on Papago), as shown in (78).

(78)

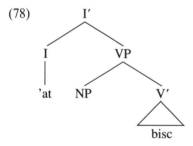

We are assuming that the D-Structure position of the grammatical subject is [Spec, VP].[14] A subject may appear in that position only if it is, in principle, forced to appear there. The predication requirement forces the appearance of a subject for verbs whose complements are inherently predicational, that is, PP or AP; this is, so to speak, a "VP-internal" motivation. Otherwise, the motivation is "external," in the sense that the appearance of a subject is forced by properties of the matrix—for example, the transitive features of a causative verb, or the Case and agreement features of I, as illustrated above. An internally motivated subject is, in an intuitively clear sense, a "part" of the lexical item with which it is associated, inasmuch as its appearance is determined by properties of the lexical item itself. In short, it enters into grammatical relations defined by the projection of the lexical head.

The appearance of a subject in [Spec, VP] is not a uniform phenomenon. In (78) we must assume that the subject appears in that position as a result of lexical insertion, since it is not forced to appear by virtue of any requirement inherent to the verbal projection itself. On the other hand, in the case of a verb of the type represented by English *clear* (79), the subject is forced by predication internal to the verbal projection, the complement of the head V being an adjective (whose incorporation results in the deadjectival verb).

(79)

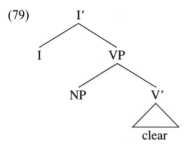

At D-Structure these subjects are identical in their structural positions. Where governed by I (as in (78–79)), both raise to [Spec, IP] to satisfy requirements of that projection and, presumably, to realize the relation, traditionally called predication, that holds between [Spec, IP] and the VP (Rothstein 1983), a relation that may or may not be distinct from the very real VP-internal relation, also called predication, that is assumed to hold of [Spec, VP] in relation to the head V and its V′ projection.

However, although internally and externally forced subjects (as exemplified by (79) and (78), respectively) are structurally indistinct, they differ in "interpretation," in the manner suggested in earlier discussions. An internally forced subject is the subject of a VP-internal predicate, that is, of the PP or AP complement of a head V. By contrast, externally forced subjects are regularly interpreted as "agents" (or some other thing appropriate to the event depicted in the verbal projection), purely as a product of the construction itself. If this interpretation is by predication, as suggested above, it is purely constructional and is not inherent to the relevant lexical items, which systematically lack internally forced, or "lexical," subjects.

Before concluding this subsection, we should say something more about the fact that English unergatives lack causative forms. If the overt causative morphology of Papago, and many hundreds of other languages, has properties (whatever these may be) that force the appearance of a subject in its immediate complement VP, why does the nonovert causative postulated for English *fail* to force that argument to appear—why is *Sneeze the child* impossible in English, while its Papago counterpart *(G)* *'ali bisckcud* is perfectly well formed? The answer lies in the nature of (certain) nonovert verbal elements. The English nonovert "causative" is fundamentally devoid of properties, apart from the category V itself (and the associated elementary semantics). In particular, it has no properties that could force the appearance of an NP in the Spec position of its complement. To all intents and purposes, the nonovert causative is simply "not there." To be sure, it could "acquire properties" through incorporation of the overt head of its complement. But this would effectively block lexical insertion, of a subject, into the lower Spec position. The result is the same: the causative of the unergative is ungrammatical.

The notion that the nonovert causative of English is devoid of properties makes sense of another fact of English: namely, the extremely free transitivity alternation found with the ergative verbs of the language. Verbs like *clear, thin, lengthen* have both transitive and intransitive (inchoative) forms.[15] This comes for free under the hypothesis that the nonovert causative verb has no properties of its own (apart from category, of course). It acquires properties through incorporation (giving the transitive variant). Thus, the observed transitivity alternation depends simply on whether head movement applies or not. The alternation is not stipulated for these verbs, since it follows directly from the essential nature of nonovert verbs.

4.3 A Summary of the Framework

The approach we have entertained here is fundamentally one that seeks to determine the extent to which it is possible to understand certain observed limitations on argument structure in terms of the essential nature of preestablished principles and elements.

The relevant constraints on argument structure are basically these: (i) the variety of relations between arguments and the head and its projections is highly restricted, a circumstance that is reflected, for example, in the correspondingly restricted range of semantic roles (thematic roles) recognized in an ample and well-informed linguistic literature; (ii) what might be termed the "depth of embedding" in lexical structures is uniformly modest, generally permitting no more than one complement VP for a given lexical entry, shunning full use of the "recursive" capacity inherent in complementation.

We have argued that the lexical categories (V, N, etc.) project unambiguous syntactic structures. Crucially, Unambiguous Projection prohibits *n*-ary branching, where *n* is greater than two, and it prohibits the projection of a phrasal category through more than one intermediate level (e.g., V projects at most V′ and VP). This accounts in large measure for constraint (i) by restricting arguments to the complement and Spec positions in LRS representations. These positions correspond to the grammatical "relations" an argument may bear in LRS: specifier of VP, complement to V, complement to P, and so on. And, in this conception of argument structure, there are no lexically determined "roles" beyond these.

Argument structure representations are also subject to Full Interpretation. This is relevant primarily in connection with the Spec position, which can be occupied only if the appearance of an argument there is internally motivated by predication. Since only AP and PP are predicates in LRS representations, VP recursion, which would be possible only if VP were a predicate, is excluded. We suggest that this is what accounts for constraint (ii), in part at least.

Notes

Like this volume, this paper is dedicated to Sylvain Bromberger, to whom we are indebted for the many ways in which he has enriched our understanding of linguistic problems. We wish also to acknowledge the helpful comments and criticisms of a number of colleagues, including Mark Baker, Robert Berwick, Maria Bittner, Noam Chomsky, Chris Collins, Abdelkader Fassi Fehri, Jeff Gruber, Morris Halle, Mika Hoffman, Richard Larson, Beth Levin, Alec Marantz, Richard Oehrle, David Pesetsky, Tova Rapoport, Tom Roeper, Susan Rothstein, Carol Tenny, and Ken Wexler. In addition, we are grateful for the comments and criticisms of students and colleagues who were present when various versions of this work were presented in the context of the MIT Lexicon Project and elsewhere. Finally, we wish to acknowledge the support of the MIT Center for Cognitive Science to the MIT Lexicon Project.

1. Notationally, the trace of a category affected by head movement is represented here as X-dominating-t, where X represents the lexical category of the trace t.

2. The issue of linguistic level (lexicon, D-Structure) will figure in our discussion only where it is directly relevant. For the most part, we will be talking about structures we assume to be present at the lexical level of linguistic structure.

3. We do not attempt to account here for the morphophonological developments (final voicing in this instance) that characterize certain denominal verbs.

4. For some remarks on English weather verbs, see Hale and Keyser 1991:21–22.

5. It could be argued that these sentences are ill formed because the adjectival secondary predicates have no overt subject. But an overt subject does not seem to be a requirement for secondary predication in general—note, for example, *We*

pick green, We ship dry (i.e., ship our cows dry), We wean young (i.e., take calves from their mothers while they are young).

6. In LRS representations, of course, we are dealing with the universal categories, whatever they turn out to be. Their realization in individual languages as nouns, verbs, and so on, is a parametric matter. Thus, the English possessive verb *have*, for example, is probably a realization of the universal category P, not V. But the Warlpiri verb *mardarni*, which most often "translates" English *have*, is clearly V, not P.

7. In assuming complex VP structures as the basis of denominal location (e.g., *shelve*) and locatum (e.g., *saddle*) verbs, we do not intend to imply that a conflation like *shelve* "means" the same thing as its analytic paraphrase *put on a shelf* (cf., *put the sand on a shelf, shelve the sand*). We maintain simply that they share the same LRS representation (a claim that could also be wrong, to be sure). We will not address here the very real linguistic problem of accounting for the fact that conflations typically do not, in the full sense, mean the same things as the expressions usually put forth as their analytic paraphrases.

8. We use the expressions *s-syntactic* and *s-syntax* for expository convenience to refer to syntax in the sense of D-Structure or S-Structure, that is, syntax in the generally received sense, in contrast to syntax in the lexicon, to which we sometimes refer as *l-syntax*.

9. This is a feature that distinguishes lexical syntactic representations from s-syntax, where causatives in many languages readily take unergative complements (see section 4.2 for discussion). We postpone for later work an analysis of prima facie LRS counterexamples represented by English "comitative" transitives such as *trot the mule, jump the horse*, and *run the hounds*; see Brousseau and Ritter 1991.

10. It is likely that the requirement of full interpretation also limits the appearance of subjects within the LRS projections of the categories other than V, an issue we will not discuss here (but see Hale and Keyser 1991).

11. The S-Structure representation (43) is simplified in relation to the lexical syntactic representation in various ways—for example, by erasure of the trace defined by head movement, together with the phrasal node projected thereby. We leave open here the important question of whether the material thus deleted is "visible" at D-Structure and S-Structure.

12. The qualification "single-complement" is necessary since, for reasons we do not understand, middles cannot be formed where an overt expression would remain behind in complement position in s-syntax. Thus, **These books put easily on shelves*, beside *These books shelve easily*.

13. The factors that force the appearance of a subject in the complement of overt causative verbs are elusive and cannot be identified exclusively with Case; if Case alone were the factor, then we would expect **with John speak for us, *consider Mary speak well*, and **get Bill leave early* to be grammatical, other things being equal.

14. We assume this simply as a temporary convenience, without argument. We do not intend to imply that the question is settled, by any means. Strong arguments

exist in favor of other alternatives (see especially Bittner 1991, Koopman and Sportiche 1987, Speas 1990, Sportiche 1988).

15. We must assume that the overt derivational ending -*en* appearing on many such verbs is associated with the "lower" (inchoative) verb and not with the "upper" (causative) verb. But see Pesetsky 1990 for detailed discussion of derivational morphology and for observations that might show our assumption to be wrong.

References

Anderson, M. 1977. NP pre-posing in noun phrases. In *Proceedings of the 8th Annual Meeting of the North Eastern Linguistic Society*, ed. M. J. Stein. GLSA, University of Massachusetts, Amherst.

Baker, M. 1988. *Incorporation: A theory of grammatical function changing*. Chicago: University of Chicago Press.

Baker, M., and K. Hale. 1990. Relativized Minimality and pronoun incorporation. *Linguistic Inquiry* 21:289–97.

Bittner, M. 1991. Case and scope. Ms., Rutgers University.

Branigan, P. 1992. Subjects and complementizers. Doctoral dissertation, MIT.

Bresnan, J., and J. Kanerva. 1989. Locative inversion in Chicheŵa: A case study of factorization in grammar. *Linguistic Inquiry* 20:1–50.

Brousseau, A. M., and E. Ritter. 1991. A non-unified analysis of agentive verbs. To appear in *Proceedings of the Tenth West Coast Conference on Formal Linguistics*.

Burzio, L. 1981. Intransitive verbs and Italian auxiliaries. Doctoral dissertation, MIT.

Carrier-Duncan, J. 1985. Linking of thematic roles in derivational word formation. *Linguistic Inquiry* 16:1–34.

Chomsky, N. 1970. Remarks on nominalization. In *Readings in English transformational grammar*, ed. R. Jacobs and P. Rosenbaum. Waltham, Mass.: Ginn.

Chomsky, N. 1981. *Lectures on government and binding*. Dordrecht: Foris.

Chomsky, N. 1982. *Some concepts and consequences of the theory of government and binding*. Cambridge, Mass.: MIT Press.

Chomsky, N. 1986a. *Barriers*. Cambridge, Mass.: MIT Press.

Chomsky, N. 1986b. *Knowledge of language: Its nature, origin, and use*. New York: Praeger.

Clark, E., and H. Clark. 1979. When nouns surface as verbs. *Language* 55:767–811.

Condoravdi, C. 1989. The middle: Where semantics and morphology meet. In *MIT working papers in linguistics 11: Papers from the Student Conference in Linguistics*. Department of Linguistics and Philosophy, MIT.

Grimshaw, J. 1990. *Argument structure*. Cambridge, Mass.: MIT Press.

Grimshaw, J., and A. Mester. 1988. Light verbs and θ-marking. *Linguistic Inquiry* 19:205–32.

Gruber, J. 1965. Studies in lexical relations. Doctoral dissertation, MIT.

Hale, K. 1986. Notes on world view and semantic categories: Some Warlpiri examples. In *Features and projections*, ed. P. Muysken and H. van Riemsdijk. Dordrecht: Foris.

Hale, K. 1989. The syntax of lexical word formation. Paper presented at the Amerindian Parasession of the Fourth Annual Pacific Linguistics Conference, University of Oregon, Eugene.

Hale, K., and S. J. Keyser. 1986. Some transitivity alternations in English. Lexicon Project Working Papers 7, Center for Cognitive Science, MIT.

Hale, K., and S. J. Keyser. 1987. A view from the middle. Lexicon Project Working Papers 10, Center for Cognitive Science, MIT.

Hale, K., and S. J. Keyser. 1988. Explaining and constraining the English middle. In *Studies in generative approaches to aspect*, ed. C. Tenny. Lexicon Project Working Papers 24, Center for Cognitive Science, MIT.

Hale, K., and S. J. Keyser. 1991. On the syntax of argument structure. Lexicon Project Working Papers, Center for Cognitive Science, MIT.

Hale, K., and S. J. Keyser. 1992. The syntactic character of thematic structure. In *Thematic structure: Its role in grammar*, ed. I. M. Roca. Berlin: Foris.

Hale, K., and T. R. Rapoport. In progress. On the licensing of subject, manner, and means in the syntactic representation of lexical argument structure. Ms., MIT.

Higginbotham, J. 1985. On semantics. *Linguistic Inquiry* 16:547–93.

Hoffman, M. 1991. The syntax of argument-structure-changing morphology. Doctoral dissertation, MIT.

Jackendoff, R. 1972. *Semantic interpretation in generative grammar*. Cambridge, Mass.: MIT Press.

Jaeggli, O. 1984. Passives, middles, and implicit arguments. Ms., MIT.

Jaeggli, O. 1986. Passive. *Linguistic Inquiry* 17:587–622.

Kayne, R. 1984. *Connectedness and binary branching*. Dordrecht: Foris.

Kearns, K. 1988. Light verbs in English. Ms., MIT.

Keyser, S. J., and T. Roeper. 1984. On the middle and ergative constructions in English. *Linguistic Inquiry* 15:381–416.

Keyser, S. J., and T. Roeper. 1992. Re: The abstract clitic hypothesis. *Linguistic Inquiry* 22:89–125.

Kipka, P. 1990. Slavic aspect and its implications. Doctoral dissertation, MIT.

Koopman, H., and D. Sportiche. 1987. Subjects. Ms., UCLA.

Lakoff, G. 1977. Linguistic gestalts. In *Papers from the Thirteenth Regional Meeting, Chicago Linguistic Society*. Chicago Linguistic Society, University of Chicago.

Larson, R. 1988. On the double object construction. *Linguistic Inquiry* 19:335–91.

Levin, B. 1983. On the nature of ergativity. Doctoral dissertation, MIT.

Levin, B. 1991. English verb classes and alternations: A preliminary investigation. Ms., Northwestern University.

Levin, B., and T. R. Rapoport. 1988. Lexical subordination. In *Papers from the Twenty-fourth Regional Meeting, Chicago Linguistic Society*. Chicago Linguistic Society, University of Chicago.

Lombard, L. B. 1985. How not to flip the prowler: Transitive verbs of action and the identity of actions. In *Actions and events*, ed. E. LePore and B. McLaughlin. Oxford: Blackwell.

Marantz, A. 1984. *On the nature of grammatical relations*. Cambridge, Mass.: MIT Press.

Mithun, M. 1984. The evolution of noun incorporation. *Language* 60:845–95.

Nwachukwu, P. A. 1987. The argument structure of Igbo verbs. Lexicon Project Working Papers 18, Center for Cognitive Science, MIT.

Oosten, J. van 1977. Subjects and agenthood in English. In *Papers from the Thirteenth Regional Meeting, Chicago Linguistic Society*. Chicago Linguistic Society, University of Chicago.

Perlmutter, D. 1978. Impersonal passives and the unaccusative hypothesis. In *Proceedings of the Berkeley Linguistics Society 4*. Berkeley Linguistics Society, University of California, Berkeley.

Pesetsky, D. 1990. Experience predicates and universal alignment principles. Ms., MIT.

Pullum, G. K. 1988. Topic . . . comment: Citation etiquette beyond Thunderdome. *Natural Language & Linguistic Theory* 6:579–88.

Rapoport, T. R. 1987. Copular, nominal, and small clauses: A study of Israeli Hebrew. Doctoral dissertation, MIT.

Rothstein, S. 1983. The syntactic forms of predication. Doctoral dissertation, MIT.

Speas, M. J. 1990. *Phrase structure in natural language*. Dordrecht: Kluwer.

Sportiche, D. 1988. A theory of floating quantifiers and its corollaries for constituent structure. *Linguistic Inquiry* 19:425–50.

Talmy, L. 1985. Lexicalization patterns. In *Language typology and syntactic description*, ed. T. Shopen. Cambridge: Cambridge University Press.

Travis, L. 1984. Parameters and effects of word order variation. Doctoral dissertation, MIT.

Walinska de Hackbeil, H. 1986. The roots of phrase structure. The syntactic basis of English morphology. Doctoral dissertation, University of Washington, Seattle.

Walinska de Hackbeil, H. 1986. Theta-government, thematic government, and extraction asymmetries in zero derivation. Report CS-R8918 April, Center for Mathematics and Computer Science, Amsterdam.

Williams, E. 1980. Predication. *Linguistic Inquiry* 11:203–38.

Chapter 3

Distributed Morphology and the Pieces of Inflection	Morris Halle and Alec Marantz

1 Morphology with or without Affixes

The last few years have seen the emergence of several clearly articulated alternative approaches to morphology. One such approach rests on the notion that only stems of the so-called lexical categories (N, V, A) are morpheme "pieces" in the traditional sense—connections between (bundles of) meaning (features) and (bundles of) sound (features). What look like affixes on this view are merely the by-product of morphophonological rules called word formation rules (WFRs) that are sensitive to features associated with the lexical categories, called lexemes. Such an a-morphous or affixless theory, adumbrated by Beard (1966) and Aronoff (1976), has been articulated most notably by Anderson (1992) and in major new studies by Aronoff (1992) and Beard (1991). In contrast, Lieber (1992) has refined the traditional notion that affixes as well as lexical stems are "morpheme" pieces whose lexical entries relate phonological form with meaning and function. For Lieber and other "lexicalists" (see, e.g., Jensen 1990), the combining of lexical items creates the words that operate in the syntax. In this paper we describe and defend a third theory of morphology, Distributed Morphology,[1] which combines features of the affixless and the lexicalist alternatives. With Anderson, Beard, and Aronoff, we endorse the separation of the terminal elements involved in the syntax from the phonological realization of these elements. With Lieber and the lexicalists, on the other hand, we take the phonological realization of the terminal elements in the syntax to be governed by lexical (Vocabulary) entries that relate bundles of morphosyntactic features to bundles of phonological features.

We have called our approach *Distributed Morphology* (hereafter DM) to highlight the fact that the machinery of what traditionally has been called morphology is not concentrated in a single component of the grammar, but rather is distributed among several different components.[2] For example, "word formation"—the creation of complex syntactic heads— may take place at any level of grammar through such processes as head movement and adjunction and/or merger of structurally or linearly adjacent heads. The theory is a new development of ideas that we have each been pursuing independently for a number of years.[3] It shares important traits with traditional morphology (e.g., in its insistence that hierarchically organized pieces are present at all levels of representation of a word), but deviates from traditional morphology in other respects (most especially in not insisting on the invariance of these pieces but allowing them to undergo changes in the course of the derivation).

As noted above, the theory of DM is in substantial agreement with lexeme-based morphology that at the syntactic levels of Logical Form (LF), D-Structure (DS), and S-Structure (SS) terminal nodes lack phonological features and that they obtain these only at the level of Morphological Structure (MS) (see (1)). DM parts company with lexeme-based morphology with regard to its affixless aspect. As discussed in greater detail below, lexeme-based theory treats inflections of all kinds as morphosyntactic features represented on nodes dominating word stems and sees inflectional affixes as the by-product of WFRs applying to these stems. Anderson (1992) motivates this position by citing violations of "the one-to-one relation between components of meaning and components of form which is essential to the classical morpheme..." (p. 70). Rather than redefine the notion of morpheme so as to allow for particular violations of the one-to-one relation between meaning and phonological form, as in DM, Anderson chooses to eliminate all affixes from morphology.

On its face, Anderson's proposal contradicts not only the traditional approaches to morphology, but also much current practice in generative syntax, where inflections such as the English tense or possessive markers are standardly treated as heads of functional categories and must therefore be terminal nodes. Since Anderson neither offers alternative analyses nor indicates any intention to revise syntactic theory, we suppose that he accepts the current view that in the syntactic representations—in LF, SS, and DS—Tense, Possessive, and other inflections constitute separate nodes. Since Anderson recognizes no affixal morphemes in the morphology or phonology, we must assume that on his account these inflectional morphemes are eliminated in the input to the morphology, and their morphosyntactic features are transferred to the stem lexemes, so that at the point at which lexical insertion applies, the terminal nodes allow for the insertion of stems exclusively. It is to these affixless stems that Anderson's

WFRs apply and insert (or change) phonological material. Anderson's theory thus crucially involves a stage where affixal morphemes are eliminated, followed by a stage where many of the same affixal morphemes are reintroduced by the WFRs.

In many cases the hierarchical structure of phonological material (affixes) added by the WFRs recapitulates the hierarchical organization of functional morphemes in the syntax. In Anderson's theory, any such parallel between the layering of syntax and the layering of phonology is just an accident of the organization of the WFRs into ordered blocks, since in his theory the ordering of the blocks creates the layering of phonological material and is essentially independent of the sorts and sources of morphosyntactic features mentioned in the rules. This direct relationship between syntax and morphology does not obtain everywhere: it is violated, for example, in cases of suppletion such as English *be, am, was,* and (as shown in section 3.2) it is with suppletion phenomena that Anderson's theory deals most readily. Since suppletion is not of central importance in the morphology of English or of any other language, the approach did not seem to us to be on the right track. Moreover, as we explain below, we find essential aspects of the approach unnecessary and even unworkable.

Lieber (1992) elaborates the traditional view that affixes are morphemes in a version that both contradicts Anderson's lexeme-based approach and deviates in important respects from DM. In Lieber's theory, affixes and stems alike are lexical items containing both phonological and morphosyntactic features. Crucially for this theory, these lexical items combine to create the words manipulated by the syntax. We agree with Lieber that both stems and affixes are lexical (for us, Vocabulary) entries that connect morphosyntactic feature bundles with phonological feature complexes. However, for DM the assignment of phonological features to morphosyntactic feature bundles takes place after the syntax and does not create or determine the terminal elements manipulated by the syntax. This difference between the theories yields two important contrasts between DM and Lieber's lexical morphology. First, since in DM syntactic operations combine terminal nodes to create words prior to Vocabulary insertion, the theory predicts that the structure of words—the hierarchical location of affixes, and so on—is determined by the syntax and not by subcategorization frames carried by each affix, as on Lieber's account. Second, since in DM none of the morphosyntactic features involved in the operation of the syntax is supplied by Vocabulary insertion, the Vocabulary entries can be featurally underspecified. On this issue, DM agrees with a major insight of Anderson's theory and diverges from Lieber's theory, where the

Vocabulary entries of affixes must carry enough features to generate the proper feature structures for the syntax and LF. This aspect of Lieber's approach leads to difficulties that are discussed in Marantz 1992c and Noyer 1992a and are therefore not included here.

2 Distributed Morphology

DM adopts the basic organization of a "principles-and-parameters" grammar, diagrammed in (1). The added level of Morphological Structure is the interface between syntax and phonology. MS is a syntactic representation that nevertheless serves as part of the phonology, where "phonology" is broadly conceived as the interpretive component that realizes syntactic representations phonologically.

(1)

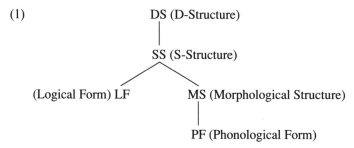

Representations at each of the five levels consist of hierarchical groupings of terminal elements graphically represented by the familiar tree diagrams. The terminal elements of the trees consist of complexes of grammatical features. These terminal elements are supplied with phonological features only after Vocabulary insertion at MS (see below). Although nothing hinges on this terminology in what follows, we have chosen to call the terminal elements "morphemes" both before and after Vocabulary insertion, that is, both before and after they are supplied with phonological features.

If hierarchical tree structures of terminal nodes (morphemes) within both words and phrases constitute the representations at every level of grammatical analysis, we might expect the organization of phonological pieces (stems and affixes) in the structure at PF to be isomorphic to the hierarchical arrangement of morphosyntactic terminal elements in the syntax. As already remarked, in many instances there seems to be no one-to-one relation between terminal elements in the syntax and phonological pieces, nor does the organization and bracketing of the phonological pieces directly reflect the syntactic bracketing. Affixless morphology constitutes one response to this observation; a different response is offered by DM. Instead of abandoning the notion that affixes are morphemes, DM recognizes that MS is a level of grammatical representation with its own principles and properties and that the apparent mismatches between the organization of the morphosyntactic pieces and the organization of the phonological pieces are the result of well-motivated operations manipulating terminal elements at this level and at DS and SS.

2.1 Mismatches between Syntax and Morphology

We examine here some of the important differences between the terminal elements and their organization in LF, SS, and DS, on the one hand, and in MS and PF, on the other. We assume that in LF, SS, and DS there is only hierarchical nesting of constituents, but no left-to-right order among the morphemes. The linear order of morphemes that all sentences exhibit at PF must therefore be established by the rules or principles that relate SS to MS (and PF). (For some discussion, see Travis 1989, 1992, Marantz 1989.) Note that we do not assume, with Lieber (1992), that the ordering of constituents within words and the ordering of words within phrases obey the same principles, with common notions of "head," "complement," and "specifier" triggering orderings of affixes with respect to stems and of phrases with respect to syntactic heads. Although we will not argue against Lieber's position here (but see Anderson 1992: chap. 2 for some relevant considerations and the critical review in Spencer, to appear), we will assume that an affix's status as a prefix, suffix, or infix is in principle independent of its syntactic role.

An additional source of the noted lack of isomorphism between PF and SS is the fact that morphemes may be inserted in MS to meet universal and/or language-specific well-formedness conditions. For example, subject-verb agreement is implemented in many languages by adjoining an Agr morpheme to the Tns node; features from the subject are then copied onto the Agr node. Case-number-gender concord in Determiner Phrases (DPs) is implemented in a similar fashion by supplying, for example, case-number suffixes to Adjective and Determiner nodes and copying features associated with the head noun of the DP onto them.[4]

This addition of terminal nodes at MS changes the number of terminal elements that might find phonological realization and thus contributes to the noted lack of isomorphism between PF and SS. Other grammatical processes also may disturb the one-to-one relation between terminal elements in the syntax and terminal elements at MS: a terminal element may be moved from one position in a tree and adjoined to a terminal element in another position by head-to-head movement; structurally adjacent nodes may be merged; sister terminal nodes may be fused into a single terminal node; and a given node may be fissioned into two. (For discussion of head movement, merger, fusion, and fission, see Baker 1988, Bonet 1991, Koopman 1983, Marantz 1984,1988,1989, 1992b, Noyer 1992a, and below.)

We distinguish here between "merger" and "fusion." Merger, like head-to-head movement, joins terminal nodes under a category node of a head (a "zero-level category node") but maintains two independent terminal nodes under this category node. Thus, Vocabulary insertion places two separate Vocabulary items under the derived head, one for each of the merged terminal nodes. Merger generally joins a head with the head of its complement XP; see the references cited above. Thus, like head-to-head movement, merger forms a new word from heads of independent phrases; but these independent heads remain separate morphemes within the new derived word. On the other hand, fusion takes two terminal nodes that are sisters under a single category node and fuses them into a single terminal node. Only one Vocabulary item may now be inserted, an item that must have a subset of the morphosyntactic features of the fused node, including the features from both input terminal nodes. Unlike merger, fusion reduces the number of independent morphemes in a tree. Since both head-to-head movement and merger form structures in which two terminal nodes are sisters under a single category node, both may feed fusion.

Examples of head-to-head movement include the movement of English auxiliary verbs to Tense (Tns), and Tns to C in questions (see section 4). Merger combines Tns with the main verb in English, as illustrated in section 4. A simple example of morpheme fusion is the single affix signaling number and case encountered in many Indo-European languages; such affixes realize a terminal node that is the result of the fusion of independent Case and Number nodes. In contrast, number and case constitute separate phonological pieces in Turkish, indicating that fusion has not applied to the Number and Case nodes here.

Morpheme fission is discussed in Marantz 1992b and Noyer 1992a. A simple example involves the pronominal proclitics of Georgian, treated by Anderson (1992) in terms of WFRs but analyzed, we believe correctly, as pronominal clitics by Nash-Haran (1992). Sample Georgian verb forms are listed in (2), in three subgroups.[5] The first subgroup (2a–f) contains the 3rd singular object forms; the second subgroup (2g–l) contains the 3rd singular subject forms; and the third subgroup (2m–q) contains forms where both subject and object are either 1st or 2nd person.

(2) With 3rd person object: X draw(s) 3rd person

a. v-xatav
   'I draw him'

b. v-xatav-t
   'we draw him'

c. ∅-xatav
   'you (sg) draw him'

d. ∅-xatav-t
   'you (pl) draw him'

e. xatav-s
   'he draws him'

f. xatav-en
   'they draw him'

With 3rd person subject: 3rd person draws X

g. m-xatav-s
   'he draws me'

h. gv-xatav-s
   'he draws us'

i. g-xatav-s
   'he draws you (sg)'

j. g-xatav-(s)-t
   'he draws you (pl)'

k. xatav-s
   'he draws him'

l. xatav-s
   'he draws them'

I-you and you-me forms

m. g-xatav
   'I draw you (sg)'

n. m-xatav
   'you (sg) draw me'

o. g-xatav-t
   'we draw you (sg or pl)' or 'I draw you (pl)'

p. gv-xatav
   'you (sg) draw us'

q. gv-xatav-t
   'you (pl) draw us'

The most salient feature of the examples in (2) is that 3rd person arguments do not surface in prestem position, nor do they (generally) determine when the plural /-t/ is inserted.[6] To capture these facts, we postulate that in prestem position these verb forms contain a Clitic cluster, which syntactically attaches as a sister to the inflected verb. The Clitic cluster incorporates under a single node all the 1st and 2nd person (pronominal) arguments (and certain special 3rd person arguments; see note 6). The terminal nodes in the Clitic cluster then fuse into a single terminal node.

After fusion, the MS structure is further modified by the MS fission rule in (3).

(3) *Fission*

Cl + Stem → [+pl] + Cl + Stem (linear order irrelevant)[7]
    |
[+pl]

    unless the [+pl] is part of a [+1], DAT argument

Rule (3) splits off a plural feature from this fused Clitic cluster and sets the feature up as a separate terminal node (direct and indirect objects in Georgian appear in the dative case). The Plural does not appear as a split-off morpheme when the Clitic cluster includes a 1st person "dative" argument (which might be an indirect object or a "dative subject" as well as a direct object). Although we have captured this fact by the exception stated in rule (3), it would have been possible to obtain the same result by writing a further fusion rule that undoes the effects of (3) for a 1st person DAT argument. Nothing in the analysis would have to be changed under this option.[8]

The splitting off of the Plural as a separate morpheme occurs prior to the insertion of the Vocabulary entries, in particular prior to the insertion of (5f), which identifies the morpheme as a suffix. The positioning of the fissioned Plural morpheme before the stem in (3) is therefore purely a matter of notational convenience: the correct placement of the Plural morpheme to the right of the stem is implemented by the Vocabulary entry (5f), an entry for a suffix.

Vocabulary insertion occurs after the application of all MS rules that modify the trees generated at SS. In the case under discussion, Vocabulary insertion applies after incorporation of 1st and 2nd person subject, object, and indirect object pronouns, the fusion of these pronouns into a Clitic terminal node, and the operation of rule (3). The preinsertion terminal nodes corresponding to some of the forms in (2) are shown in (4); the letters in (4) refer back to the corresponding examples in (2).

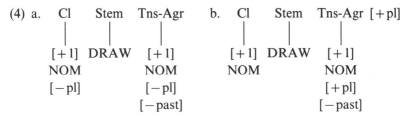

(4) a. Cl   Stem   Tns-Agr   b. Cl   Stem   Tns-Agr [+pl]
        | | | | | | |
      [+1] DRAW [+1]   [+1] DRAW [+1]
      NOM   NOM   NOM   NOM
      [−pl]   [−pl]   [+pl]
                  [−past]   [−past]

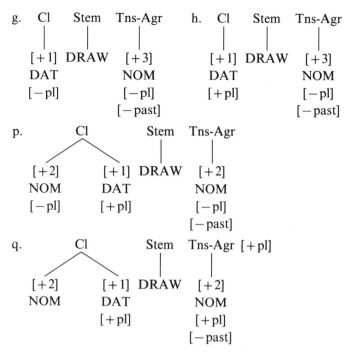

In addition to the fused Clitic cluster and the Stem, the forms in (4) include a fused Tns-Agr node. This Agr agrees with the NOM (or Ergative) argument in person and number. The Vocabulary items that are inserted in the Tns-Agr node are traditionally organized into what are called "screeves." For the examples under discussion, when the Agr is 1st or 2nd person, the Tns-Agr is ∅. For 3rd singular, the Tns-Agr is /-s/, for 3rd plural /-en/. A readjustment rule (see section 2.3) deletes 3rd singular /-s/ before plural /-t/. An impoverishment rule (see the end of this section and section 5) deletes the Plural terminal node when it follows any 3rd plural Tns-Agr node.

The main function of Vocabulary insertion is to supply phonetic features to the different morphemes in (4). The Vocabulary entries for the Clitic node and the [+ pl] (fissioned) node involved in the derivation of the forms in (2) are given in (5).

(5) *Clitic*

   a. [+1], DAT, [+pl] ↔ /gv-/
   b. [+1], DAT   ↔ /m-/
   c. [+2], DAT   ↔ /g-/
   d. [+1]   ↔ /v-/
   e. [+2]   ↔ ∅

Plural

f. [+pl]   ↔ /-t/

The Vocabulary entries in competition for insertion in a particular terminal node automatically organize themselves into blocks like that illustrated in (5), where entries are ordered by the principle that the most specified entry takes precedence over entries that are less specified. As noted by Kiparsky (1973), this ordering by decreasing complexity was explicitly recognized already in Pāṇini's Aṣṭadhyāyī. A consequence of this ordering principle is that in (5) the affix marked, for example, [+1], DAT, [+pl] (5a) will take precedence over those marked simply [+1], DAT (5b) and [+1] (5d). Similarly, the affix marked [+2], DAT (5c) will take precedence in insertion over the affix marked simply [+2] (5e).

The Pāṇinian elsewhere principle as now understood fails to determine the precedence between (5b) and (5c) or between (5d) and (5e). Competition between these pairs could arise, in principle, because the Clitic morpheme incorporates and fuses the features of subject, object, and indirect object arguments. The representation in (4q) indicates how two sets of agreement features can coexist under a single Clitic node in Georgian. Both sets in principle might be DAT. Noyer (1992a) has argued that hierarchical relations among particular morphosyntactic features impose further ordering relations among the competing entries above and beyond those that are imposed by complexity. These considerations may provide the required ordering. If this should turn out not to be the case, the correct output can be obtained by imposing an extrinsic order of precedence between the two Vocabulary entries in question, as was done in (5) and elsewhere in this paper. What is crucial here is that in the syntax we are dealing with bundles of morphosyntactic features, which are not *from* the Vocabulary in any important sense, and that for their phonological realization the Vocabulary must be searched for the underspecified entry that best matches the morphosyntactic features supplied by the syntax. Once that entry is found, its phonological and other idiosyncratic features are copied into the morpheme.

Fusion and fission of morphemes affect the correspondence between pieces at SS and pieces in the phonology. In addition, at any level of grammatical analysis, the feature composition of a morpheme may be changed in particular contexts, leading again to apparent mismatches between the syntax and the phonological affixes. For example, quite generally, features are deleted at MS in what Bonet (1991) calls "impoverishment." We will consider several examples of impoverishment in the analysis of Potawatomi in section 5.[9]

2.2   Vocabulary Insertion Examined

We have shown that in DM the ordering, number, feature composition, and hierarchical positioning of terminal nodes may change in the derivation of MS, but only in highly constrained and fairly well understood ways. We emphasize that the operation of morphology is constrained by substantive universals (a theory of features) and locality conditions on merger, fusion, fission, and feature interactions between morphemes; in the absence of such motivated constraints, the theory loses its empirical content. Although the terminal nodes may change at MS, perhaps the most striking difference between SS and MS derives from the systematic difference in the type of features found in the terminal nodes in the two structures. As noted above, in conformity with the "separation" theory of Beard (which finds traces back to Chomsky's (1965) treatment of inflectional morphology), it is assumed here that at LF, DS, and SS terminal nodes consist exclusively of morphosyntactic/semantic features and lack phonological features.[10] The morphosyntactic features at these levels are drawn from a set made available by Universal Grammar (we are unaware of any arguments that language-specific features are necessary at these syntactic levels). The semantic features and properties of terminal nodes created at DS will also be drawn from Universal Grammar and perhaps from language-particular semantic categories or concepts.

We assume that the Vocabulary of a language plays no role in the creation of terminal nodes at DS. That is, the particular set of universal and/or language-particular semantic and syntactic features chosen for a terminal node is not constrained by whether or not that set of features appears in any Vocabulary entry in the language. The bundles of morphosyntactic and semantic features that constitute morphemes at DS, SS, and LF are more or less freely formed. Although the feature complexes at these three levels must satisfy all universal and language-specific constraints on combining such features, they are not necessarily identical with the feature complexes of actually occurring Vocabulary items of the language. This, however, will not prevent Vocabulary insertion from taking place, since insertion requires only that the feature bundle of the Vocabulary item be nondistinct from the features of the terminal node at MS that serves as the site of insertion. The competition among different Vocabulary items nondistinct from the features of a terminal node at MS ensures that the Vocabulary item that matches the most features of the node will be inserted.

Vocabulary items may therefore be underspecified for the morphosyntactic feature complexes that they realize (see Lumsden 1992 on this point). For example, the Vocabulary entry for the English verb *sink* is featurally not specified for the distinction between its transitive (causative) and intransitive (inchoative) variants, although at LF, SS, and DS a given sentence may have the features corresponding to either the one or the other. Similarly, as discussed below, the English past participle ending /-d/ in *I had played tennis all day* will correspond only to the feature [+past] in its Vocabulary entry although in the example just given it is inserted at a node with the feature [+participle] in addition to the feature [+past].

It is assumed here that the entries that make up the Vocabulary of a language are each composed of two distinct sets of features: phonological and morphosyntactic/semantic. Thus, phonological features are supplied to morphemes only at MS and the mechanism responsible for this is Vocabulary insertion. As noted above, for a given Vocabulary entry to be "inserted" in some SS morpheme, none of its morphosyntactic features can conflict with a morphosyntactic feature present in SS; the Vocabulary entry must contain a subset of the morphosyntactic features of the terminal node. Like the operation of feature copying crucial to agreement and concord at MS, Vocabulary insertion at MS is subject to the constraint that it cannot modify already existing feature values.

On this view, as in Anderson's model, the phonological affixes and stems that make up complex words are underspecified with respect to morphosyntactic features. Since, unlike in the lexicalist models of Lieber and others, in DM the phonological pieces are not required to carry all the features necessary to explain the syntactic behavior of the words they create, they may be specified only for those features that determine which morpheme is inserted at which terminal node.[11] However, as in Lieber's model but not in affixless theories, the Vocabulary items might come with categorial and subcategorial information that is not part of the morphosyntactic representation prior to Vocabulary insertion and that affects the further phonological realization in the word. For example, inserted affixes or stems might belong to inflectional classes that condition the insertion of other affixes or the operation of morphologically conditioned phonological rules (here called "readjustment rules"; for examples, see below).

Since Vocabulary entries differ from morphemes at LF, DS, and SS in that, in addition to morphosyntactic features, they possess a set of phonological features, the Vocabulary can be regarded as the repository of the knowledge that speakers have about the interrelationship between the morphosyntactic feature bundle characterizing a morpheme and its phonological features, that is, about the mapping of morphosyntactic features onto complexes of phonological features.

2.3 Allomorphy

As we have just noted, a variety of changes can affect morphemes in the course of deriving the MS representation, creating a hierarchical structure of terminal elements related in a principled manner to, but not identical with, the hierarchical structure of such elements at SS. Vocabulary items, listed according to their morphosyntactic categories, compete to realize the resulting terminal elements in Vocabulary insertion. This immediately raises the issue of how to determine the winner in any such competition. Two types of competition can be distinguished in Vocabulary insertion: context-free and context-dependent (or *conditioned allomorphy*). We discuss the two in turn.

In context-free insertion, we find the Vocabulary entries whose category is compatible with the category of the terminal element being phonologically realized and whose features are compatible with the set of morphosyntactic features that the syntax and morphology have generated on this terminal element. As noted, this search will in some instances involve competition among different entries for the chance to spell out a particular set of features, where the entries differ only in the features they realize (that is, in their "substantive" features).

Like context-free Vocabulary insertion, conditioned allomorphy also involves a choice among alternative Vocabulary items. However, the choice in this case is not among items that differ in their substantive morphosyntactic features, but among items that differ in their stated insertion contexts and phonological features. For example, in English the past tense suffix $\emptyset$ is selected by the so-called *strong* verb stems (e.g., *put, beat*), whereas *weak* verbs select the suffix /-t/ or /-d/ (e.g., *dwelt, played*). The substantive features ([+past], etc.) of the /-t/, /-d/, and $\emptyset$ allomorphs are the same; they differ only in contextual features. As in context-independent insertion, the choice among competing allomorphs in conditioned allomorphy is again determined by the Pāṇinian principle, understood here as giving precedence to the allomorph appearing in the most complex, most highly specified context over allomorphs appearing in less complex contexts. The past tense allomorphs are therefore ordered as in (6). (These entries will be revised in (8).)

(6) *Tns*

[+past] ↔ ∅   / [+strong] _____
[+past] ↔ /-t/ / [−strong] _____
[+past] ↔ /-d/

Here the ∅ and /-t/ allomorphs of the past tense have precedence over the /-d/ allomorph, because ∅ and /-t/ impose conditions on the verb stem, whereas /-d/ is inserted elsewhere. The /-d/ is thus literally the default entry for [+past] Tns. (As the entries in (6) are currently written, the ordering between the ∅ and /-t/ allomorphs is not determined by complexity.)

For many terminal nodes (e.g., the English Tns node; see section 3), the competition among Vocabulary items will include competition among items with the same features and different environments, as in (6), and simultaneously among items with different features, as in (5). We propose that consideration of the substantive features realized by a Vocabulary entry takes precedence in the competition over contextual considerations so that all Vocabulary items that realize the same features (e.g., the three in (6)) are ordered in a block together relative to Vocabulary items that realize different features. Within each such block, the specificity of the environment determines relative ordering, as just explained.

3   Vocabulary Insertion versus Readjustment

3.1   English Verb Inflection

The phonological information contained in the Vocabulary entries is not sufficient to ensure that in all cases the correct phonological output will be generated. As suggested in Halle 1990 and elsewhere, the remaining part of the information about the phonological form of morphemes is provided by a set of *readjustment rules*.[12] This distinction between these two sources of phonological information parallels the traditional distinction between morphophonemic alternations (i.e., allomorphs related by a set of morphologically conditioned phonological rules), on the one hand, and suppletion and conditioned allomorphy, on the other. To clarify the nature of this distinction, we examine the inflection of English verbs.

The inflectional affixes of the English verb are, in part, surface manifestations of the different complexes of morphosyntactic features that may be generated at the terminal I(nflection) node in the IP constituent (or, more specifically, at the terminal T(ense) node of the TP constituent; for an example showing the position of this node in sentences and some discussion, see (13)). Disregarding here and below the verb *be*, the five principal parts of the English verbal inflection are illustrated in (7).

(7) Past participle   beat-en   put   dwel-t   play-ed
    Past finite   beat   put   dwel-t   play-ed
    Nonpast finite 3rd sg   beat-s   put-s   dwell-s   play-s
    Nonpast participle   beat-ing   putt-ing   dwell-ing   play-ing
    Nonpast finite   beat   put   dwell   play

The feature complexes that can occupy the I node at the point of Vocabulary insertion are made up at least of the morphosyntactic features [±past], [±participle], to which in [−participle] bundles are added the six number-person complexes (Chomsky's ϕ-features) that express subject-verb agreement in English (1st, 2nd, and 3rd person in singular and plural). Specifically, an Agr morpheme is added to [-participle] I nodes at MS, and the Agr morpheme is fused with the I morpheme into a single node. The fused I node can thus accommodate 2 [+participle] bundles ([±past]) and 2 ([±past]) × 6 (for agreement features) [−participle] bundles, for a total of 14 different feature bundles.

Examination of (7) reveals that there are three phonetically distinct suffixes in the nonpast forms: /-ing/, /-z/, and $\emptyset$. And there are four phonetically distinct suffixes in the past forms: /-n/, $\emptyset$, /-t/, and /-d/. These seven suffixes compete for insertion into the I node, which will contain one of the 14 feature bundles just described.

As shown by the forms in the first line of (7), there are four distinct past participle suffixes: /-n/, $\emptyset$, /-t/, and /-d/. The last three are identical with the finite past suffixes. It is worth noting that of the 58 English verbs that take /-n/ in the past participle, 9 have the default /-d/ suffix in the finite past (*do, ^hew, ^prove, ^sew, ^shear, show, ^sow, ^swell, ^strew*), 1 takes the /-t/ suffix (*go-ne*/*wen-t*), and 48 form the finite past tense with the $\emptyset$ suffix.[13] In other words, although verbs that take the /-n/ suffix in the past participle manifest a preference for the $\emptyset$ finite past suffix, the preference is not absolute. Since the verbs that take /-n/ in the past participle share no other grammatical, morphological, or semantic property, there is no justification for treating these verbs as belonging to a special inflectional class of their own, as was done in (6).[14] The list of verbs that choose the /-n/ suffix in the past participle will therefore be included in the Vocabulary entry of this suffix as a disjunctive list in a contextual feature for the suffix (see (8)). The fact that in almost all other verbs the past participle form is identical with the finite past form is expressed in (8) indirectly, by the absence of a separate past participle entry other than /-n/. In most cases, then, a node with the features [+past], [+participle] will be realized by an affix with only the [+past] feature.

Several of the verbs that take the /-n/ suffix in the past participle have an alternative form with the default /-d/ suffix, where the alternation is manifested sometimes by different speakers, sometimes by a single speaker. We have listed such stems with the diacritic ^ to indicate that they optionally take /-d/. Whenever Vocabulary insertion fails to insert the /-n/ suffix after such ^ stems, the default /-d/ suffix will automatically be inserted, unless the stem appears among those listed with one of the other past suffixes in (8). We leave open the questions of whether there is true optionality within the grammar of an individual speaker and of what the formal treatment of optionality should be; we emphasize here only that if the first (most highly specified) Vocabulary item—/-n/—competing for the Tns node is not chosen for one of the "optional" ^ stems, the remaining Vocabulary items in (8) will yield the correct "alternative" past participle form. The seven Vocabulary items competing for insertion under the fused Tns-Agr node are all suffixes and have the representations in (8).[15]

(8) I (= *fused Tns and Agr*)

$\quad$ [+participle, +past] $\quad \leftrightarrow \quad$ /-n/ / X + _____
$\qquad\qquad\qquad\qquad\qquad\qquad$ where X = ^*hew, go, beat,* ...
$\quad$ [+past] $\qquad\qquad\quad \leftrightarrow \quad \emptyset$ / Y + _____
$\qquad\qquad\qquad\qquad\qquad\qquad$ where Y = *beat, drive, bind, sing,* ...
$\quad$ [+past] $\qquad\qquad\quad \leftrightarrow \quad$ /-t/ / Z + _____
$\qquad\qquad\qquad\qquad\qquad\qquad$ where Z = *dwell, buy, send,* ...
$\quad$ [+past] $\qquad\qquad\quad \leftrightarrow \quad$ /-d/
$\quad$ [+participle] $\qquad\quad \leftrightarrow \quad$ /-ing/
$\quad$ [3sg] $\qquad\qquad\qquad \leftrightarrow \quad$ /-z/
$\qquad\qquad\qquad\qquad\qquad\quad \leftrightarrow \quad \emptyset$

The entries in (8) are listed in the order of decreasing complexity of the conditions on their insertion, where this can be determined. Recall that substantive features take precedence over contextual features for determination of complexity, so an entry with the features [+past, +participle] would take precedence over any entry with the feature [+past] even if the former were inserted in any environment and the latter restricted to certain stems. Since the $\emptyset$ and /-t/ past suffixes are of equal complexity, both containing the [+past] substantive feature and an environment feature, they are not ordered by complexity. Since each contains a different set of verbs in its environment, no ordering is required. The ordering among past suffixes as a group, [3sg] /-z/, and [+participle] /-ing/ is also not determined by complexity. Here, though, the ordering matters. We do not want to insert the [+participle] /-ing/ in a [+past, +participle] node. Nor do we want to insert /-z/ in a [+past] node that is [3sg]. Perhaps a universal hierarchy of tense > aspect > agreement might order these affixes; otherwise, their ordering must be stipulated in the manner shown in (8).

As noted above, the fact that a given terminal node contains morphosyntactic features that are absent in a particular Vocabulary entry will not block insertion of this item as long as the additional morphosyntactic features are nondistinct from the features in the Vocabulary entry. For example, the [+past] /-d/ will be inserted in a [+past, +participle] node as long as the stem is not listed in any of the [+past, +participle] or [+past] entries in (8). After insertion, the node will still be [+past, +participle] although the Vocabulary entry itself had only the feature [+past].

Since in language there is an arbitrary relation between the morphosyntactic and phonological features of a Vocabulary item (Saussure's *arbitraire du signe*), it is not surprising that the relationship between morphosyntactic and phonological features is many-to-many. Thus, phonological ∅ is the phonological realization of two distinct sets of features in (8), and the [+past] morpheme is represented by ∅, /-t/, and /-d/.

As the examples in (9) show, the past participle and past forms frequently differ from nonpast forms and/or from each other in the phonological composition of the stem.

(9) a. i.   beat – beat – beat-en   break – broke – brok-en
            drive – drove – driv-en   fall – fell – fall-en
        ii. put – put – put   bind – bound – bound
            sing – sang – sung   come – came – come
    b.   dwell – dwel-t – dwel-t   send – sen-t – sen-t
            leave – lef-t – lef-t   buy – bough-t – bough-t
    c. i.   prove – prove-d – prove-n   do – di-d – do-ne
        ii. yell – yell-ed – yell-ed   tell – tol-d – tol-d

The suffixes in (8) differ in the extent to which they trigger phonological changes in the stems. For example, the /-n/ suffix triggers changes in 56 of the 58 stems that take it, whereas for ∅ and /-t/ the figures are 103 out of 131 and 16 out of 40, respectively. By contrast, of the several thousand stems that take the /-d/ past suffix, only 13 undergo stem changes. Specifically, as shown in (10), the /-d/ past suffix replaces the stem rime with short /u/ in four verbs (*should, would, could, stood*), with short /i/ in one verb (*did*), and with short /e/ in one verb (*said*). The same suffix rounds and backs the syllabic nucleus in two instances (*sol-d, tol-d*), but shortens the nucleus in only three stems (*fle-d, hear-d, sho-d*). Finally, the stems *make* and *have* lose their final consonant before the /-d/ suffix. Unlike allomorphy resulting from the choice of contextually distinguished Vocabulary entries, the stem allomorphies under discussion here result from the operation of readjustment rules that have the form of phonological rules and apply to morphemes after Vocabulary insertion. The readjustments described above are given more formally in (10).

(10) a. Rime → /u/ / X ____ [+past]
$$|$$
x

where X-Rime = *shall, will, can, stand*

b. Rime → /i/ / Y ____ [+past, −participle]
$$|$$
x

Rime → /ʌ/ / Y ____ [+past, +participle]
$$|$$ [−past, 3sg]
x

where Y-Rime = *do*

c. Rime → /e/ / Z ___ [+past]
$$|$$ [−past, 3sg]
x

where Z-Rime = *say*

d. V → [+bk] / W ____ U [+past]
   [+rd]

where WVU = *sell, tell*

e.   V   → V / T ____ S [+past]
      ⟋ ⟍ |
     x   x   x

where TVS = *flee, hear, shoe*

f. C → ∅ / Q ____ [+past]
                  ⟨[−past, 3sg]⟩

where QC = *make,* ⟨*have*⟩

The readjustments induced in the stem by the /-t/ suffix are somewhat less varied than those summarized in (10). Here stems ending in /d/ delete the stem-final consonant—*send* → *sen∅-t*—and stems with rimes ending in a dorsal (velar) obstruent (or that historically derive from such stems) replace the rime with the low vowel /ɔ/—*bring* → *brough-t*. None of the other stems is subject to stem readjustment before the /-t/ suffix, once account is taken of the fact that stem vowel shortening and final obstruent devoicing in forms such as *mean-t, kep-t, lef-t, los-t* are due to general phonological rules whose effects in English are also found outside verb inflection—for example, in *bread-th, dep-th, wid-th*.

The readjustment rules triggered by the /-n/ past participle and the ∅ past suffixes are considerably more complex than those triggered by /-d/ or /-t/. Since these facts add little to an understanding of the issues under discussion, they have been omitted here.[16]

There are two verbs for which the relationship between the allomorphs in the [−past] and [+past] is entirely arbitrary. These are *go/wen-t* and the archaic and highly literary *work/wrough-t* (/rɔt/). For these verbs, two different Vocabulary entries with the same substantive features will be listed; they will differ in that one will contain the contextual feature [__[+past, −participle]]. With the exception of these two verbs, the relations among variants of a given stem in the different morphological contexts can be characterized by means of readjustment rules like those in (10), rules that satisfy the same formal constraints as ordinary phonological rules (and might even be ordered among the phonological rules; see the discussion of "allomorphy rules" in Davis 1991).

3.2   English Inflection and Affixless Morphology

In the theory of affixless morphology, the terminal string at the input to the morphology consists exclusively of lexemes, that is, of word stems. Such information as that a noun is plural is represented at this stage by features assigned to the nonterminal node dominating the noun. Ultimately, the plural features are spelled out by WFRs.[17]

The WFRs constitute a homogeneous set. This is an important respect in which affixless morphology differs from DM, where the phonological shapes of words are accounted for by rules and processes belonging to different classes subject to different constraints. As illustrated above, Vocabulary insertion is responsible for certain phonological aspects of an utterance, whereas other aspects are accounted for by the rather different set of impoverishment and readjustment rules. In this section we examine the way in which the homogeneity of WFRs in the affixless theory affects the treatment of the familiar facts of English noun inflection.

Anderson notes that WFRs "operate to map . . . lexical stems onto fully inflected surface words" (p. 122). This procedure, however, fails to "provide an account of the complementarity of regular and irregular modes of inflectional marking. For instance, we must avoid applying a rule for a regular formation such as the English plural in /-z/ to an item which is already lexically specified for the same properties. Thus, since the (irregular) plural of *ox* is *oxen* we must not produce **oxes* or **oxens*" (p. 123).

To achieve this complementarity between regular and irregular inflection, Anderson introduces two special principles. He explains that

[o]ften . . . more than one phonological stem will share the same syntax and semantics. . . . Where more than one stem makes up the lexical stem set of a given lexical item, the principle in (19) governs the choice among them.

(19) In interpreting a given Morphosyntactic Representation M, from among the stems in the lexical set S of a given lexical item, only that stem S_i which is characterized for the maximal subset of the features compatible with M may serve as the basis of an inflected form $\{S, M\}$. (p. 133)[18]

Anderson notes that principle (19) allows him

to account for the absence of forms like **oxes* in English. Such a form, if it existed, would be the result of applying the regular plural rule so as to add /-z/ to the stem /aks/. But in fact the stem /aks/ is not available to interpret the position whose Morphosyntactic Representation contains the features [+ Noun, + Plural], because the only stem set containing /aks/ also contains /aksən/. Since this latter stem is characterized for a larger subset of the features [+ Noun, + Plural] than is /aks/, the principle in (19) requires us to use only /aksən/ and not /aks/ to interpret such a position. (p. 133)

By entering *oxen* as a stem with the features [+ Noun, + Plural], Anderson has in effect accounted for this irregularity by means of suppletion, because there is no way in which his solution takes account of the partial identity of *oxen* and *ox*. Instead of being composed of the latter two stems, the stem set could equally well have contained *ox* and any phonetically well formed string of phonemes. It is an accident of English that it contains no truly suppletive pairs of singular-plural noun stems.

Although principle (19) rules out **oxes*, it fails to rule out **oxens*. According to Anderson,

[t]his suggests that another principle of disjunction (or "blocking") is at work here. This principle . . . shares an obvious family resemblance with the principles in (18) and (19), since all of these conditions enforce the precedence of specific cases over general ones.

(20) When a rule R of the grammar would apply to a stem S on the basis of the features F of a given position to be interpreted, application of R is blocked, if F constitutes a subset of the lexical specifications of S.

The absence of *oxens*... then follows directly. In interpreting a position with the morphosyntactic features [+ Noun, + Plural], we have already seen that only the stem /aksən/ is available. In order to derive /aksənz/ it would be necessary to apply the regular plural rule to append /-z/ to /aksən/. This is prevented by (20), however, since the features that this rule refers to are precisely [+ Noun, + Plural], a subset of the lexical features of /aksən/. (p. 134)

Principle (20) rules out forms where a special stem allomorph is selected for insertion in the context of a particular feature while a second WFR affixes something to the stem in the context of the same feature. Anderson remarks, "If genuine cases of such 'double marking' do indeed exist, this would imply that the scope of the principle proposed here as (20) must be limited in some way that is not yet understood" (p. 134).

In fact, forms with such "double marking" are widely attested. Several examples from English are found in (11).

(11) a.   live-s   bath-s   house-s
     b.   broke-n   froze-n   drive-n   go-ne   do-ne
     c. i. bough-t   caugh-t   taugh-t   though-t
       ii. buil-t   sen-t   wen-t   len-t

In (11a) the stem-final consonant is voiced before the plural suffix. In (11b) the stem vowel is modified and the suffix /-n/ is added as well. In (11c) the past /-t/ is suffixed; in addition, the rime is replaced by /ɔ/ in (11ci) and the stem-final consonant /d/ is deleted in (11cii).

Since genuine cases of "double marking" are quite common, Anderson's principle (20) cannot be maintained. Without (20), however, his account of English plural formation will not work.

It should be noted that nothing in Anderson's theory prevents him from dealing with the three sets of examples in (11) as instances of suppletion. As noted above, he proposes to treat *ox/oxen* as an instance of suppletion, that is, as a set of "phonologically distinct stems... each associated with its own (partial) set of morphosyntactic properties" (p. 133). In the case of *ox/oxen* this treatment obscures the fact that except for the /n/ the two forms are phonologically identical. Since only two or three nouns in the language take such non-∅ irregular plural endings, one might be inclined to sweep these examples under the proverbial rug. The point made by the examples in (11) is not only that there are additional cases that must be similarly swept under the rug, but also that phonological "modifications" produced by what we have called Vocabulary insertion (the addition of phonological material) are separate from and independent of those produced by readjustment rules (which may change and delete features, as well as add them). An approach such as Anderson's, which denies the existence of this distinction, is unable—as a matter of principle—to distinguish cases of total suppletion such as *be/were* from cases of partial suppletion such as *go/wen-t*, from different stem readjustments such as *goose/geese, life/live-s*, and from cases of irregular suffixation such as *ox/ox-en* and *child/childr-en*, and is therefore forced to subsume all of these clearly different cases under the rubric of suppletion.

We have shown, then, that one of Anderson's principles of disjunction for morphology, his principle (20), incorrectly rules out the choice of a suppletive stem or a stem readjustment in the context of a feature that also triggers affixation. In our terms, the features of a terminal node (e.g., [+past] on a Tns node) may form the context for choice of a stem allomorph or trigger a readjustment rule in addition to serving as a crucial feature for the insertion of a Vocabulary item at the node. Anderson proposes a principle similar to (20)—his "elsewhere" principle (18) (p. 132)—that prohibits a WFR in one rule block from applying if its triggering features are a proper subset of those for a WFR that has applied in an earlier block. Since Anderson treats stem allomorphy and affix allomorphy as completely distinct phenomena (incorrectly in our view), he cannot combine his two disjunction principles. In section 5 we will show that this additional disjunctive principle (18), like principle (20), cannot be maintained, and for the same reasons. Readjustment rules apply to affixes as well as to stems. A readjustment rule for one affix triggered by a feature of a terminal node to its right simply does not block the insertion of phonological material—that is, Vocabulary insertion—at the location of the triggering feature. As we will show, Anderson's own analysis of Potawatomi, as well as our analysis, clearly illustrates this lack of disjunctivity.

4 Null Morphemes

As shown in (8), among the English Vocabulary items that compete for assigning phonological features to the Tns-Agr node there are two that assign phonological zero to the node. Anderson (1992) has questioned the reality of zero morphs of this kind. Thus, he remarks that "these obviously have no content at all. . . . the assumption that any information which is not overtly signalled nonetheless corresponds to some zero morpheme leads to the formal problem of assigning a place in the structure (and in linear order) to all these zeros. Thus, the free positing of zero morphs allows us to say that Latin *amo* 'I love' represents 'LOVE +

CONJ1 + INDIC + ACTIVE + PRES + 1PERS + SG', but in which order (from among the 7! or 5040 possible orders)?" (p. 61).

In Anderson's Latin example each morphosyntactic feature is assumed to constitute a single morpheme. This assumption is surely not logically necessary, and Anderson offers neither evidence nor argument for it. Once it is admitted—as the large majority of workers in this area have done— that several morphosyntactic features can (and sometimes must) coexist in a single morpheme, Anderson's example loses much of its combinatorial absurdity and with it also its negative force. Without question, morphology must include a theory of features that determines when they must cluster in morphemes and when they may surface in separate terminal elements. For example, the feature "CONJ1" in Anderson's Latin example clearly is a classificatory feature that partitions the general class of verb stems. Thus, not only must this feature be a feature of the stem, and not a separate morpheme; as a classificatory feature it would be unable under any circumstances to split from the stem and form its own terminal node. The person, number, and gender features of 1st and 2nd person arguments arguably form a constituent. Thus, Anderson's 1PERS and SG features would belong to a single morpheme. We do not yet have a solid understanding of how tense features are distributed among the functional heads in the syntax (for one view, see Giorgi and Pianesi, to appear), but it is not unreasonable to suppose, in the absence of any arguments to the contrary, that the features that Anderson identifies as PRES, INDIC, and ACTIVE, if they are really operative features in Latin, are features of a single Tns node. We have assumed that subject Agr attaches to Tns at MS, so Tns and Agr form a unit in the Latin verb that is attached to the Verb stem marked for its conjugation class. The only complexity faced by the child learning Latin, then, is the fusion of the Tns and Agr nodes before Vocabulary insertion, a possibility left open but not required by Universal Grammar. Thus, Anderson's Latin example sheds no light on the issue of zero morphemes.

We recognize at least two types of zero morphemes, leaving open the question of whether these are actually distinct. One type was illustrated by the ∅ English past tense chosen by a particular set of stems (see (8)). Here the zero past tense suffix blocks the default past tense /-d/. Thus, we find *drove* but not *drive-d* or *drove-d*. The English tense system (8) illustrates the second sort of zero morpheme as well. For the [−past, −participle] ending when the subject is not 3rd person singular, the suffix is also ∅. However, in this case the ∅ suffix is a default for the [−past] feature, in fact, for the Tns node as a whole. It may be that Universal Grammar provides a zero spell-out as the default phonological realization of a morpheme in the unmarked case. This possibility in no way undermines the existence of zero morphemes.

To see the linguistic reality of zero morphemes such as the zero realizations of the English Tns-Agr node, consider the sentences in (12).

(12) a. They sleep late.
      b. Do they sleep late?
      c. They do not sleep late.

Somewhat simplified DS and SS trees for (12a) are given in (13). In English, main verbs, unlike auxiliary verbs, do not raise to Tns at SS. Thus, unlike auxiliary verbs, English tensed main verbs are ordered in the sentence in the position of verbs, not in the position of Tns. This is seen by comparing *They definitely seem old* with *They are definitely old*. The first contains an inflected main verb that must follow adverbs like *definitely* that come before the VP; the second contains auxiliary BE that raises out of the VP to Tns and thus occurs before the adverb.

Although main verbs do not raise to Tns, Tns does appear on the verb in sentences like (12a). The joining of Tns with main verbs is sometimes attributed to a "lowering" head movement analogous to upward head movement. However, we believe that this joining is an example of merger under structural adjacency of a type discussed by Marantz (1988, 1989). If Tns merges with the main verb (as opposed to the verb adjoining to Tns), the resulting inflected verb should pattern with verbs rather than with Tns (and auxiliary verbs), as required. The result of merger is shown in (13b).

(13) a.

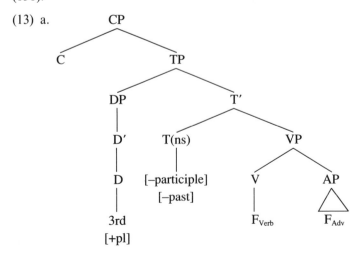

b.

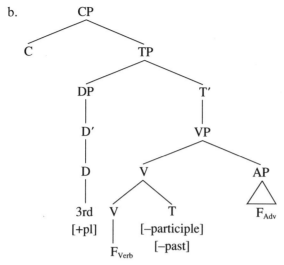

In the preceding discussion we have assumed that the values of the different morphosyntactic and semantic features under terminal nodes are almost entirely specified in the syntax but that no actual Vocabulary items are present in these trees. In particular, although the features of the main verb in (13) need not single out the verb *sleep*, at least the feature that distinguishes main from auxiliary verbs in English must be present in the trees. At MS, the Vocabulary is consulted to find items whose features are nondistinct from those of the terminal nodes in the tree and that therefore can be inserted, providing phonological features for the nodes.

In many languages—for example, Spanish, Russian, Latin, Latvian—word stems must have a Theme suffix, which has no syntactic or semantic role (see, for example, Halle 1991). It is natural to assume that such affixes are introduced by the rules that relate SS to MS. By placing them in this part of the grammar, we account for their lack of effect in the syntax or at LF. It has been argued by Marantz (1992a) that, like the Theme, Case and Agr morphemes are added to heads at MS in accordance with language-particular requirements about what constitutes a morphologically well formed word in that language. In addition to the Theme suffix, languages like Russian, Latvian, and Latin require a case suffix for well-formed nouns and adjectives. English differs from these languages in that it requires neither a theme nor a case suffix for nouns or adjectives. English, Latin, Russian, and Latvian are alike in that they require an Agr morpheme for well-formed finite verbs. The insertion of the Agr morpheme, onto which the appropriate features of the subject have been copied, transforms tree (13b) into tree (14).

(14)

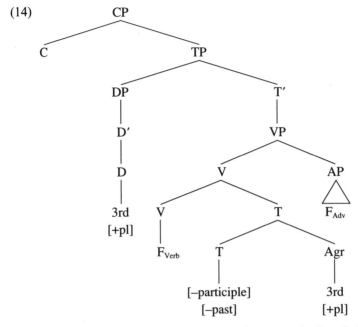

The fusion of sister morphemes into a single terminal node is a widely attested phenomenon. For example, the Case and Number morphemes that appear separately in an agglutinative language like Turkish are fused into a single morpheme in Latin, Latvian, and Russian. Similarly, Tns and Agr fuse into a single morpheme—terminal node—in English, but remain separate in German and Russian.

After merger and fusion of terminal nodes, phonological features are supplied to the different morphemes by consulting the Vocabulary; that is, at this point Vocabulary insertion takes place. In addition to phonological features, Vocabulary insertion supplies morphological features that signal idiosyncratic properties of specific Vocabulary items.

We assume that the insertion operation has available the entire syntactic tree so that insertion at a given node may make reference to features at other—primarily adjacent—nodes. For example, the verb stem *wend* will be inserted at a V node with the syntactic and semantic features of "go" if the adjacent Tns node dominates [+past, −participle], whereas *go* will be inserted elsewhere. Similarly, /-t/ will be inserted next to *wend* under the [+past, −participle] node since *wend* is a verb on the list subcategorized for by /-t/. (Recall that the final /-d/ of *wend* will delete before /-t/ as in *send/sent*.)

Concerning English inflection, it is essential to note that even when spelled out as ∅, the Tns-Agr morpheme is present among the terminal nodes at MS. Consider the derivation of (12b). Question formation in English involves the raising of Tns to C or to some functional head between CP and TP; the identity of this head is irrelevant for present purposes. If an auxiliary verb moves to Tns, then this derived Tns moves to C (e.g., *Are you sleeping?*). Main verbs in English do not raise to Tns; thus, in (12b) only Tns moves to C, via head-to-head movement, as shown in (15).

(15)

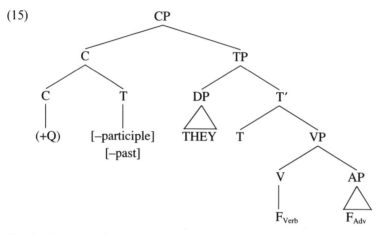

To the Tns morpheme in (15) at MS must be added an Agr node, as in (13b), that will pick up the features of the subject DP.

It is a morphological fact about the English Tns morpheme that it requires a V to make a well-formed MS word. Note that it is *not* a property of English verbs that they require Tns; the morphological requirement is on Tns itself (English verbs appear tenseless, for example, in causative constructions such as *I made him leave*). This requirement holds regardless of the affix—regardless of the Vocabulary entry—inserted as the Tns morpheme. As first noted by Chomsky (1957), whenever a Tns morpheme is stranded without a verbal stem to which it may suffix, the dummy verb *do* is inserted, and this applies when the Tns morpheme is phonetically ∅ as well as when the Tns morpheme is readily isolated as a piece in the phonetic string. In (12b) the Vocabulary item chosen for [−participle] [−past] Tns + Agr will be phonologically ∅, yet a verb must be adjoined to Tns in (15) to meet the morphological well-formedness conditions on Tns in English. We assume that the morphological well-formedness condition is met by the minimal disruption in the structure, that is, by the insertion of a V node without any features other than its category identification. There is a Vocabulary entry for the V *do* in English that has no features other than its category, making *do* the unmarked Verb, chosen to phonologically realize the V node when the other verbs lose out in the competition by being overly specified.

Thus, the ∅ Tns morpheme is just as much a morpheme as any other Tns morpheme in English. In (12c), when negation is included, the existence of the null Tns morpheme is revealed yet again. A Neg functional head blocks the merger of Tns with a main verb (the intervention of a NegP with a filled head between TP and VP prevents the Tns head of TP from being structurally adjacent to the V head of VP). Since Tns, regardless of its realization, requires a sister V as a morphological property, an empty V node must be inserted at MS and realized as *do* in (12c) even though the spell-out of Tns will be ∅. Note that the presence of the negation *not* is not a sufficient condition for *do* insertion, as shown by the absence of the dummy verb *do* in a tenseless clause such as the bracketed one in *John made [them not work]*. What is required for *do* insertion is the presence of a stranded Tns morpheme, regardless of whether or not the Tns morpheme will have a nonnull phonetic realization.

5   Complex Inflectional Systems: The Potawatomi Independent Verbal Inflection

Anderson (1992) illustrates his approach to inflectional morphology with an analysis of some inflectional paradigms from Hockett's description of the Algonquian language Potawatomi (in particular, Hockett 1966).[19,20] From Anderson's analysis of Potawatomi, one might conclude (i) that the disjunctive relations among competing affixes should follow from disjunctive relations among WFRs in arbitrary rule blocks, (ii) that multiple exponence is possible in the form of repeated and arbitrary reference to the same features in multiple rule blocks, and (iii) that readjustment and impoverishment should not be distinguished from the choice of affixal material—both are simply consequences of the WFR blocks.

In the analysis of Potawatomi to follow, we will show that these claims are not warranted. In particular, the evidence reviewed below shows (i) that each "disjunctive rule block" of the correct analysis corresponds to a terminal node from the syntax or morphology (or some terminal node that results from the merger and fusion of other nodes) and that the blocks therefore are featurally coherent, (ii) that there is no "multiple exponence" of features from a single syntactic or morphological node, and (iii) that readjustment and improverishment (the influence of one morpheme on others) need to be distinguished from the choice of a phonological form for a terminal node (as argued in section 3).

We make the strong claim that many of the terminal nodes that find phonological realization in affixes are syntactic heads; the rest are added or created at MS in principled and predictable ways, as described in section 2. Thus, it is not possible to go far with any morphological analysis without also doing syntax. Although our knowledge of Potawatomi syntax is limited and the literature on Potawatomi itself and on related Algonquian languages grossly underdetermines the analysis, we can motivate each of the morphemes relevant to the analysis, even while leaving a great deal undecided about both syntax and morphology.

5.1 Features and Affixes

Potawatomi verbs are inflected for tense, negation, and agreement in two general patterns, called the *independent* and *conjunct* patterns or *orders* ("orders" because the order of negation and the verb differs in independent and conjunct inflected verbs). In the two examples given in (16) the verb is inflected for a 2nd person plural subject and a 3rd person plural object. The conjunct order verb in (16a) shows a negative prefix before the verb stem. Following the stem is an Agr morpheme whose phonological realization is sensitive to the features of both subject and object; see table 1. The last suffix realizes a preterit Tns morpheme. The independent order verb in (16b) begins with a pronominal clitic never found in the conjunct, here signaling the 2nd person subject. The verb stem is immediately followed by an Agr morpheme agreeing with the 3rd person object, also not found with the conjunct order. Following this agreement suffix is the negative suffix characteristic of the independent order, as opposed to the negative prefix found in the conjunct order verb shown in (16a). The negative suffix is followed by a second Agr morpheme that occupies the same structural position as the conjunct Agr and signals that the subject is 2nd person plural. This Agr is followed by the same preterit Tns morpheme found in the conjunct order, which is in turn followed by a third Agr morpheme agreeing in plurality with the 3rd person object.

(16) a. *Conjunct order*

      pwa- min -kwa   -pun
      Neg V   Agr   Tns
             give 2plNOM.3plACC preterit
      'you (pl) didn't give them (something)'

b. *Independent order*

k- wapm -a   -s'i -m -wapunin -uk
Cl V   Agr   Neg Agr Tns   Agr
2   see   3ACC   2pl preterit 3pl
'you (pl) didn't see them'

The independent order is generally used with main clauses in declarative styles; the conjunct order is used, for example, in embedded contexts and for participles (see Hockett 1966 for details). Anderson discusses only the independent order without negation and without the preterit (past) suffix—important omissions, it will turn out.

In the Potawatomi clause, all arguments are pronominal; that is, they consist of DPs containing only features for person, number, and so forth, on the D (see Jelinek 1984, Speas 1990, and Baker 1991 (on Mohawk) for a discussion of such languages). Full DPs—phrases such as 'John' or 'the canoe by the river'—are adjoined to the clause and bind (thus, "double") the pronominal arguments within the clause. This striking difference between Potawatomi and, say, familiar Indo-European languages is not clearly brought out by Anderson. An understanding of the issues and of the exposition below depends on keeping this feature of Potawatomi clearly in mind.

With independent order verb inflection, 1st, 2nd, and certain 3rd person pronominal DPs (the [−obv] DPs; see immediately below) cliticize to the front of the CP and are realized as proclitics in this position. The remaining 3rd person pronominal DPs are small pro's that are identified by Agr on the inflected verb. Since the tensed verb also agrees with the 1st and 2nd person arguments, what looks like multiple exponence results: phonological material corresponding to 1st, 2nd, and certain 3rd person arguments appears as both proclitic and agreement suffix (as in Georgian; see section 2). However, this is the standard type of agreement found everywhere in language; that is, we commonly see both the arguments and the agreement that agrees with these arguments, as in the English *She* sleeps. The Potawatomi pronominal proclitics are not part of the verb: they need not appear immediately before the verb stem or even as part of the same phonological word as the verb; their location depends on what else occurs within the CP. The examples in (17) show that the clitics appear at the front of CP on phonological words that are independent from the inflected verb, clearly indicating that these clitics are not (directly) part of the inflectional system.

(17) a. n̠-ku   wapm-a
         1st-OK see
         'OK I'll see him'

     b. n̠-kuko?   ns'-a
         1st-quickly kill
         'I kill him quickly'

     c. n̠-wep   ns'-a
         1st-incep kill
         'I start to kill him'

The Potawatomi verb shows agreement with both subject and object, for person, number, and "obviation" of 3rd person arguments. Obviative marking distinguishes 3rd person arguments in discourse and allows the listener to track 3rd persons across clauses. The details of obviation in discourse, although ultimately important for the correct analysis of Pota-watomi, will be ignored here. We will assume a three-way division among DPs (more precisely, among Ds): [+obv], [−obv], and unmarked for obviation. 1st and 2nd person pronouns, here treated as Ds, are always marked [−obv]. 3rd person DPs may be marked [+obv] for discourse reasons or left unmarked. In a particular syntactic environment to be described below, 3rd person DPs may be marked [−obv]; these [−obv] 3rd person DPs behave like 1st and 2nd person DPs. Potawatomi nouns are classified into two genders: animate and inanimate. Although 1st and 2nd persons and nouns referring to people are animate, the division of other nouns into the two genders is fairly arbitrary.

For animate nouns, as in (18)–(19), the marking on the nouns (18) and the agreement pattern on intransitive verbs (19) show one suffix /-k/ for nonobviative plural (18b)/(19b) and another suffix /-n/ for [+obv], either singular or plural (18c)/(19c).

(18) *Antimate noun*

     a. waposo   'rabbit'
     b. waposo-k̠   'rabbits'
     c. waposo-n̠   'rabbit(s) (obv)'

(19) *Verb with an animate subject*

     a. kaskumi   'he starts running'
     b. kaskumi-k̠   'they start running'
     c. kaskumi-n̠   'he/they (obv) start running'

Inanimate nouns as in (20) have a plural marking (20b) but no obviative suffix; the singular and plural forms in (20) are both ambiguous between obviative and nonobviative.

(20) *Inanimate noun*

    a. čiman   'canoe' (obv or not)
    b. čiman-<u>un</u> 'canoes' (obv or not)

Although the suffixes on inanimate nouns do not distinguish between [+obv] and nonobviative, the distinction must nonetheless be marked by a morphosyntactic feature on inanimate nouns because intransitive verbs with inanimate subjects have the same pattern of agreement for plural and [+obv] as intransitive verbs with animate subjects, as shown in (21). Compare (21) with (19). In both cases a [+obv] subject triggers a particular suffix, /-n/ for animates, /-nun/ for inanimates, regardless of the plurality of the subject. Nonobviative [+pl] subjects trigger a different affix, /-k/ for animates, /-ton/ for inanimates.

(21) *Verb with an inanimate subject*

    a. wawyeya   'it (not obv) is round'
    b. wawyeya-<u>ton</u>   'they (not obv) are round'
    c. wawyeya-<u>nun</u> 'it/they (obv) is/are round'

Although 3rd person arguments are generally either [+obv] or unmarked for obviation in Potawatomi, a 3rd person D may be marked [−obv] in certain environments.[21] In particular, in clauses with 3rd person DPs as both subject and object arguments, one of the 3rd person DPs must be specially marked [−obv] and the other must be marked [+obv]. Only animate DPs may be marked [−obv]. Exactly the same sort of morphosyntactic marking occurs inside possessed DPs, with a 3rd person possessor specially marked [−obv] and the possessed argument marked [+obv]. Although either a subject or an object DP may be [−obv] when the other argument of a transitive verb is [+obv], within possessive DPs only the possessor, not the possessed, may bear the [−obv] feature.

To illustrate the distribution of this special [−obv] marking for 3rd persons, we compare in (22)–(23) 2nd person [−obv] possessors or transitive subjects with 3rd person possessors or transitive subjects. In both sets of examples the possessed argument or the direct object is 3rd person. Note that for both 2nd and 3rd person possessors or subjects in these examples, there is a proclitic showing the person of the possessor or subject—/k-/ for 2nd person and /w-/ for 3rd person—and an agreement suffix /-wa/ when the possessor or subject is plural. Since Potawatomi proclitics are limited to [−obv] arguments, the data in (22)–(23) support the proposal that a 3rd person DP is marked [−obv] in opposition to another 3rd person argument in the DP/IP—either a subject or object in the case of a transitive verb or the possessed NP in the case of a possessed DP.

(22) a. ḳ-čiman   'your (sg) canoe'
     b. ḳ-čiman-wa   'your (pl) canoe'

     c. w̱-čiman   'his canoe'
     d. w̱-čiman-wa   'their canoe'

     e. ḳ-os'   'your father'
     f. ḳ-os'-un   'your father (obv)'

     g. w̱-os'-un   'his father (obv)' (/w/ → /ʔ/ by phonological rule)

     h. w̱-os'-wa-n   'their father (obv)'
     i. *w̱-os'   'his father (not obv)'

(23) a. ḳ-wapm-a   'you (sg) see him'
     b. ḳ-wapm-a-wa   'you (pl) see him'

     c. w̱-wapm-a-n   'he sees him/them (obv)'
     d. w̱-wapm-a-wa-n   'they see him/them (obv)'
     e. *w̱-wapm-a-wa   'they see him'

There is one major difference between the structures involving a 3rd person [−obv] DP and those involving a 1st or 2nd person DP (which are automatically [−obv]), a difference that shows up in the possessed form of an animate noun (22e–i) or in the transitive verb pattern with an animate direct object (23). (22e) shows that an animate noun possessed by a 2nd person need not be marked [+obv], whereas the ungrammaticality of (22i) shows that an animate noun possessed by a 3rd person (by hypothesis, [−obv]) DP must be so marked. (23a–b) show that the 3rd person object with a 2nd person subject also need not be marked [+obv], whereas the ungrammaticality of (23e) indicates again that the 3rd person object with a [−obv] 3rd person subject must be marked [+obv].

The examples in (24) should be compared to those in (23).

(24) a. w̱-wapm-uko-n   'he/they (obv) sees him'
     b. w̱-wapm-uk-wa-n   'he/they (obv) sees them'
     c. *w̱-wapm-uk   'he (not obv) sees him'

In (24), as in (23), both subject and object of the transitive verb are 3rd person. In (23c–e) the subject was marked [−obv] and the object [+obv].

(24) shows that the other option is also possible; the object is marked
[−obv] and the subject [+obv]. The difference is signaled by the morpheme immediately after the stem, /-a/ in (23) and /-uko/ in (24). As will
be explained in more detail below, this morpheme agrees in case with a
3rd person argument that is not [−obv]—/-a/ for an accusative argument
as in (23) and /-uko/ for a nominative argument, as in (24). The ungrammaticality of (24c) again shows that when one 3rd person argument
is [−obv], the other must be [+obv].

5.2 Identifying the Morphemes

The syntactic structure of independent order clauses is summarized in
(25).

(25)

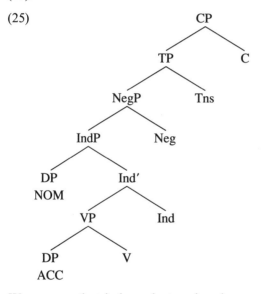

We assume that independent order clauses contain a functional head,
here represented as "Ind," that forms a particular "participle"-like phrase
under T(ense)P. Given that independent order clauses have a special distribution in discourse, we might suppose that there is a selection relation
in (25) between C and Tns, and between Tns and Ind. Recall that all the
DPs in argument positions in Potawatomi are pronominals, consisting
solely of features on the head D. Full DPs "doubling" these pronominal
arguments will be adjoined to the CP when they occur. [−obv] Ds—1st,
2nd, and some 3rd person Ds—are true pronominals and will cliticize to
the front of CP at MS. Other Ds—[+obv] 3rd person Ds and Ds unmarked for [obv]—must be small pro's. We have placed the "NOM"

subject in [Spec, IndP] and the "ACC" object in the VP in (25); however, the subject might move to [Spec, TP] in the syntax if TPs need subjects.

In the syntax, the verb will raise via head-to-head movement to Ind, Neg, Tns, and then C. Each time the verb raises, it adjoins to the next head up in the tree. At MS the Agrs are added to the appropriate functional heads, Agr_1 to Ind, Agr_2 to Tns, and Agr_3 to C, yielding the structure in (26).

(26) *Inflected independent order verb at MS*

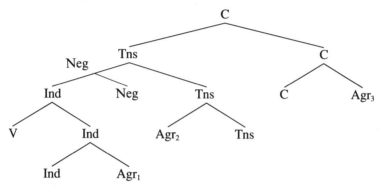

Recall that if both DP arguments are 3rd person, one must be marked [−obv] and the other [+obv]. Agr_1 will agree in all features, including case, with a pro DP—non-[−obv]—argument in the government domain of V + Ind, after V raises (see Marantz 1992a for elaboration on the mechanisms of agreement). Agr_2 agrees in person and number with all [−obv] DP arguments in the government domain of V + Ind(+Neg) + Tns after V-raising. Agr_3 is a Gender (animacy)/Number/Obviation concord morpheme, much like the Gender/Number/Case morpheme assumed to be added at MS to Russian adjectives, as explained in footnote 4. Agr_3 will agree, via concord, in [+pl] and [+obv] with the Agr_1 on Ind, which independent C selects. The characteristics of the various Potawatomi Agr morphemes are summarized in (27).

(27) *Agr*   *Adjoins to X at MS*   *Agrees with Y in Z features*

Agr	*Adjoins to X at MS*	*Agrees with Y in Z features*
Agr_1	Ind	Agrees with a pro DP argument (a non-[−obv] argument) in animacy, case, [±pl], and [±obv]
Agr_2	Tns	Agrees with [−obv] arguments in person, [±pl], and case
Agr_3	C	Agrees (via concord) with Agr_1 in animacy, [±pl], and [±obv]

We assume that the determination of government relations in word structures like (26) follows the same principles as for government relations in the syntax. In particular, when A is adjoined to B, as Agr_2 is adjoined to Tns in (26), A c-commands everything that B c-commands; that is, A c-commands everything c-commanded by both the "segment" of B to which A is adjoined and every segment of B formed via adjunction. Thus, in a structure like (26) Agr_2 c-commands all constituents c-commanded by its sister Tns node (here, Neg and the constituents dominated by Neg) and all constituents c-commanded by the highest Tns node (here, constituents dominated by C).

The major problem in the analysis of the independent order verb is that the agreement for $[-obv]$ arguments (Agr_2) is in a different (suffixal) morpheme from that of other arguments. Example (16b), repeated here as (28), is a typical instantiation of the independent order verb structure (26) with its three agreement suffixes, labeled Agr_1, Agr_2, and Agr_3.

(28) k-   wapm -a   -s'i   -m   -wapunin -uk
     Cl- V Agr_1 Neg Agr_2 Tns Agr_3
     2   see   3ACC   2pl   preterit   3pl

'you (pl) didn't see them'

Agr_1 reflects the subject versus object contrast of a non-$[-obv]$ 3rd person argument (a pro argument) of the verb (the /-a/ in (28) is for an ACC argument (direct object)). The obviation and number features of this argument are assigned to Agr_3, (the /-k/ in (28) signals plural). Sandwiched between Agr_1 and Agr_3, and between Neg and Tns, is the Agr_2 morpheme, which marks the person, number, and case features of all and only the $[-obv]$ arguments of the verb, the /-m/ affix standing for 2nd person plural. In sentences with a 1st or 2nd person argument as subject and object, Agr_2 will contain two sets of agreement features, one with NOM and one with ACC case. Similarly, the Clitic complex will contain two sets of features, one for each of the arguments.

In Marantz 1992a it is argued that Agr always attaches to some head at MS to pick up the features of DPs governed by that head. For the analysis of Potawatomi to follow from general principles, we need to motivate the terminal nodes that the various Agrs in (28) are attaching to.

The Agr_2 next to Tns presents no conceptual difficulty. The usual situation cross-linguistically is for Agr to attach to Tns and agree with one or more arguments in the government domain of $[V+Tns]$ (see Marantz 1992a). In the conjunct order inflection (see (16a)) all arguments, includ-

Table 1
Potawatomi "conjunct order" Agr$_2$ (for transitive animate stems)

	OBJECT							
	1	2	3	3obv	1incl	1excl	2pl	3pl
SUBJECT								
1		unan	uk				unuko	ukwa
2	yun		ut			yak		utwa
3	t	uk		at	unuk	yumut	unak	
3obv			ukot					ukwat
1incl			at					
1excl		unak	uko				unak	
2pl	yek		ek			yak		ukwa
3pl	wat	uk'wa		awat	unuk	yumut	unak	

ing non-[−obv] 3rd person ones, show agreement in this position in the verb.

The various manifestations of this Agr$_2$ for transitive verbs with animate objects in the conjunct order are shown in table 1 (from Hockett 1948). Note that the repetition of phonological pieces within the various cells of table 1 suggests that some splitting of features of the Agr$_2$ morpheme into independent terminal nodes might be justified, just as we split the plural feature from the proclitics in Georgian in section 2.1. However, as a whole, the conjunct Agr$_2$ node agrees simultaneously with both subject and object in person, number, and case.

Recall that in contrast, Agr$_2$ in the independent order agrees only with the [−obv] arguments. The question, then, is to determine what is special about the independent order inflection that splits [−obv] arguments off into a special class and employs two extra morphemes, one on the stem (Agr$_1$) and one outside all the other morphemes (Agr$_3$), that show agreement with different features of the non-[−obv] arguments.

Since independent order inflection goes with main clauses, the choice of such inflection must involve the Complementizer system in some way, or at least some functional category higher than TP that may be governed from C. For present purposes, we will identify as a C this functional category that contains the information that the clause is independent. The independent C chooses the morpheme that appears on the verb stem and shows agreement with non-[−obv] (the pro) arguments in case; that is, independent C chooses the morpheme to which Agr$_1$ attaches. This morpheme appears only in the independent order, not in the conjunct order.

We call the form of the verb stem chosen by independent C the *independent* or *Ind* stem.

Since the agreement on the functional category that creates this Ind stem (Agr_1) agrees in case with a pro 3rd person argument, as shown in (29), it would be tempting to call the form that agrees with a subject as in (29a,b,f,i) the "active" participle and the one that agrees with the object as in (29c–e,g,h) the "passive" participle. However, cross-linguistically passive and active participles have aspectual implications not exhibited by these forms. Moreover, passives and actives are not generally restricted to 3rd person arguments. We therefore leave the nature of these stem forms open for further investigation, emphasizing again that the only unusual thing about them is that the agreement on them targets non-[−obv] arguments only. (See Johns 1992 for speculations about Inuit that might suggest that the Ind stem forms should be treated as nominalizations of the verb root.)

(29) a. k-wapm-<u>uk</u>   'he sees you (sg)'
     b. k-wapm-<u>uko</u>-k   'they see you (sg)'
     c. k-wapm-<u>a</u>   'you (sg) see <u>him</u>'
     d. k-wapm-<u>a</u>-k   'you (sg) see <u>them</u>'
     e. n-wapm-<u>a</u>   'I see <u>him</u>'
     f. n-wapm-<u>uk</u>   'he sees me'
     g. n-wapm-<u>a</u>-n   'I see <u>him</u> (obv)'
     h. w-wapm-<u>a</u>-n   'he [−obv] sees <u>him</u> (obv)'
     i. w-wapm-<u>uko</u>-n   '<u>he</u> (obv) sees him [−obv]'

Agr_1 and Ind fuse into a single terminal node prior to Vocabulary insertion. The data in (29) are consistent with there being two Vocabulary items that compete for spelling out the fused Agr_1 + Ind node, as in (30).

(30) [Agr_1 + Ind]

NOM ↔ /-ukO/ / [+trans] _____

         ↔ /-a/   / [+trans] _____

We have included the stipulation that the Vocabulary items in (30) are inserted only on [+trans] stems, where the [+trans] stems comprise an inflectional class in Potawatomi that does not conform exactly to the syntactic class of transitives. The [Agr+Ind] node is always zero with intransitive animate stems ([−trans] stems with an animate subject); see (19). However, the /−a/ appears on transitive inanimate stems ([+trans] stems with an inanimate object) in addition to the transitive animate stems of (29), agreeing with a pro, [−anim] object in these cases; see (38).

Whereas Agr_1 agrees in case with a pro argument and appears in the position of Ind, Agr_3 agrees in obviation and number with such an argument and appears in the position of what we now identify as the C node. (31) shows examples of this Agr_3 agreeing with either the subject, when Agr_1 is NOM as in (31c–d), or the object, when Agr_1 is ACC, as in (31a–b). (31e–f) are a reminder that the Vocabulary items that spell out [+pl] and [+obv] in the $Agr_3 + C$ node are the same as those that spell out these features on animate nouns.

(31) a. n-wapm-a-<u>k</u>   'I see <u>them</u>'

     b. n-wapm-a-<u>n</u>   'I see him (<u>obv</u>)'

     c. n-wapm-uk   'he sees me'

     d. n-wapm-uko-<u>k</u>   '<u>they</u> see me'

     e. n-os'-<u>uk</u>   'my father<u>s</u>'

     f. n-os'-<u>un</u>   'my father (<u>obv</u>)'

Recall that there is a selection relation between independent C and the Ind node creating the independent stem. This node carries agreement—Agr_1—with a pro argument. If there is concord agreement for animacy, [±pl], and [±obv] between C and the Ind node that it selects, we would have the features we want in the correct place in the verb. The agreeing features from Agr_1 appear on the Agr_3 node, which fuses with C to yield a single terminal node for Vocabulary insertion. The competing Vocabulary items for [$Agr_3 + C$] in (32) will yield the correct results. We have also included the Vocabulary items for a D within the DP, which agrees in animacy, [±pl], and [±obv] with the head N of its NP complement. For animate nouns and animate pro's, the Vocabulary items for fused [$Agr_3 + C$] and [$Agr + D$] are the same, (32d–e). For inanimate nouns and inanimate pro's, the Vocabulary items are different. Agreement with pro on a C for inanimates requires the items in (32a–b), illustrated in (21).[22] Agreement on D for inanimates involves the plural suffix (32c).

(32) [$Agr_3 + C$] ($Agr + D$)

     a. C $\leftrightarrow$ /-ton/

       [+obv]

       [−anim]

     b. C $\leftrightarrow$ /-nun/

       [+pl]

       [−anim]

     c. [+pl]

       [−anim] $\leftrightarrow$ /-n/[23]

d. $[+\text{obv}]$ $\leftrightarrow$ /-n/
   $[+\text{anim}]$

e. $[+\text{pl}]$ $\leftrightarrow$ /-k/

Recall that the DP subject in [Spec, IndP] in (25) and the DP object in the VP will be pronominal, consisting only of features under the D node. Overt DPs (adjuncts) outside the CP may bind the pronominal arguments. Non-[−obv] arguments are phonologically null pro's ("identified" by Agr_1). As explained above, the [−obv] argument pronominals in independent order cliticize to the front of CP, before certain adverbials that may appear inside the CP and before the verb, as in (17). The clitics fuse together (as explained in section 2.1 for Georgian), and the Vocabulary items in (33) compete to spell out the resulting node. Again, the difference between [−obv] and other DP arguments is that the [−obv] arguments have Vocabulary items to spell them out whereas the non-[−obv] arguments must be pro.

(33) *Clitic*

$[+2]$ $\leftrightarrow$ /k-/
$[+1]$ $\leftrightarrow$ /n-/
$[-\text{obv}]$ $\leftrightarrow$ /w-/[24]

These competing items must be ordered as shown in (33), either explicitly or because of language-specific or universal priority relations among the features involved. If $[\pm 1]$ universally takes priority over $[\pm 2]$, the same results could be ensured by giving /n-/ the feature $[-2]$ as well, making it come first in the ordering, as suggested by Noyer (1992a).

The need for the ordering in (33) becomes particularly clear when we examine the form of verbs with 1st person inclusive arguments, that is, arguments meaning 'you and I'. A slightly simplified MS structure for such a verb prior to Vocabulary insertion is shown in (34a). In (34b) we show the individual Vocabulary items that are inserted in the different terminal nodes. The positions in the word will still be fully specified with the features shown in (34a) after Vocabulary insertion even though the Vocabulary items themselves are underspecified, since insertion is "feature-filling" rather than "feature-changing."

(34) 'You and I (we) see him.'

a. Cl-	[[V	Agr_1]	Agr_2]
$[+1], [+2]$		$[-1], [-2]$	$[+1], [+2]$
NOM, $[+\text{pl}]$		ACC, $[-\text{pl}]$	NOM, $[+\text{pl}]$

b. k-   wapm   -a   -mun
    Cl-   V   -Agr$_1$ -Agr$_2$
    [+2]   ACC   [+1], pl

As shown in (34a), the Clitic position for [−obv] arguments contains the features [+1] and [+2] for a 1st person inclusive subject; the Agr$_2$ agrees with this [−obv] argument in all features. The competition among the morphemes in (33) for insertion in the Clitic node must end with the [+2] prefix /k-/ as the winner. However, the competition among the Agr$_2$ affixes, which are shown in (35), ends with the [+1]-carrying /-mun/ as the winner. In particular, the prefix with the [+2] feature must win over the prefix with the [+1] feature even when both are present. This outcome is ensured by the ordering in (33). As is shown in (35) and in many examples below, the form for Agr$_2$ without the [+1] feature in a string like (34) would be /-wa/, not /-mun/. The choice of /-mun/ for Agr$_2$ in (34b), then, indicates the presence of the [+1] feature on both Clitic and the Agr$_2$ that agrees with the Clitic argument.

There is a great deal of allomorphy for the affixes inserted under the Agr$_2$ node, as partially indicated by the Vocabulary items that compete for this node listed in (35).

(35) *Agr$_2$*

    a. [+1]   ↔   /-nan/   / ϕ ____
        [+pl]
        [ACC] or [GEN]

    b. [+1]   ↔   /-mun/   / Ind ____
        [+pl]

    c. [−obv]   ↔   /-wa/   / ϕ ____[25]
        [+pl]
        [case]
        add /na/ before /-wa/ for verbal stems when ϕ includes [−anim]

    d. [−obv]   ↔   /-m/   / Ind ____
        [+pl]

    e. [−obv]   ↔   /-n/   / Ind ____
                                          [−anim]
        deletes before [+preterit]

Note that the Vocabulary entries in (35) will compete for the Agr$_2$ node with the affixes whose phonological forms are given in table 1, where the realizations of Agr$_2$ in conjunct order are listed. To ensure that the items in (35) will only be inserted in independent order verbs, the suffixes in (35) are explicitly marked to occur either next to ϕ-features (person, number, and gender) or next to the Ind morpheme. The ϕ-features mentioned in (35a,c) are the person, number, and gender (animacy) features that either Agr_1, found only on Ind, or a noun stem might have. By mentioning these ϕ-features in the Vocabulary entries here, we explain why the affixes /-nan/ and /-wa/ are limited in the verbal inflection to independent order verbs where a pro subject or object occurs and Agr_1 therefore has ϕ-features. In addition, we explain why these same affixes occur as the agreement form for plural possessive agreement, as shown in (36).

(36) a. n-čiman-<u>nan</u>   '<u>our</u> canoe'
     b. k-čiman-<u>wa</u>   '<u>your</u> (<u>pl</u>) canoe'
     c. w-čiman-<u>wa</u>   '<u>their</u> [−<u>obv</u>] canoe'

In the case of the possessed nouns, it is the noun stem itself that carries the ϕ-features that serve as the environment for the insertion of (35a) or (35c). Thus, the forms in (35a,c) will compete for the Agr on N in DPs that agrees with the (genitive) [−obv] possessor. The possessors are also pronominal proclitics that cliticize to the front of the possessed N and are realized with the same Vocabulary items that compete for the pronominal proclitics on independent order verbs (see (33)).

The ordering of the affixes in (35) deserves some comment. The ordering of (35b) before (35c) does not clearly follow from general principles, although the ordering is required unless the features assigned to the affixes are modified, as noted above. The issue of which entry is more fully specified, (35b) or (35c), hinges on decisions made about hierarchies of features, as explored by Noyer (1992a). If case features are dependent on person features, for example, and [+1] is more specific than [−obv], then on one view, (35b) would be more specific than (35c).

For the sake of completeness, we have included a few elements in (35) that have not yet been encountered in examples. At this point we will illustrate the basic use of each of the Vocabulary items in (35). In the next section we will illustrate how the interaction between morphemes affects both the distribution of these Vocabulary items and their phonological form.

The examples in (37) show the basic uses of the [+pl] affixes (35a–d).

(37) a. n-wapm-uk-<u>nan</u>   'he sees us'
     b. n-wapm-a-<u>mun</u>   'we see him'
     c. k-wapm-a-<u>wa</u>   'you (pl) see him'
     d. k-wapm-a-<u>m</u>-wapun   'you (pl) saw him'

The suffix /-nan/ is used for a 1st person plural Agr$_2$ with ACC case in (37a), inserted next to /-uk/, which has ϕ-features agreeing with a pro subject. The suffix /-mun/ appears in (37b) in place of /-nan/ since the 1st person plural Agr$_2$ in (37b) is NOM, not ACC or GEN. We will discuss the different environments for the suffixes /-wa/ and /-m/ in the next section; we note here only that /-wa/ occurs for a plural Agr$_2$ in (37c), whereas /-m/ occurs in (37d) before the preterit /-(wa)pun/. We will propose an impoverishment rule that removes the case features of Agr$_2$ before the preterit Tns, causing the choice of /-m/ rather than /-wa/ before /-wapun/.

What remains to be introduced from (35) are elements involved with inanimate verb stems, which we have not yet discussed; these are illustrated in (38).

(38) a. w-wapt-a-<u>na</u>wa   'they see it (inanim)'
  b. k-wapt-a-<u>n</u>   'you see it (inanim)'
  c. k-wapt-a-∅-napun   'you saw it (inanim)'

The form *waput* 'see' in (38) is morphologically related to the verb *wapum* 'see' that we have been using in most of our examples. The former is used for inanimate direct objects, the latter for animate direct objects. The situation described under the Vocabulary item (35c), in which the expected /-wa/ shows up as /-nawa/, is illustrated in (38a). Here Agr$_1$ is [−anim] and thus Agr$_2$ is next to ϕ-features containing [−anim]. (The /na/ could be added by a readjustment rule; see section 5.3 for a discussion of such rules in Potawatomi.) The Vocabulary item in (35e), like /-nawa/, is restricted to transitive inanimate stems. (38b) illustrates this /-n/ suffix. Although /-n/ occurs with inanimate object verbs in the independent order, it does not occur on inanimate possessed nouns. For that reason, the restriction to stems with the Ind morpheme is included among its features in (35e). If we used the context, ϕ-features including [−anim] for (35e), this Vocabulary item would attach to inanimate possessed nouns, which have ϕ-features including [−anim]. The disappearance of /-n/ before the preterit suffix, as described by the "deletes before [+preterit]" in (35e), is shown in (38c). (This deletion could be written as a readjustment rule.) The appearance of the preterit as /-napun/ rather than /-pun/ will be discussed below.

Continuing with this survey of Potawatomi affixes, we turn to the preterit and negative morphemes of the independent order. As mentioned above, the preterit Tns affix is /-pun/, with some allomorphs (/napun/,

/wapun/, /napunin/, /wapunin/) to be discussed below. The negative affix
for independent order verbs is /-s'i/.

5.3   Affixes as Morphemes

We have shown that the positioning of phonological pieces in the Potawatomi inflected verb is plausibly the result of the insertion of Vocabulary
items into terminal nodes derived from the syntax. Each "position" in the
Potawatomi verb can be related to a featurally coherent terminal node
whose syntactic and morphological function is fairly straightforward. On
this analysis, there is no reason to appeal to arbitrarily ordered blocks of
WFRs, as on Anderson's analysis, to derive the Potawatomi verb.

In addition to determining the location of the phonological realization of inflectional features, the Potawatomi inflectional morphemes show
their presence by influencing the realization of structurally adjacent morphemes. It will be recalled from the discussion of English verb inflection
in section 3.1 and the Georgian inflections in section 2.2 that such contextual influences fall into three categories. First, there are instances of conditioned allomorphy, where the choice of one item in Vocabulary insertion
is determined by an adjacent morpheme, as, for example, in the English
past participle forms *take-n* and *put-∅*. Parallel examples from Potawatomi were discussed in the preceding section in connection with the choice
of affixes for Agr$_2$ in (35). Second, English also has alternations such
as *freeze–froze-n* or *break–brok-en* where the phonetic composition of a
morpheme is modified in a position adjacent to another morpheme. Alternations of this kind were handled by readjustment rules like (10). In this
section we discuss some readjustment rules of Potawatomi, which differ
from those in (10) in applying to affixes rather than stems. Finally, as
discussed briefly in connection with the Georgian plural /-t/ suffix in section 2.2, there are rules of impoverishment that delete morphosyntactic
features of morphemes in the context of other morphemes. We discuss
rules of impoverishment from Potawatomi in this section as well. As
pointed out below, the facts captured by readjustment and impoverishment
constitute a major sort of problem for affixless theories like Anderson's.

Consider first a simple example of the interaction of morphemes in
Potawatomi. The /-mun/ suffix (35b) for 1st person plural subject agreement in Agr$_2$ appears to block the further affixation of the Agr$_3$ suffixes
/-n/ and /-k/. This is shown in (39a–b), where the expected forms with
final /-n/ and /-k/ are ungrammatical and must be replaced by the forms
without /-n/ and /-k/ for the same arrangement of arguments. We will
argue that this blocking effect is the result of the deletion—impoverish-

ment—of Agr$_3$ in the environment of the features on Agr$_2$ that trigger the insertion of /-mun/. It is not just any suffix under Agr$_2$ that forces deletion of Agr$_3$. Unlike /-mun/, /-nan/ (35a), which realizes Agr$_2$ with the features of 1st person plural objects, does not block /-n/ and /-k/, as shown in (39c–d). (39e–f) show that 2nd person plural subject Agr$_2$ /-wa/ (35c) does not block /-n/ or /-k/ either.

(39) a. *n-wapm-a-<u>mun-uk</u>   'we see them'   n-wapm-a-<u>mun</u>
     b. *n-wapm-a-<u>mun-un</u>   'we see him (obv)'   n-wapm-a-<u>mun</u>
     c. n-wapm-uk-<u>nan-uk</u>   'they see us'
     d. n-wapm-uk-<u>nan-un</u>   'he (obv) sees us'
     e. k-wapm-a-<u>wa-k</u>   'you (pl) see them'
     f. k-wapm-a-<u>wa-n</u>   'you (pl) see him (obv)'

As shown by the examples in (40), adding the preterit morpheme *wapunin* appears to complicate the analysis of Agr$_3$ deletion.

(40) a. *n-wapm-a-<u>mn</u>-(w)apunin-<u>uk</u>   'we saw them'
        n-wapm-a-<u>mn</u>-apun
     b. *n-wapm-a-<u>mn</u>-(w)apunin-<u>un</u>   'we saw him (obv)'
        n-wapm-a-<u>mn</u>-apun
     c. k-wapm-a-<u>m</u>-wapunin-<u>uk</u>   'you (pl) saw them'
     d. k-wapm-a-<u>m</u>-wapunin-<u>un</u>   'you (pl) saw him (obv)'

Although the preterit Tns morpheme appears between /-mun/ and the Agr$_3$ /-k/ or /-n/, still the presence of /-mun/ blocks the /-k/ and /-n/ even "over" the preterit, which has the allomorph /-(w)apun/ after /-mun/ and /-(wa)punin/ before /-k/, /-n/ (see the discussion of Potawatomi readjustment below). (40a–b) show the blocking effect of /-mun/ over /-wapunin/, and (40c–d) show that it is not the combination of any Agr$_2$ suffix and the preterit that blocks /-k/, /-n/ but only /-mun/. Note in (40c–d) that the 2nd person plural subject Agr$_2$ shows up as /-m/ (35d) instead of /-wa/ before /-wapun(in)/, as it did in (39e–f).

To avoid an analysis in which an affixal morpheme with certain features, Agr$_2$, deletes another morpheme, Agr$_3$, one might propose that the deletion or blocking of the /-n/ and /-k/ suffixes is triggered by the phonological sequence /-mun/, not by a particular morpheme. However, a further set of facts defeats this proposal. The distinction between /-nan/ and /-mun/ is lost before /(w)apun(in)/; even with a 3rd person subject and 1st plural object, we find /-mun/ for Agr$_2$, not /-nan/, before the preterit, as shown in (41). Compare (41a–b) with (39c–d). This /-mun/ for 1st person plural objects, like the 1st person plural object affix /-nan/ but unlike the 1st person plural subject affix /-mun/, does not block further affixation of /-n/, /-k/, as shown in (41). Thus, it is not the phonological piece /-mun/ that blocks the /-n/ or /-k/ realization of Agr$_3$; rather, it is the presence of a 1st person plural *subject* Agr$_2$.

(41) a. n-wapm-uk-<u>mun</u>-(w)apunin-<u>uk</u>   'they saw us'
     b. n-wapm-uk-<u>mun</u>-(w)apunin-<u>un</u>   'he (obv) saw us'

Although Agr$_2$ (subject /-mun/) seems to affect Agr$_3$ (/-k/, /-n/) non-locally, over the Tns (/-pun/) morpheme, when the hierarchical structure of the inflected verb is examined, it becomes clear that Agr$_2$ governs Agr$_3$ in the technical sense. Consider the relevant portion of an independent order inflected verb from (26), reproduced as (42).

(42)

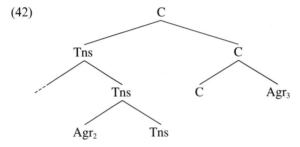

On the technical definition of c-command used, for example, in Chomsky 1993, Agr$_2$ c-commands Agr$_3$; since Agr$_2$ is adjoined to Tns, it is not dominated by every segment of Tns and may c-command constituents dominated by C. Since Agr$_3$ is adjoined to C, it is not dominated by every segment of C and C may not serve as a barrier to government of Agr$_3$ by Agr$_2$. The adjunction structures that result from head movement and adjunction in the syntax and from the adjunction of Agr to functional heads at MS allow for more government relations among terminal nodes than the linear string of morphemes might suggest.

We propose that the effect of /-mun/ on Agr$_3$ is a form of impoverishment—the deletion of certain morphosyntactic features in the presence of other such features in the same or in a governing morpheme. In particular, we tentatively propose the radical impoverishment rule in (43).

(43) Agr$_3$ → ∅ / governed by Agr$_2$

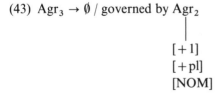

$$[+1]$$
$$[+pl]$$
$$[\text{NOM}]$$

Although we now have an account of why Agr$_3$ is not realized in the presence of 1st person plural subject /-mun/, we have not explained why 1st person object Agr$_2$ shows up as /-nan/ in (39c–d) but as /-mun/ before the preterit affix in (41). It seems that /-mun/ is the unmarked form for a 1st person plural Agr$_2$, and we have given it just the features [+1], [+pl] in (35); thus, the change from /-nan/ to /-mun/ represents a retreat to the general case. There is another special form for 1st person plural Agr$_2$ that disappears before the preterit; for 1st person plural objects when the subject is 2nd person, there is a special form /-ymun/ that also retreats to /-mun/ before the preterit, as shown in (44).

(44) a. k-wapm-uymun   'you (sg or pl) see us'
     b. k-wapm-umn-(w)apum   'you (sg or pl) saw us'

Suppose that /-nan/ carries the feature [ACC], as in (35a), and that the /y/ of /-ymun/ in (44a) is inserted by a readjustment rule, (45), that is triggered by the same [ACC] feature.

(45) $\emptyset \rightarrow$ /y/ / _____ /mun/
                  [ACC]

We can now propose an impoverishment rule as in (46) to delete the feature [ACC] from a [1] Agr$_2$ next to [+preterit]. This impoverishment rule will take /-nan/ out of the competition for the phonological realization of Agr$_2$ before a preterit Tns, since /-nan/ depends on the presence of [ACC] in Agr$_2$. In addition, (46) will bleed the readjustment rule in (45).[26]

(46) [ACC] $\rightarrow \emptyset$ / _____ [+preterit]
         [+1]

One other alternation was observed above to occur before the preterit: the alternation /-wa/ $\sim$ /-m/ for the 2nd person plural Agr$_2$. /-wa/ occurs for [−obv] plural subjects or objects as long as they exclude the 1st person (recall that the 1st person affixes for plural Agr$_2$ are ordered before those for the plain [−obv] affixes in (35)). The distribution of /-wa/ is illustrated in (47).

(47) a. k-wapm-a-wa   'you (pl) see him'
     b. w-wapm-a-wa-n   'they [−obv] see him (obv)'
     c. k-wapm-uk-wa   'he sees you (pl)'
     d. w-wapm-uk-wa-n   'he (obv) sees them [−obv]'

Elsewhere the unmarked form for a [−obv] plural Agr$_2$ is /-m/. Where otherwise we would expect /-wa/, Agr$_2$ reverts to /-m/ before [+preterit] for plural subjects, but not for plural objects, as shown in (48). (48c–

d) exhibit an additional feature: /-wa/ deletes before the /-wa/ part of /-wapun/ in a type of haplology, since the /-wa/ of /-wapun/ is also a plural /-wa/, as shown in (53).

(48) a. k-wapm-a-m̲-wapun   'you (pl) saw him'
     b. w-wapm-a-m̲-wapunin-un   'they [−obv] saw him (obv)'
     c. k-wapm-uk-(wa̲)-wapun   'he saw you (pl)'
     d. w-wapm-uk-(wa̲)-wapunin-un   'he (obv) saw them [−obv]'

If we suppose that the /-wa/ spell-out of plural Agr$_2$ requires a case feature (either [NOM] or [ACC]; see (35c)), then the impoverishment rule in (49) will account for the examples in (48a–b). Note that this rule is very similar to (46) except that it deletes [NOM] instead of [ACC].

(49) [NOM] → ∅ / _____   [+ preterit]
                         [− obv]
                         [− 1]

In our analysis of the influence that individual morphemes have on other morphemes, we have thus far proposed mainly impoverishment rules that take place before the insertion of Vocabulary items (the exception is the readjustment rule in (45) that must occur after the insertion of /-mun/). The impoverishment rules delete features of terminal nodes in the presence of other morphosyntactic features; obviously, the deletion of such features in a morpheme affects the set of Vocabulary items that might compete for the phonological realization of that morpheme. Deleting the [ACC] feature of Agr$_2$ before the preterit in (46), for example, takes /-nan/ out of the running for the Agr$_2$ node. By contrast, the readjustment rule (45), which changes the phonological features of a morpheme, must be ordered after Vocabulary insertion, which provides phonological features for morphemes.

To complete the analysis, we need some additional readjustment rules, rules that change the phonological form of morphemes after Vocabulary insertion. The first rule adds /-n/ (or /-non/ after Neg) to Agr$_2$ when Agr$_2$ contains two sets of ϕ-features (i.e., when both the arguments of a transitive verb are [−obv]) and the subject is 1st person. The output of this rule can be seen in (50), and we have attempted to formulate it in (51). The curious addition of another /-n/ to the basic /-n/ (or to the /-non/ after Neg) when the mentioned ϕ-features include plural is illustrated in (50b,e) and produced by the second set of angled brackets in rule (51).

(50) a. k-wapm-u̲n̲   k-wapm-u̲n̲-napun
         'I see you'   'I saw you'

    b. k-wapm-<u>un</u>um   k-wapm-<u>unn</u>um-wapun
       'I see you (pl)'   'I saw you (pl)'
    c. k-wapm-<u>un</u>mun   k-wapm-<u>un</u>mun-wapun
       'we see you (sg/pl)'   'we saw you (sg/pl)'
    d. k-wapm-us'-<u>non</u>   k-wapm-us'-<u>non</u>-napun
       'I don't see you'   'I didn't see you'
    e. k-wapm-us'-<u>non</u>um   k-wapm-us'-<u>nonn</u>um-wapum
       'I don't see you (pl)'   'I didn't see you (pl)'
    f. k-wapm-us'-<u>non</u>mun   k-wapm-us'-<u>non</u>mun-wapum
       'we don't see you (sg/pl)'   'we didn't see you (sg/pl)'

(51) $\emptyset \rightarrow /\langle no \rangle_1\text{-n}\langle n \rangle_2/ \ / \ \langle Neg \rangle_1$ _____ Agr_2 $\langle \text{preterit} \rangle_2$

$$\overset{\displaystyle [+1] \qquad \phi}{\overset{\displaystyle \diagup \diagdown}{}}$$

NOM $\langle pl \rangle_2$

In addition to readjusting Agr_2 in some cases, we need to account
for the appearance of the preterit /-pun/ in various environments. First,
/-pun/ becomes /-punin/ before /-k/ or /-n/. More generally, Hockett
claims the addition of /-in/ occurs before any suffix.

(52) $\emptyset \rightarrow /\text{in}/ \ / \ \text{pun}$ _____ /segment/

Second, /wa/ is added before /-pun/ when Agr_2 is [+pl]. Recall that
haplology appears to delete one of two /wa/'s in a row if such a sequence
is produced by (53).

(53) $\emptyset \rightarrow /\text{wa}/ \ / \ [+\text{pl}]$ _____ pun

Finally, /-pun/ shows up as /-wapun/ or /-napun/ after a phonologically
overt Agr_2 (for examples of /-napun/, see (38c), (50a,d)). We have shown
that /-wapun/ occurs after an *overt* [+pl] Agr_2. The examples in (54a–b)
from the animate transitive paradigm and the examples in (54c–f) from
the intransitive animate paradigm would suggest that /-napun/ occurs
after a *nonovert* [−obv] Agr_2 as well. Compare these examples with the
intransitive examples in (54g–j) where there is no [−obv] argument—
and thus no [−obv] Agr_2—and the preterit is /-pun(in)/ rather than
/-napun(in)/.

(54) a. k-wapum-$\emptyset$ 'you see me'
     b. k-wapm-$\emptyset$-<u>unapun</u>   'you saw me'
     c. n-kaskumi-$\emptyset$ 'I start running'
     d. k-kaskumi-$\emptyset$ 'you start running'

    e. n-kaskumi-Ø-<u>napun</u>   'I started running'
    f. k-kaskumi-Ø-<u>napun</u>   'you started running'
    g. kaskumi   'he starts running'
    h. kaskumi-n   'he (obv) starts running'
    i. kaskumi-<u>pun</u>   'he started running'
    j. kaskumi-<u>punin</u>-un   'he (obv) started running'

Although a $[-\text{obv}]$ Agr$_2$ in the singular (even one that is phonologically null) seems to trigger /-napun/ in (54b,e,f), when Agr$_1$ has ϕ-features (i.e., in transitive contexts where one of the arguments is 3rd person pro), an agreeing $[-\text{obv}]$ Agr$_2$ will not trigger /-napun/, as shown in (55).

(55) a. n-wapm-a-Ø-pun   'I saw him'
    b. n-wapm-uk-Ø-pun   'he saw me'

If we propose another impoverishment rule (56) that deletes the $[-\text{obv}]$ feature of a singular Agr$_2$ adjacent to animate ϕ-features (i.e., after an agreeing Agr$_1$ for transitive animate verbs), then we could add the readjustment rule in (57) to account for the distribution of /-napun/. For transitive inanimate verbs, singular Agr$_2$ spells out as /-n/ (35e) and we get /-napun/ for $[+\text{preterit}]$ rather than /-pun/; see the examples in (38). This indicates that we do not want to delete Agr$_2$ when the ϕ-features of Agr$_1$ include $[-\text{anim}]$; rather, with inanimate Agr$_1$ we want to trigger (57).

(56) $[-\text{obv}] \rightarrow \emptyset \ / \ [+\text{anim}]$ ___
$$[-\text{pl}]$$

(57) $\emptyset \rightarrow /\text{na}/ \ / \ [-\text{obv}]$ ___ pun

5.4 Anderson's Analysis of Potawatomi and Georgian

The phenomena treated above by recourse to readjustment and impoverishment constitute a major stumbling block for Anderson's (1992) theory. Some of these difficulties were noted in section 3.2 with regard to English inflections. Equally serious problems arise from the facts of Potawatomi and Georgian.

Recall that Anderson does not recognize the existence of affixal morphemes; all the features that we have attributed to affixes in Potawatomi, Anderson would consider features of the verbal stem (after the syntax). The only mechanism Anderson's theory has available for the phonological realization of these features is the ordered sets of WFRs. The effects of impoverishment, Vocabulary insertion, and readjustment alike must be handled through these rule blocks. Since the mechanism of WFRs is unconstrained, Anderson could in principle mirror our analysis of

Potawatomi using such rules, some of which would simply delete morpho-syntactic features (impoverishment) without changing the phonology of the stem. However, Anderson's own analysis of allomorphy in Potawa-tomi follows a rather different tack. Noting that /-mun/ blocks the affixation of /-n/ and /-k/ for obviative and plural of a 3rd person argument, Anderson includes in the block of rules that adds /-n/ and /-k/ a zero affixation rule, /Xmun/ → /Xmun/. We reproduce this rule block from Anderson's analysis (1992:169) in (58).

(58) a. $\begin{bmatrix} +\text{Verb} \\ +\text{me} \quad [\ ] \\ +\text{pl} \end{bmatrix}$ /XmUn/ → /XmUn/

    b. $\begin{bmatrix} -\text{me} \\ -\text{you} \\ +\text{anim} \\ +\text{pl} \end{bmatrix}$ /X/ → /Xk/

    c. $\begin{bmatrix} \begin{bmatrix} -\text{me} \\ -\text{you} \end{bmatrix} \\ \begin{Bmatrix} +\text{pl} \\ +\text{obv} \end{Bmatrix} \end{bmatrix}$ /X/ → /Xn/

The rule (58a) does nothing to a stem; it is a zero affixation rule. How-ever, since it occurs as the first rule in a disjunctive rule block, it prevents the application of the other rules in the block whenever its features are met. Anderson adds features to this rule to limit it to the cases in which /-mun/ has been added by a previous WFR in the environment of 1st person plural subjects. In particular, the [+Verb] feature and the empty square brackets in (58a), interacting with other rules, will ensure that (58a) applies only when there is a 1st person plural subject and a 3rd person object.

The blocking effect of /-mun/ across an intervening /-pun/, as demon-strated in (40a–b), indicates that Anderson should have omitted /-mun/ from rule (58a), replacing it with simply /X/ → /X/; a stem need not end in /-mun/ for it to block further affixation of /-n/ or /-k/. However, now it is clear that it is the features 1st person plural subject that are blocking the remaining rules in (58), not /-mun/. Anderson's framework would allow any arbitrary set of features to trigger a zero affixation rule like (58a) and thus block all the other rules in any disjunctive rule block. He makes clear the blocking potential of any morphosyntactic features in his theory: "we posit such a formally empty rule just in case some set of rules must be precluded from applying in the presence of certain morphosyntactic features" (p. 169).

In DM, *random* morphosyntactic features may not trigger deletion (impoverishment) of features and thereby block the insertion of affixes bearing the deleted features. Impoverishment and other rules of the morphology are subject to locality constraints; they involve structurally adjacent morphemes (i.e., a morpheme may act as the context for the impoverishment of another morpheme if it governs the latter morpheme). We showed earlier that Agr_2 does govern Agr_3, yielding the proper relation between the morphemes for the impoverishment rule (43). Interactions between structurally adjacent morphemes are widespread cross-linguistically, but since Anderson does not recognize that affixes are morphemes, his theory cannot capture this fact but instead must resort to the notation of $/X/ \rightarrow /X/$ rules that allow it to express blocking relations between random sets of features and random rule blocks.

Anderson's treatment of what amounts to allomorphy triggered by adjacent morphemes runs counter to his analysis of blocking across rule blocks, introduced in his analysis of Georgian in Anderson 1986 and repeated in Anderson 1992. To account for the sort of Georgian data we briefly surveyed in (2), Anderson's theory requires that when a particular WFR changes $/X/ \rightarrow /gvX/$ in Georgian in the presence of 1st person plural object features, this WFR blocks a rule in a later rule block that changes $/X/ \rightarrow /Xt/$ in the presence of a plural feature (recall the analysis in section 2.1). His version of the "elsewhere" principle that has this blocking effect across rule blocks is given in (59).

(59) *"Elsewhere" Principle*

Application of a more specific rule blocks that of a later more general one. (p. 132)

According to this principle, a WFR in a later rule block whose features are a subset of those of a WFR from an earlier block will be blocked by that earlier rule, even though the rules are not in the same disjunctive block.

The general problem for this principle in the analysis of conditioned allomorphy will be illustrated with another example from Potawatomi. We have shown that $[-obv]$ plural /-wa/ does not occur before the preterit when the $[-obv]$ argument is the subject; instead, we find the /-m/ allomorph of Agr_2. Some relevant examples are repeated in (60). Anderson's WFR introducing /-wa/ $(/X/ \rightarrow /Xwa/)$ must be prevented from applying by another WFR in the same rule block that changes $/X/ \rightarrow /Xm/$

when the [+pl] feature mentioned in the latter rule is a feature of the subject and the verb is [+preterit]. Note that the /wa/ in (60a–b) corresponds to the /m/ before the preterit /wapun(in)/ in (60c–d).

(60) a. k-wapm-a-<u>wa</u>   'you (pl) see him'
     b. w-wapm-a-<u>wa</u>-n   'they see him (obv)'
     c. k-wapm-a-<u>m</u>-wapun   'you (pl) saw him'
     d. w-wapm-a-<u>m</u>-wapunin-un   'they saw him (obv)'

The problem for Anderson's theory is best illustrated by the form in (60c). Although the Agr_2 in (60c) takes on a special form /m/ with the feature [+preterit], this same feature finds its unmarked spell-out following a [+pl] Agr_2 in (60c). Thus, in the rule block that adds the phonological material /wapun/, Anderson's analysis will have a WFR something like /X/ → /Xwapun/ when there is a [+preterit] and a [pl] feature. But, by Anderson's version of the elsewhere condition, this rule must be blocked by the WFR that spells out /m/ in the previous block because this previous rule will mention [+preterit] plus [pl] and a few other features while the [+preterit] rule will mention only [+preterit] and [pl], a proper subset of the features of the earlier rule. In general, Anderson's approach to situations in which one morpheme influences the phonological realization of an adjacent morpheme will fall victim to this type of difficulty since the features of the influencing morpheme will be mentioned in the WFR that spells out the conditioned allomorph of the morpheme being influenced, in many cases blocking the spell-out of the influencing morpheme itself.

Anderson's own analysis of Potawatomi repeatedly violates his principle (59). For example, to account for the /-ymun/ form of Agr_2 that occurs with 1st person plural subjects and 2nd person objects (see (44a)), this analysis has the WFR (61a) in one block to add the /y/ and the WFR (61b) in a later block to add the /mun/ (compare our (35b) and (45)).

(61) a. $\left[\left[\begin{matrix} +\text{me} \\ +\text{pl} \end{matrix}\right]\right]$

     /X/ → /Xy/

     b. $\left[\begin{matrix} +\text{me} \\ +\text{pl} \end{matrix}\right]$

     /X/ → /Xmun/

Clearly the rule in (61a) is more specific than the rule (61b) and should block it. However, both rules are required to apply. We leave it to the reader to verify that Anderson's analysis requires other violations of (59).

Anderson's analyses of Georgian and Potawatomi are intended as the major empirical support for the affixless theory. In examining these analyses, we discover that Anderson's account of Georgian crucially relies on the "elsewhere" principle (59) to capture the distribution of the plural /-t/ suffix. However, as we have just shown, his account of Potawatomi relies just as crucially on violating this very same principle. Jointly, then, his analyses of Georgian and Potawatomi fatally undermine the theory that they were intended to support.

5.5   What's in Paradigm?

A chief issue for a word-and-paradigm approach such as Anderson's is what forms to include in the paradigms that are accounted for by a particular set of ordered blocks of WFRs. On a strict "lexeme-based" theory, one would presumably put together all and only the rules that apply to particular lexemes, that is, to particular N, V, and A stems. The leading idea behind this approach is that the rules relate forms of a word, not different words. These basic intuitions behind a word-and-paradigm approach call Anderson's Potawatomi analysis into question for what it includes and what it excludes. As we have illustrated, Potawatomi distinguishes a number of verb classes; these classes determine the form of inflectional morphology as well as the syntax of sentences in which the verbs occur. Intransitive verbs with animate subjects, intransitive verbs with inanimate subjects, transitive verbs with animate objects, and transitive verbs with inanimate objects all constitute separate classes. One could argue that there are often derivational relations between, say, transitive animates and transitive inanimates (e.g., *wapum* 'see' (animate object) in most of the examples vs. *waput* 'see' (inanimate object) in (38)) or between transitive animates and intransitive animates; therefore, the same stems may be involved in more than one class and the different inflectional paradigms for the different classes might be considered forms of the same word (stem) in some general sense. However, some argument must be made for including the inflectional rules for all these classes in the same rule blocks, as Anderson does. It is not sufficient to point out that much of the inflectional morphology is similar across these classes (although the similarities between, say, intransitive inanimates and the rest are slight here; see the examples in (21)). Moreover, Anderson includes the WFRs for nouns in the same rule blocks as the WFRs for the various verb classes. If nouns and verbs are in the same blocks, why not all the WFRs of the language? These choices make a significant difference in Anderson's theory, since numerous issues—how the WFRs are formulated, how they are ordered, which features they must mention, and what sort of blocking can occur between rules in different blocks—all depend on particular details of the full range of morphology under consideration.

Although Anderson mixes verb classes and nouns and verbs in his WFR blocks, he leaves out negation and the preterit, both central to allomorphy and the final phonological form of the Potawatomi independent order verb. He also leaves out the conjunct order inflection. Clearly the negative, preterit, and various conjunct inflections constitute different "forms of a verb" and are more obvious candidates for the verbal inflectional rule blocks than the nominal inflections that Anderson does include.

This is not an idle point. Adding these other inflections does not simply add more rules to the analysis; it changes the analysis entirely. In particular, in Anderson's analysis of Potawatomi, the disjunctive rule blocks do not correspond to morphemes we have identified in our analysis. Two of his blocks in particular seem to spell out heterogeneous sets of inflectional features. Once we add the negative and preterit affixes to the paradigms, however, we find that Anderson's blocks must be split, resulting more or less in a one-to-one correspondence between his blocks and the morphemes of our analysis. For example, Anderson includes spell-outs of pieces of Agr_2 affixes in the same block as what we have identified as phonological realizations of Agr_1. The /a/ and the /uk/ of Agr_1, shown in (62a,b), are put in the same rule block as the highlighted /n/ in (62c) and the highlighted /y/ in (62e). However, the Neg morpheme comes *after* Agr_1 (62a–b), whereas it comes *before* these /n/ and /y/ pieces of Agr_2 (62d,f).

(62) a. n-wapm-a̱-s'i   'I don't see him'
      Cl-see-Agr_1-Neg

   b. n-wapm-u̱k-s'i
      Cl-see-Agr_1-Neg   'he doesn't see me'

   c. k-wapm-u̱n   'I see you'
      Cl-see-Agr_2

   d. k-wapm-us'-<u>non</u>   'I don't see you'
      Cl-see-Neg-Agr_2

   e. k-wapm-u̱ymun   'you see us'
      Cl-see-Agr_2

   f. k-wapm-us'-i̱mun   'you don't see us'
      Cl-see-Neg-Agr_2

Thus, the unusual grouping of features in Anderson's disjunctive rule blocks is a function of the limited range of paradigms that he included in his analysis. No child acquiring Potawatomi could make such arbitrary and limiting decisions about which "forms of a word" to include in his or her grammar of the language.

6 Summary and Postscript: Distributed Morphology and "Checking Theory" within Chomsky's "Minimalist" program

In DM, a verb stem is assumed to pick up inflectional features, bundled in terminal nodes, through various mechanisms that are either syntactic or rely on syntactic structure. Head movement and adjunction, a syntactic operation, may affix an inflectional morpheme to a stem. In addition, head merger under structural adjacency, also a syntactic operation, may affix inflectional morphemes to verbs. The addition of Agr and other morphemes at MS, followed by the copying of features in agreement, depends on the syntactic structure. In all cases, these manipulations of structure operate on terminal nodes organized into hierarchical structures and yield terminal nodes organized into hierarchical structures. Relations between terminal nodes in these hierarchical structures, relations such as government and structural adjacency, are syntactic relations. All terminal nodes—lexical and functional, those present at DS and SS and those added at MS, those whose integrity has been maintained in the grammar and those that have been subject to fusion or fission—are subject to Vocabulary insertion at MS in exactly the same way.

In general, then, DM claims that inflectional features are picked up in prepackaged morpheme bundles in the grammar, not in the "lexicon" or Vocabulary, and that word formation is syntactic and postsyntactic, not lexical. By having the terminal nodes containing inflectional features obey the same structural principles as other terminal nodes and undergo the same Vocabulary insertion, DM accounts for the distribution of syntactic/semantic and phonological information in words and in sentences. The correlation between the distribution of syntactic/semantic information and of phonological information is mediated by Vocabulary items in all cases; the Vocabulary entries are responsible for assigning phonological and morphophonological information to sets of syntactic/semantic features. All information is bundled into terminal nodes that are realized phonologically in the same way. In the grammar, the bundles of information inside words interact in the same manner as the word-size bundles of information in phrases.

In contrast to the picture presented by DM, Chomsky (1993) suggests that the interface between a verb's internal morphological structure and the syntax involves a system of feature checking rather than feature addition. Such a theory is perhaps most comfortably wed with a Lieber-style lexical morphology (although, technically, words are not actually formed in the lexicon under Lieber's theory; still, the inflected verbs are built up, featurally and phonologically, from lexical pieces, not from head movement, merger, and so on, in the syntax). On the simplest view of a "checking theory," all the features of an inflected verb float around in one pot (unordered set) of features. As the verb raises to functional heads in the syntax, it matches and checks features from this pot with the features of the functional heads to which it adjoins. Affixation in the lexicon prior to lexical insertion would provide the inflected verb with all the features for its pot but would not impose any particular structure on the organization of these features.

Immediately, the question arises for Chomsky's proposal that arises for affixless theories: why does the internal hierarchy of inflectional affixes on a verb seem to reflect a bundling of features into morphemes, some of which correspond to functional heads in the syntax? Recall that in a checking theory, an inflected verb could be an amorphous mass of features; the connection between the internal phonological structure of the verb (the internal structure of stem and affixes) and the inflectional features of the verb has no consequences for the rest of the grammar.

For the checking theory, the worst possible state of affairs would be for some strict version of Baker's (1985) Mirror Principle to accurately describe the relation between affixes on a verb and the hierarchy of functional categories in the syntax that check the features of these affixes (Noam Chomsky, personal communication). Baker's principle implies that the order of affixes is just the order that would be derived by raising the verb to each dominating functional head in turn and affixing that functional head to the verb. Since checking theory insists that the functional heads to which a verb raises are not the inflectional affixes on the verb—the affixes are added in the lexicon—checking theory would lack an account for the fact that head-to-head raising in the syntax recapitulates affixation in the lexicon, were the Mirror Principle accurate.

Chomsky (1993) claims that, even were this worst-case scenario (accuracy of the Mirror Principle) to hold, checking theory could provide an acount: "Suppose that Baker's Mirror Principle is strictly accurate. Then we may take a lexical element—say, the verb V—to be a sequence V = $(\alpha, \text{Infl}_1, \ldots, \text{Infl}_n)$, where α is the morphological complex [R-Infl$_1$-...-

Infl$_n$], R a root and Infl$_i$ an inflectional feature. The PF rules only 'see' α. When V is adjoined to a functional category F (say, Agr$_O$), the feature Infl$_1$ is removed from V if it matches F; and so on." (p. 28).

In other words, Chomsky is proposing that inflected words come from the lexicon with a structure like that in (63).

(63)

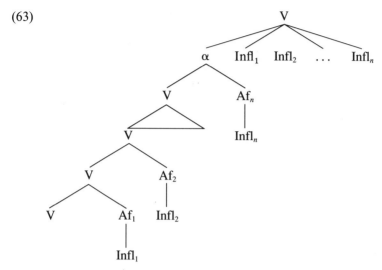

The node α is the hierarchical structure derived by affixing prefixes and suffixes to stems in the lexicon. These prefixes and suffixes come with inflectional features in bundles—Infl$_i$—and phonological forms. Therefore, "α" is the familiar inflected Verb, ready for phonological interpretation of its phonological structure. The inflectional feature bundles of the affixes attached to the Verb are arranged in a sequence with "α" itself, with the features of the most deeply embedded affix Infl$_1$ coming first in the sequence and the order of the rest of the features following the embedding structure of the affixes. The last affix (Af$_n$) added to the Verb in the lexicon provides the last features (Infl$_n$) for the sequence.

This sequence, considered a lexical item in its entirety, is inserted in the syntactic derivation of a sentence. The functional heads in the syntax (e.g., Tns and Agr) do not contain lexical items but only inflectional features. As the Verb sequence raises to functional heads in the course of a derivation, it checks the inflectional features in its sequence bundle by bundle, starting with the first bundle (Infl$_1$)—that is, starting with the bundle contributed by the most deeply embedded affix on the inflected Verb. Thus, by stipulation in a checking theory, features are checked in the order in which they were provided to the verb via affixation in the lexicon, the features of the innermost affix being checked first.

Crucial to the success of such an analysis of Mirror Principle effects is that Baker's Mirror Principle be "strictly accurate." However, as our discussion should have made clear, Baker's principle is not strictly accurate. If head-to-head movement and adjunction were the only process of inflectional affixation, then Baker's principle would appear to be more or less accurate and Chomsky's checking solution to mirroring would seem sufficient. We have shown, however, that in addition to head-to-head movement and adjunction, the interaction between the syntax and morphology includes head merger, the insertion of morphemes at MS, morpheme fusion, and morpheme fission. All these processes are sensitive to syntactic structure and obey strict locality conditions. Moreover, Vocabulary insertion (i.e., the assignment of phonological form to morphosyntactic features) must follow all the changes to morphological structure that lead to violations of a strict Mirror Principle.

A checking theory could, of course, mimic DM's account of the distribution of information within inflected verbs. In place of the inflectional affixes in (63), we could add within α terminal nodes that include just the syntactic/semantic features of the functional heads that will check them in the syntax (if we add the wrong terminal nodes, the derivation will crash). Now checking proceeds as Chomsky describes in the quotation above. However, within α—within the combination of the verbal stem and the terminal nodes containing inflectional features—we perform the various syntactic and MS operations that would be required under the DM account, followed by Vocabulary insertion into the resulting terminal nodes.

This checking version of DM enforces a disturbing split among terminal nodes in the grammar. The functional heads that contain checking features (e.g., Tense and Agr) are never phonologically instantiated via Vocabulary insertion but bear a special relation with respect to a set of terminal nodes within a verb that do undergo Vocabulary insertion. Otherwise, all terminal nodes behave alike with respect to such operations as head raising and adjunction, merger, fusion, and fission. In fact, the functional heads are also subject to head raising and adjunction, while the terminal nodes within the verb that they check (within α) are subject to everything else that terminal nodes might be subject to, including Vocabulary insertion. This checking version of DM, then, fails to capture the central claim of DM: that terminal nodes mediate the connection between syntactic/semantic information and phonological information in a uniform manner, regardless of the source or identity of the terminal node—a morpheme is a morpheme is a morpheme. Even if the Mirror Principle were strictly correct and the mechanism Chomsky outlines were sufficient to account for the connection between the hierarchical structure of affixes and the hierarchical structure of functional heads in the syntax, the checking theory would be making a distinction between the terminal nodes of the inflectional system, which implicate a set of nodes that never correspond to Vocabulary items, and the remaining terminal nodes in the grammar. DM locates its main dispute with checking theory in the latter's nonuniform treatment of the connection between terminal nodes and Vocabulary items.

Of course in addition to these perhaps conceptual differences between the theories, a major contrast in analyses separates them along lines that should lead to an empirical confrontation. According to checking theory, since a verb need not pick up its inflectional affixes on the way from DS to PF, the verb may remain separate from a functional head at PF but nevertheless bear an affix that contains features to be checked by this functional head. In this case, raising of the verb to the functional head at LF will allow for feature checking. On the other hand, since the functional heads in DM carry the features that serve as the locus of Vocabulary insertion, the verb in DM must join with a functional head on the way from DS to PF in order to bear the affix that instantiates the features of this functional head.

This difference between LF raising in a checking theory and affixation between DS and PF in DM shows up in the analysis of English tense. It is a fact that main verbs in English do not raise to the Tns node on the path between DS and PF. Under a checking theory, Tns need not be lowered onto or merged with main verbs to account for the fact that the tense affix appears on such verbs in English. Rather, English main verbs may raise to Tns at LF and check the tense features of the affix. In DM, on the other hand, as described in section 4, the Tns morpheme must be assumed to merge with English main verbs at MS. Here we appeal to the theory of merger developed in Marantz 1984, 1988, 1989. If merger is not a possible operation between terminal nodes or if the principles of merger prove inappropriate for English tense on main verbs and other similar structures, then DM loses out to the checking theory. Clearly research should be focused on those constructions that require raising to a functional head at LF in a checking theory, but necessitate head merger at MS within DM.

Notes

We thank Eulàlia Bonet, Noam Chomsky, Rolf Noyer, and especially Sylvain Bromberger for inciting and clarifying many of our thoughts on morphology. Mark Aronoff, Robert Beard, Andrew Carstairs-McCarthy, Norbert Hornstein, and Rolf Noyer contributed crucial comments on an earlier draft of this paper.

1. The term *Distributed Morphology* and the general view that it incorporates resulted from discussions with David Pesetsky; see also Pesetsky, to appear.

2. Here we are in general agreement with similar approaches presented in Baker 1988 and Borer, to appear.

3. For this work, see Marantz 1984, 1988 and Halle 1990, 1991.

4. In some of the Indo-European languages (e.g., Russian) case and number are copied onto the adjectival suffix whereas gender and animacy are copied onto the adjective stem. It is worth noting at this point that the feature-copying operation appears to be subject to the constraint that it cannot modify already existing feature values; it can only add new ones. This constraint on the formal power of concord rules has interesting empirical consequences. For example, as detailed in Halle's (1990) discussion of concord in Russian number phrases, in Russian the numerals 1–4 are adjectives whereas the numerals 5–20 are singular class III (feminine) nouns. Being class III singular nouns, the numerals 5–20 have inherent gender, animacy, and number, and cannot be supplied with any of these features by concord. As a result, these numerals agree with the head noun of the phrase only in case. By contrast, the numerals 1–4, being adjectives, have no inherent gender, animacy, or number. These numerals therefore agree with the head noun not only in case, but also in number ($1 = $ sg, 2–$4 = $ pl), animacy, and gender (which for morphophonological reasons is not overtly expressed in 3, 4).

5. Some of the mechanisms employed in this analysis will be explained at greater length in the sections to follow.

6. In "inversion" contexts, a 3rd person dative subject may trigger the plural /-t/. We believe that in the correct analysis of Georgian a rule assigns to 3rd person subjects of verbs whose object is also 3rd person a morphosyntactic feature otherwise carried only by 1st and 2nd person arguments; see the analysis of Potawatomi in section 5, where a similar solution is required. Given independently motivated interactions among morphemes, this analysis correctly predicts that a 3rd person argument will trigger the plural /-t/ only when the 3rd person argument is a dative subject and there is a 3rd person nominative object in the clause.

7. We assume here that fission of a morpheme M that is a sister to a stem S yields a ternary-branching structure with the two pieces of M and S as sisters under the original mother node. Thus, if a prefix is inserted under one piece of M and a suffix under the other, as in Georgian, a phonological "circumfix" results. Other assumptions about fission are possible.

8. Noyer (1992a) defends a different theory of morpheme splitting, one that allows the Vocabulary entries themselves to control the splitting in some instances.

9. In addition to deleting features, it may be necessary to allow morphosyntactic features to be changed at MS, leading, for example, to the generation of appar-

ently "wrong" cases, where the appearance of the anomalous case has no effect on the syntax. For example, in Russian the (syntactically motivated) accusative case is implemented as genitive if the stem is animate, and as nominative if the stem is inanimate. This happens in all nouns and adjectives in the plural and in nouns and adjectives of the second (masculine-neuter) declension also in the singular. These genitive- and nominative-marked objects behave alike syntactically, as do the objects that are marked with the "real" accusative case. (For discussion, see Halle 1990, 1992.)

10. We of course extend this separation to stems (lexemes) as well as affixes. An important difference between the current version of DM and the one outlined in Halle 1990, 1991, 1992 is that in the latter theory inflectional affixes are "inserted" at MS but other morphemes are inserted, with their phonological features, at DS. We believe that this procedure encounters conceptual difficulties that arise primarily in connection with morphemes generated in the course of the derivation of MS from SS. In DM all insertion of Vocabulary items takes place at MS; no Vocabulary items appear at DS, only bundles of features in terminal nodes.

11. Technically, in a lexicalist model an affix need not carry all the features necessary to explain the syntactic behavior of the words created by the affix; some of these features might be provided via default rules. See Noyer 1992a for some discussion on this point.

12. In this paper we distinguish two sorts of readjustment rules treated as a single class in Halle 1990. One class manipulates morphosyntactic features in the environment of other such features. When these rules delete features, we have called them *impoverishment rules*, after Bonet 1991. These rules are logically prior to Vocabulary insertion, which finds Vocabulary items with morphosyntactic features nondistinct from those of the already "readjusted" terminal nodes. The second set of readjustment rules, to which we will now apply that term exclusively, change the phonological form of already inserted Vocabulary items and thus logically follow Vocabulary insertion.

13. Here and below we have utilized the convenient data collection found in Bloch 1947. On the diacritic " ^ ," see the text below.

14. For a different view on the inflectional classes of English verbs, see Noyer 1992b.

15. Two verbs that optionally take a ∅ suffix in the past finite take the default /-d/ suffix in the past participle: *crew* or *crowed*, *had crowed*, *dove* or *dived*, *had dived*. As with the optionality of the /-n/ participle with some stems, it is not clear here whether the different past forms occur in the dialects of individual speakers and in the same semantic/syntactic contexts.

16. For some details, see the Appendix in Halle and Mohanan 1985. Although the changes induced by the different verbal inflections of English do not straightforwardly fall into classes, the individual stem changes are phonetically plausible. The majority of the changes affect only the stem vowel or the stem-final consonant; in a minority of cases the entire rime is replaced. Neither of these processes would justify the "bizarre conclusions" alluded to by Anderson (1992:61–62) in his brief discussion of the English irregular verbs.

17. Carstairs-McCarthy has published critiques of Anderson's theory that overlap with the remarks made in this section. See Carstairs-McCarthy 1992 and the references cited there.

18. It is readily seen that, with proper generalization to all morphemes, both affixes and stems, Anderson's principle (19) is equivalent to the Pāninian principle we have assumed governs the competition among Vocabulary items for insertion at a given terminal node (with "Morphosyntactic Representation M"). We contend that this is the only morphological principle of "disjunction" or complementarity that UG contains.

19. We follow Hockett's transcription of Potawatomi in using /u/ for what is phonetically [ə]. The appearance of these /u/'s is apparently predictable; see Hockett's and Anderson's clear discussions of this issue. For the most part, we have given the phonological form of Vocabulary items without these or other vowels that come and go in various forms. It might be necessary to include a vowel, perhaps a vowel unspecified for other features, in the Vocabulary entries in some cases to predict the surface distribution of vowels in the language. The distribution of vowels in Potawatomi is not critical for any of the following discussion.

20. Anderson chose Potawatomi primarily to support his treatment of "inversion" in Georgian; specifically, he claims that the proper analysis of Potawatomi involves manipulating the agreement features on verbs much the same way as for Georgian. Although our analysis shows why "inversion" of agreement features is unmotivated in Potawatomi, this will not be the main thrust of our remarks.

21. We thank Rolf Noyer for suggesting this analysis to replace one in an earlier version of this paper.

22. The ordering of these inanimate Agr_3s and the preterit suffix /-pun/ is not straightforward. We leave this problem to further research.

23. There are various ways to collapse the Vocabulary entries (32c–d); however, no such attempt will be made here.

24. Here the [−obv] feature would not be necessary if the presence of a Clitic node is dependent on the presence of a [−obv] argument in the clause.

25. In (35c–e) the [−obv] feature would be unnecessary if an Agr_2 node appears only when there is a [−obv] argument in the clause.

26. Rule (46) thus changes the grammatical case realized on Agr_2. This effect of (46) is similar to the case changes of the Russian accusative mentioned in note 9.

References

Anderson, S. 1986. Disjunctive ordering in inflectional morphology. *Natural Language & Linguistic Theory* 4:1–31.

Anderson, S. 1992. *A-morphous morphology*. Cambridge: Cambridge University Press.

Aronoff, M. 1976. *Word formation in generative grammar*. Cambridge, Mass.: MIT Press.

Aronoff, M. 1992. Morphology by itself. Ms., SUNY, Stony Brook.

Baker, M. 1985. The Mirror Principle and morphosyntactic explanation. *Linguistic Inquiry* 16:373–416.

Baker, M. 1988. *Incorporation: A theory of grammatical function changing*. Chicago: University of Chicago Press.

Baker, M. 1991. On some subject/object non-asymmetries in Mohawk. *Natural Language & Linguistic Theory* 9:537–76.

Beard, R. 1966. The suffixation of adjectives in contemporary literary Serbo-Croatian. Doctoral dissertation, University of Michigan.

Beard, R. 1991. Lexeme-morpheme base morphology. Ms., Bucknell University.

Bloch, B. 1947. English verb inflection. *Language* 23:399–418.

Bonet, E. 1991. Morphology after syntax: Pronominal clitics in Romance languages. Doctoral dissertation, MIT.

Borer, H. To appear. *Parallel morphology*. Cambridge, Mass.: MIT Press.

Carstairs-McCarthy, A. 1992. *Current morphology*. London: Routledge.

Chomsky, N. 1957. *Syntactic structures*. The Hague: Mouton.

Chomsky, N. 1965. *Aspects of the theory of syntax*. Cambridge, Mass.: MIT Press.

Chomsky, N. 1993. A minimalist program for linguistic theory. In *The view from Building 20: Essays in linguistics in honor of Sylvain Bromberger*, ed. K. Hale and S. J. Keyser. Cambridge, Mass.: MIT Press [This volume.]

Davis, R. 1991. Allomorphy in Spanish. Doctoral dissertation, University of North Carolina, Chapel Hill.

Giorgi, A., and F. Pianesi. To appear. Toward a syntax of temporal representations. *Probus*.

Halle, M. 1990. An approach to morphology. *Proceedings of NELS 20*, 150–84. GLSA, University of Massachusetts, Amherst.

Halle, M. 1991. The Latvian declension. In *Yearbook of morphology 1991*, ed. G. Booij and J. van Marle, 33–47. Dordrecht: Kluwer.

Halle, M. 1992. The Russian declension: An illustration of distributed morphology. To appear in *The organization of phonology: Features and domains*. CSLI, Stanford University.

Halle, M., and K. P. Mohanan. 1985. Segmental phonology of Modern English. *Linguistic Inquiry* 16:57–116.

Hockett, C. F. 1939. Potawatomi syntax. *Language* 15:235–48.

Hockett, C. F. 1948. Potawatomi III. The verb complex. *International Journal of American Linguistics* 14.3:139–49.

Hockett, C. F. 1966. What Algonquian is really like. *International Journal of American Linguistics* 32.1:59–73.

Jelinek, E. 1984. Case and configurationality. *Natural Language & Linguistic Theory* 2:39–76.

Jensen, J. 1990. *Morphology: Word structure in generative grammar.* Amsterdam: John Benjamins.

Johns, A. 1992. Deriving ergativity. *Linguistic Inquiry* 23:57–87.

Kiparsky, P. 1973. "Elsewhere" in phonology. In *A festschrift for Morris Halle*, ed. S. Anderson and P. Kiparsky, 93–106. New York: Holt, Rinehart and Winston.

Koopman, H. 1983. *The syntax of verbs.* Dordrecht: Foris.

Lieber, R. 1992. *Deconstructing morphology.* Chicago: University of Chicago Press.

Lumsden, J. S. 1992. Underspecification in grammatical and natural gender. *Linguistic Inquiry* 23:469–86.

Marantz, A. 1984. *On the nature of grammatical relations.* Cambridge, Mass.: MIT Press.

Marantz, A. 1988. Clitics, morphological merger, and the mapping to phonological structure. In *Theoretical morphology*, ed. M. Hammond and M. Noonan, 253–70. San Diego, Calif.: Academic Press.

Marantz, A. 1989. Clitics and phrase structure. In *Alternative conceptions of phrase structure*, ed. M. Baltin and A. Kroch, 99–116. Chicago: University of Chicago Press.

Marantz, A. 1992a. Case and licensing. In *ESCOL '91*, 234–53. The Ohio State University.

Marantz, A. 1992b. How morphemes are realized phonologically. Paper presented at DIMACs workshop, Princeton University, February 1992.

Marantz, A. 1992c. What kind of pieces are inflectional morphemes? Paper presented at the Berkeley Linguistics Society, February 1992.

Nash-Haran, L. 1992. La catégorie AGR et l'accord en Géorgien. *Recherches Linguistiques* 21:65–79.

Noyer, R. 1992a. Features, positions, and affixes in autonomous morphological structure. Doctoral dissertation, MIT.

Noyer, R. 1992b. Paradigm economy without paradigms. Ms., Princeton University.

Pesetsky, D. To appear. *Zero syntax.* Cambridge, Mass.: MIT Press.

Speas, M. 1990. *Phrase structure in natural language.* Dordrecht: Kluwer.

Spencer, A. To appear. Review of *Deconstructing morphology: Word structure in syntactic theory* by R. Lieber. *Language.*

Travis, L. 1989. Parameters of phrase structure. In *Alternative conceptions of phrase structure*, ed. M. Baltin and A. Kroch, 263–79. Chicago: University of Chicago Press.

Travis, L. 1992. Parameters of phrase structure and verb-second phenomena. In *Principles and parameters in comparative grammar*, ed. R. Freidin, 339–64. Cambridge, Mass.: MIT Press.

Chapter 4

Integrity of Prosodic Constituents and the Domain of Syllabification Rules in Spanish and Catalan	James W. Harris

Strings of linguistic elements are characteristically organized into a hierarchy of groups called constituents. The study of constituent structure has been a prominent topic in syntax for centuries. The investigation of constituents in phonological structure, on the other hand, has come to the fore as a central theoretical issue only within the last few years, and robust debate on numerous questions continues. I focus here on the abstract property of constituents that I will call *integrity*. To study the integrity of phonological constituents is to ask to what extent and under what conditions constituency, once assigned, can be altered in the course of a derivation. Within the two core "prosodic" domains of phonology—domains in which strings of phonological segments are grouped into hierarchical structures—this question has received more attention in the investigation of accentuation than of syllabification.[1] In this paper I intend to demonstrate that syllabic as well as accentual structures resist alteration in the course of a phonological derivation under well-defined conditions. The empirical basis of the investigation is provided by well-studied segmental and prosodic phenomena in Spanish and Catalan.

1 Theoretical Underpinnings

1.1 The Formal Representation of Syllabic Constituents

A theory of constituency in syllable structure was worked out in detail in Levin 1985, which I assume now as a basis for discussion of syllabification.[2] The last syllable of the Spanish word *silabificación* 'syllabification' is shown in (1a) to illustrate the type of representation postulated by Levin.

The *prosodic skeleton* identifies the syllabifiable elements in the *segmental string*. (These elements and units of the prosodic skeleton need not

(1) a.

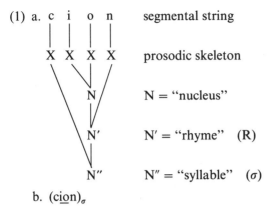

      c i o n   segmental string

      X X X X   prosodic skeleton

          N   N = "nucleus"

            N′   N′ = "rhyme" (R)

              N″   N″ = "syllable" (σ)

  b. $(c\underline{io}n)_\sigma$

match one to one, as they do in this example.) The vowel *o* is the most
sonorous element in the segmental string. This sonority peak is the head
of the constituent called the *nucleus*, which in turn is the head of the
rhyme constituent, which in turn is the head of the entire *syllable*, or
equivalently, the maximal projection N″. For typographical convenience
in numerous examples below, structures like (1a) are pared down to the
notation shown in (1b): the syllable is enclosed in parentheses and nuclear
elements are underlined; the rhyme constituent can be inferred as containing the nucleus and any following segments.

    Rules that generate structures like (1) are illustrated in (2).

(2) a. *Nucleus Projection*

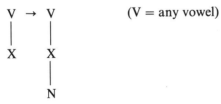

     V → V   (V = any vowel)

     X   X

           N

  b. *σ Projection*

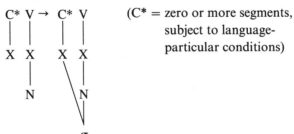

   C* V → C* V   (C* = zero or more segments,

   X X   X X   subject to language-

               particular conditions)

     N   N

             σ

c. *Rhyme Projection*

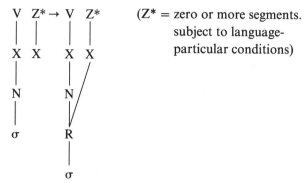

(Z* = zero or more segments. subject to language-particular conditions)

Universal Grammar makes these rules available to the grammar of all languages, where they are modulated by parochial conditions (as on C* and Z* in (2b) and (2c)) and perhaps supplemented by language-particular rules. For example, the grammar of Spanish contains the Complex Nucleus rule shown in (3), which is responsible for the formation of nuclei like the *io* of the syllable *cion* illustrated in (1).[3]

(3) *Complex Nucleus (Spanish)*

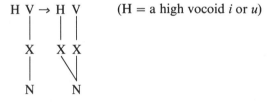

(H = a high vocoid *i* or *u*)

1.2 Phonological Derivations

The internal organization of the phonological component that I assume here is shown in (4).[4]

(4)

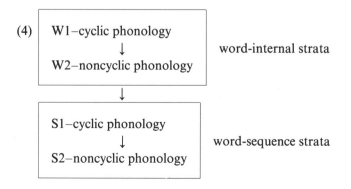

Phonological rules are organized into four ordered strata: W1, W2, S1, S2. The rules in the first pair of strata apply within the confines of individual words, while those in the second pair apply to domains larger than single words. Within each of the two pairs, the first stratum is cyclic and the second is noncyclic.[5] The rules of the cyclic stratum W1 apply to each cyclic constituent of a word in turn. The rules of the noncyclic stratum W2 apply after all passes through W1 are completed; they apply exactly once to the entire word, regardless of the number of noncyclic affixes in the word, including the case of words with no noncyclic affixes. Similarly, the rules of stratum S1 apply to successively more inclusive specifically designated domains that are larger than a single word. The rules of stratum S2 operate after all S1 applications are completed; they apply exactly once to the entire phonological phrase whatever its size or constituency, including the case of single-word phrases.

In Spanish and Catalan (and other well-studied languages), stems form cyclic word-internal domains whereas affixes can form either cyclic or noncyclic constituents.[6] In general, phrase-level rules apply (noncyclically) in S2. I argue below, however, for a pass through S1 for constituents formed by verbal clitics and their hosts in Catalan.[7] The Spanish and Catalan material examined below motivate the distribution of syllabification rules over all four strata, whereas the particular segmental rules involved in this material can all be assigned to the final stratum S2.

1.3 Constituent Integrity

Extending Prince 1985, Steriade 1988, Poser 1989, and related work, Halle (1990) and Halle and Kenstowicz (1991) identify the situations illustrated in (5), among others, in which existing instances of a particular accentual structure—the stress "foot"—cannot be altered by rules that create that structure. In the following display, the integers 123 ... indicate elements to which foot-forming rules apply, square brackets enclose morphological constituents, parentheses enclose rule-constructed stress feet, and angled brackets enclose extrametrical elements.

(5) a. *"Opacity"*

    [[12 3] 4]

12	3		input to cyclic rules
12	⟨3⟩		assign extrametricality[8]
(12)			formed in cyclic stratum
(12)	3	4	input to noncyclic rules
(12)	3	⟨4⟩	assign extrametricality
	(3)		formed in noncyclic stratum
*(2	3)		blocked

  b. *"Closure"*

    [[1 2] 3]

1	2		input to cyclic rules
1	⟨2⟩		assign extrametricality
(1)			formed in cyclic stratum
(1)	2	3	input to noncyclic rules
(1)	2	⟨3⟩	assign extrametricality
(1)	(2)		formed in noncyclic stratum
*(1	2)		blocked

Assume that two rules apply in both the cyclic and the noncyclic strata in (5a): (i) a rule E that marks the rightmost element extrametrical, and (ii) a rule BF that generates (maximally) binary feet from right to left. In the second stratum, when element 4 becomes available and 3 thereby loses its extrametricality (since it is no longer peripheral), BF cannot generate the binary foot *(23) since element 2 is already incorporated into the constituent (12). The only possible output of reapplying BF to the intermediate structure is (12)(3)4.

Assume that the prosodic structure of (5b) is assigned by the same rules E and BF. The unary foot (1) formed in the cyclic stratum cannot expand to form *(12) when element 2 becomes available in the next stratum, even though (12) would be pattern-conforming (binary). The constituent (1), once generated, is inalterable. The only possible output is (1)(2)3, even though (12)3 would be legitimate had elements 1 and 2 been accessible to rule BF simultaneously.

In sum, the integrity effects illustrated in (5) hold for rules that create constituents of a particular type out of metrically "free" elements, that is, elements that are not yet incorporated into a constituent of the type in question. These effects do not constrain other kinds of rules, for example, the widely attested Resyllabification rule shown in (6).[9]

(6) *Resyllabification*

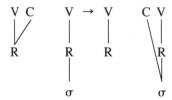

This rule is free to modify syllabic constituency as shown since it does not incorporate unsyllabified ("free") segments into new constituents. The characterization of conditions under which integrity effects do and do not hold will be sharpened below.

2   Syllable-Sensitive Segmental Phenomena in Spanish

The phenomena of aspiration and velarization are manifested in numerous dialects of Spanish in both Spain and Latin America.[10] Examples are given in (7), where the first column is standard orthography and the second column gives phonetic representations in which periods indicate syllable boundaries.

(7) a. la tos   [la.toh]   'the cough'
       las toses   [lah.to.seh]   'the coughs'

    b. sin fin   [siŋ.fiŋ]   'without end'
       fines   [fi.neh]   'ends'

Aspiration and velarization are both clearly dependent on syllable structure: /s/ is aspirated and /n/ is velarized in the rhyme but not in the onset. For present purposes the corresponding rules can be formulated as in (8).[11]

(8) a. *Aspiration*

   $s \rightarrow h / \underset{R}{\top}$

    b. *Velarization*

   $n \rightarrow ŋ / \underset{R}{\top}$

The outputs of Aspiration and Velarization can appear in syllable-initial position, however, if they are word-final and precede a vowel-initial word in the same phrase, as in (9).

(9) las osas   [la.ho.sah]   'the bears' (feminine)
    sin eso   [si.ŋe.so]   'without that'

Such outputs are evidently the result of Resyllabification (6) at the level of the phrase (word-sequence stratum S2). Illustrative derivations are given in (10).[12]

(10)

	[las]	[[[os]a]s]	[sin]	[eso]	morphological structure
W1:	[la]	[os]	[sin]	[eso]	inputs
	(la)	(o)	(si)	(e)(so)	Nucleus & σ Projection (2a–b)
W2:	[(la̲)s]	[(o̲) sas]	[(si̲)n]	[(e̲)(so̲)]	inputs
		(sa̲)			Nucleus & σ Projection (2a–b)
	(las)	(sas)	(sin)		Rhyme Projection (2c)
S2:	[(la̲s)	(o̲)(sa̲s)]	[(sin)	(e̲)(so̲)]	inputs
	h	h			Aspiration (8a)
			ŋ		Velarization (8b)
	(la̲)	(ho̲)(sah)	(si̲)	(ŋe)(so̲)	Resyllabification (6)

Rules are assigned to strata as follows: Nucleus Projection and σ Projection, W1 and W2; Rhyme Projection, W2; Aspiration, Velarization, and Resyllabification, S2. The motivation for these assignments will become clearer as the exposition progresses.[13]

For the moment, I point out two properties of (10). First, the application of Rhyme Projection (2c) in W2 to the strings (o̲)(sa̲)s and (e̲)(so̲) does not produce *(os)(as) and *(es)(o̲), though s is a valid rhyme segment. This (natural and expected) result is explained by the "opacity" effect (5a) of metrical integrity: the s in question is not a free element. No separate principle of maximization of onsets need be invoked, nor is any stipulative restriction on Rhyme Projection (2c) necessary. Second, the word-level syllabification shown provides the correct environment (rhyme position) for application of Aspiration and Velarization in las and sin, though the affected segments are resyllabified as onsets at the phrase level.

Surprisingly, [h] and [ŋ] can appear in syllable onsets within a single word, as in (11).

(11) desecho vs. deseo   [de.he.čo]/[de.se.o]   'waste'/'desire'
     enamora vs. enano   [e.ŋa.mo.ra]/[e.na.no]   'enamors'/'dwarf'

The key to these striking contrasts is that the first word of each pair contains a prefix: [des [echo]] (cf. ech- 'throw (away)') and [en [amora]] (cf. *amor* 'love') versus unprefixed [deseo] and [enano]. The surface forms are thus derived as shown in (12).[14]

(12)

	[des [ečo]]	[en [amora]]	[deseo]	[enano]	morph.
W1:	[ečo]	[amora]	[deseo]	[enano]	inputs
	(e)(čo)	(a)(mo)(ra)	(de)(se)(o)	(e)(na)(no)	(2a–b)
W2:	[des(e̲)(čo̲)]	[en (a̲)(mo̲)(ra̲)]	[(de̲)(se̲)(o̲)]	[(e̲)(na̲)(no̲)]	inputs
	(de̲)	(e̲)			(2a–b)
	(des)	(en)			(2c)
S2:	[(de̲s)(e̲)(čo̲)]	[(e̲n)(a̲)(mo̲)(ra̲)]	[(de̲)(se̲)(o̲)]	[(e̲)(na̲)(no̲)]	inputs
	h				(8a)
		ŋ			(8b)
	(de̲)(he̲)(čo̲)	(e̲)(ŋa̲)(mo̲)(ra̲)			(6)

The crucial observation is that in the first step in W2, the syllables (e̲) in [des(e̲)(čo̲)] and (a̲) in [en(a̲)(mo̲)(ra̲)] do not expand to incorporate the preceding consonants /s/ and /n/ as their onsets. If they did, the contrasts under discussion would be eliminated. Obviously, however, the syllables that would be produced by this incorporation, (se̲) and (na̲), are well formed: these are the second syllables in [(de̲)(se̲)(o̲)] and [(e̲)(na̲)(no̲)]. The property of prosodic integrity, specifically the "closure" effect (5b), blocks the step s(e̲) → (se̲) and n(a̲) → (na̲). The correct outputs are then yielded by application of Aspiration, Velarization, and Resyllabification in stratum S2 in the normal way, without appeal to any unmotivated stipulation.

3 Syllable-Sensitive Segmental Phenomena in Catalan

The Catalan material to be discussed is more intricate. I begin with data that are similar in principle to those discussed in the preceding section.[15] Consider the contrasts in syllabification, voicing, and continuancy in the realization of the phoneme /b/ in the examples in (13).[16]

(13) sublim   [su.βlím]   'sublime'
     sublunar   [sub.lu.nà]   'sublunar'
     subeditor   [su.pe.ði.tó]   'assistant editor'

What needs to be explained is (i) why the string /bl/ is syllabified as a complex onset in the first example but not in the second, and (ii) why /b/ is realized three different ways—as [β], [b], and [p]—in the three examples. As in (12), morphological structure is crucial here: *sublim* is monomorphemic, but the other examples contain prefixes, [sub [lunar]] and [sub [editor]].[17] Syllabification in Catalan is not significantly different from Spanish. Thus, the syllable structure of the example words is derived as shown in (14), where segmental effects are temporarily factored out.

(14)

	[sublim]	[sub [lunar]]	[sub [editor]]	morph.
W1:	[sublim]	[lunar]	[editor]	inputs
	(su)(bli)	(lu)(na)	(e)(di)(to)	(2a–b)
W2:	[(su̲)(bli̲)m]	[sub(lu̲)(na̲)r]	[sub (e̲)(di̲)(to̲)r]	inputs
		(su̲)	(su̲)	(2a–b)
	(blim)	(sub) (nar)	(sub) (tor)	(2c)
S2:	[(su̲)(bli̲m)]	[(su̲b)(lu̲)(na̲r)]	[(su̲b) (e̲)(di̲)(to̲r)]	inputs
			(su̲)((be̲)(di̲)(to̲r)	(6)

We now factor in the segmental effects.[18] All of the rules in (15) have abundant motivation independently of the material in question.

(15) a. *Devoicing* (obstruents are devoiced syllable-finally)[19]

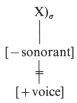

b. *Spirantization* (voiced obstruents are continuants after continuants)[20]

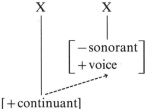

c. *Voicing Assimilation* (consonants voice before a voiced consonant)[21]

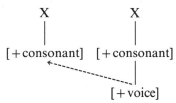

These rules apply across word boundaries as well as within words; they are thus assigned to the word-sequence stratum S2. Their operation is illustrated in (16), whose initial representations are those shown as the input to stratum S2 in (14).

(16) (su̱)(bli̱m) (su̱b)(lu̱)(na̱r) (su̱b)(e̱)(di̱)(to̱r)

	p		p	
β				Devoicing (15a)

β Spirantization (15b)

           b   Voicing Assimilation (15c)

                          (su̱)(pe̱)   Resyllabification (6)

(su̱)(βli̱m) (su̱b)(lu̱)(na̱r) (su̱)(pe̱)(di̱)(to̱r) outputs

Parallel to (12), word-level syllabification in (14)/(16) provides the representations necessary for the correct operation of Devoicing, Spirantization, and Voicing Assimilation. In particular, syllable-final position of prefixal /b/—unlike the /b/ of *sublim*—makes it a target for Devoicing, whose application makes Spirantization inapplicable. Then-voiceless p is predictably revoiced in *su*[b]*lunar* and resyllabified in *su*[p]*editor*. These word-level syllabic outputs are guaranteed by metrical integrity in W1 and W2. In particular, the "closure" effect (5b) prevents the stem-initial syllables of *lunar* and *editor* formed in W1 from expanding to capture prefixal b in W2 even though (blu̱) and (be̱) are well-formed syllables.

The examples in (17) add a new dimension to the investigation.

(17) rebre   [rè.βre]   'to receive'
       rep-la   [rèb.la]   'receive her'
       rep-ho   [rè.βu]   'receive it'
       rep això   [rè.pa.šò]   'receive that'

The contrast in syllabification of the $b + L$ (L = liquid) string in *rebre* versus *rep-la* is puzzling, as is the contrast in voicing in *rep-ho* versus *rep això*. The solution is very simple, however, once morphology and syntax are taken into account. In (17) *això* is an independent monomorphemic word, /rèb/ is the verb root, -*re* is the infinitival suffix, and *ho* and *la* are verbal clitics.[22] I propose that Catalan verbal clitics—*ho* and *la* in particular—form a larger-than-single-word domain subject to a pass through stratum S1, which phrases without clitics do not undergo. I assign Resyllabification (6) to S1 as well as to S2. Clitic groups of course subsequently undergo the rules of S2, as do all phonological phrases. Illustrative derivations are given in (18).

(18)	[[rèb]re]	[rèb] [u]	[rèb] [la]	[rèb][ašò]	morph.
W1:	[rèb]	[rèb] [u]	[rèb] [la]	[rèb][ašò]	inputs
	(rè)	(rè) (u)	(rè) (la)	(rè) (a)(šò)	(2a–b)
W2:	[(rè)bre]	[(rè)b][(u̲)]	[(rè)b][(la̲)]	[(rè)b][(a̲)(šò̲)]	inputs
	(bre̲)				(2a–b)
		(rèb)	(rèb)	(rèb)	(2c)
S1:		[(rèb) (u̲)]	[(rèb) (la̲)]		inputs
		(rè) (bu)			(6)
S2:	[(rè)(bre̲)]	[(rè) (bu̲)]	[(rèb) (la̲)]	[(rèb)(a̲)(šò̲)]	inputs
			p	p	(15a)
	β	β			(15b)
			b		(15c)
				(rè)(pa̲)	(6)
	(rè)(βre̲)	(rè)(βu̲)	(rèb) (la̲)	(rè)(pa̲)(šò̲)	outputs

The two puzzling aspects of these examples are explained in the above derivations as follows.

First, the /b + r/ of the single word *rèb + re* forms a (tautosyllabic) complex onset since the two elements of the cluster are syllabified simultaneously in stratum W2.[23] On the other hand, the /b + l/ of the word sequence *rèp-la* is syllabified in two stages, the /l/ into (1a̲) in W1 and the /b/ into (rèb) in W2 The motivation for not allowing Rhyme Projection to apply in W1 (cf. (14)) can now be seen clearly: if root-final *-b* in [[rèb] re] were syllabified in W1, the "opacity" effect (5a) of metrical integrity would prevent this metrified element from subsequently joining the onset of the following syllable (re̲), and the contrast with *rèp-la* would be lost.[24]

Second, the voicing contrast in the two-word sequences *rep-ho* and *rep això* is explained by the fact that Resyllabification applies in S1 to the /b/ in the clitic group *rep-ho*, thus removing this segment from the input to Devoicing (15a) in S2. The cliticless phrase *rep això*, on the other hand, does not take a detour through S1; its /b/ thus does undergo Devoicing in S2.

4 Summary and Conclusions

I list in table 1 all the rules mentioned in this paper, along with their stratal assignments.[25] *S* and *C* flag rules or stratal assignments particular to Spanish or Catalan, respectively; rules not so flagged apply in both languages.[26]

Table 1

	W1	W2	S1	S2
Nucleus Projection (2a)	√	√	√	√
(S) Complex Nucleus (3)	√	√	√	√
σ Projection (2b)	√	√	√	√
Rhyme Projection (2c)		√	√	√
(S) Aspiration (8a)				√
(S) Velarization (8b)				√
(C) Devoicing (15a)				√
Spirantization (15b)				√
Voicing Assimilation (15c)				√
Resyllabification (6)			(C)	√

Of the rules listed, those that incorporate an unsyllabified ("free") seg-ment into a syllabic constituent are Nucleus Projection (2a), Complex Nucleus (3), σ Projection (2b), and Rhyme Projection (2c). Every set of illustrative derivations provided above supplies evidence that the last two of these constituent-building rules are governed by the "opacity" and "closure" effects of metrical integrity (5).[27] The derivations in (10), (12), (14), and (18) show that segments incorporated as onsets are protected by the "opacity" factor from subsequent inclusion by Rhyme Projection into the preceding syllable. For example, once *sublim* reaches the stage (su̱)(bli̱)*m* (14), Rhyme Projection can produce only (su̱)(bli̱m) and not *(su̱b)(li̱m), although the latter contains no ill-formed syllables. The deri-vations in (12) and (14) show that a vowel-initial syllable, once formed, is prevented by the "closure" factor from subsequently absorbing even a "free" segment to serve as its onset For example, once *desecho* reaches the stage *des*(e̱)(čo̱) (12), σ Projection cannot produce *de*(se̱)(čo̱), although the syllable (se̱) is perfectly well formed. Of course, exactly these results could in principle be achieved by other means.[28] Given, however, that the integrity effects seem to be well established in the building of accentual structure, the normal canons of science dictate that we extend their sphere of influence to the other core prosodic phenomenon—namely, syllabicity —in the absence of contrary evidence.

In conclusion, it is worth emphasizing that the basic data investigated here, uncontroversially documented in the descriptive literature, involve a number of quite surprising and subtle distinctions the basis of whose systematicity has not been uncovered casually or quickly—for example, the contrasts in syllabification, voicing, and continuancy in the realization of /b/ in sets like *rebre* [rè.βre], *rep-la* [rèb.la], *rep-ho* [rè.βu], and *rep això* [rè.pa.šò]. I would like to believe, optimistically, that it can be seen as the hallmark of developing theoretical maturity that such phonetic minutiae can be accounted for on the basis of general principles such as the constraints on the integrity of accentual and syllabic constituents

Notes

Sylvain discovered the wonders of phonology late in life, but he learned fast, in part because he had such excellent teachers (mainly Morris Halle, me, and numerous TAs and students in 24.900). I now realize, too late, that I shouldn't have kept this paper hidden as a surprise for the festschrift; if I had shown it to Sylvain, it would have profited enormously from his comments.

1. See, for example, Prince 1985, Steriade 1988, Poser 1989, Halle 1990, Halle and Kenstowicz 1991, Harris 1991, and related work.

2. It is widely thought that the "moraic" theory of syllable structure (Hayes 1989, Itô 1986, 1989) has supplanted the "X-slot" or "segmental" syllabification theory articulated by Levin. I do not share this view: most recently and most compellingly, Sloan (1991) presents an extremely strong case in favor of "X-slot" over "moraic" syllabification.

3. It is no accident that the segment H in the input to this rule lacks a skeletal X position. Motivation for this representation is provided in Harris, in preparation.

4. This organization has been discussed at length in Halle and Vergnaud 1987, Halle, Harris, and Vergnaud 1991, and other works.

5. Not all rules assigned to the cyclic strata necessarily manifest the characteristic of applying repeatedly in successively more inclusive domains. Rather, cyclic rules are those that apply only in specifically designated cyclic domains and are subject to the Strict Cycle Condition (Mascaró 1983 and much subsequent work).

6. Watanabe (1991) argues that stems in Japanese are unpredictably either cyclic or noncyclic, and, more generally, that it does not make sense to restrict the cyclic/noncyclic distinction to affixes in any event.

7. Host-clitic combinations are "word sequences" in that clitics have the syntactic distribution of independent words. The phonological behavior of clitics, on the other hand, is like that of affixes in that they are prosodically dependent on a (nonclitic) host.

8. Extrametrical elements are invisible to prosodic rules when peripheral in a morphological constituent.

9. Intermediate nodes in (6) are suppressed in the interest of legibility.

10. The literature on these topics is vast García de Diego 1959 and Zamora and Guitart 1982 are convenient references. Hualde 1991 is a recent study in which the relationship of aspiration and velarization to syllable structure is highlighted. A particular subset of dialects is the object of inquiry here; there are many other dialects in which the facts are different and which do not provide evidence relevant to the issues at hand.

11. In the dialects at issue, [h] and [ŋ] are not underlying segments: [h] occurs only as the product of Aspiration, and [ŋ] occurs only as the product of Velarization or of assimilation to a following velar consonant. In terms of articulation, aspiration is the suppression of supraglottal constriction in the voiceless continuant obstruent /s/, as first suggested in Goldsmith 1981. The phonetic nature of velarization is discussed in detail in Trigo 1988. Here we are concerned only with the conditions under which these phenomena occur, not with their phonetic properties, their proper formal representation, their sociolinguistic aspects, and so on.

12. In *osas*, *os-* is the root, *-a-* is a declensional-class suffix (realizing feminine gender in this case), and *-s* is the plural morpheme. Only the root is a cyclic domain. I ignore possible internal structure in the other words in (10).

13. In many dialects, Aspiration and Velarization can follow Rhyme Projection in W2.

14. I disregard suffixes in (11) and (12) since they are irrelevant to the point at issue.

15. These data have been studied from other perspectives in Mascaró 1984, 1987 and Bonet 1990. I am indebted to Eulàlia Bonet for fruitful discussion.

16. Stress is not relevant to the discussion, but (in a modified version of standard Catalan orthography) I use acute and grave accent marks in phonetic representations as easy-to-type indicators of certain contrasts: *é* and *ó* represent stressed tense mid vowels, *è* and *ò* the corresponding lax vowels; *à* indicates stressed *a*; unstressed (here, unmarked) *e* and *a* are both realized as schwa.

17. As in the Spanish examples above, I ignore suffixes when they are not relevant to the topic at hand.

18. The deletion of final *-r* seen in *lunaŧ* and *editoŧ* has quirky lexical conditions and will not be taken into account. The other segmental data have been discussed extensively in the literature. I will make slightly different generalizations from the traditional ones, however.

19. This rule is commonly but mistakenly seen as word-final rather than syllable-final devoicing.

20. Mascaró (1984) stipulates that Spirantization does not apply to coda segments. This restriction can be eliminated if rule (15a) is generalized from a word-final to a syllable-final operation (see note 19).

21. Mascaró (1987) gives a more adequate formulation.

22. Actually, the infinitive marker is simply /r/; the final schwa is epenthetic. This is not critical to the discussion (see note 23). Bonet (1991) provides a detailed study of the syntax and morphology of verbal clitics in Catalan and other languages.

23. A technical detail: the infinitival suffix *-r* is presumably a cyclic affix (for reasons I will not go into here) and thus triggers a second pass through cyclic W1. Stem-final *b-* and infinitival *-r* still cannot be incorporated into syllable structure until word-level W2, however, since it is only at this level that *e*-epenthesis provides a nucleus for them to syllabify with.

24. Similarly in Spanish, words like [[padr] ino] 'godfather', syllabified as (pa̱)(dri)(no̱), show that Rhyme Projection must not apply in the root cycle, given integrity. The output would be uncorrectable *(pa̱d)(ri̱)(no̱), all of whose syllables are well formed under other circumstances. Examples of this sort pose no problem if Rhyme Projection is delayed until W2. The location of the application of Rhyme Projection in (10) and (12) is thus strongly motivated.

25. Myers (1991) argues for an interpretation of the Strong Domain Hypothesis—according to which, "a level can be specified *after* which the rule cannot apply, but no rule can be restricted so that it cannot apply *before* a given level" (p. 383)—whereby this hypothesis "cover[s] restrictions on segments and syllables, as well as phonological rules" (p. 383). It would be interesting to see how Myers would analyze the material under investigation here so as to avoid the conclusion that the rule of Rhyme Projection (2c) must be restricted so that it cannot apply *before* stratum W2, and so on.

26. It is well known that Spirantization (15b) and Voicing Assimilation (15c) operate in Spanish as well as Catalan, although this fact plays no role in this paper. Stratal assignments may be different in dialects other than those explicitly described herein.

27. Nucleus Projection and Complex Nucleus have not been illustrated here in sufficient detail to support any conclusions about integrity. However, I argue in Harris, in preparation, that these rules, too, are governed by this property.

28. For example, in an analysis of Spanish cases similar to (but simpler than) those in (13), Hualde (1991) stipulates ad hoc morphological structure in order to provide a separate lexical domain of rule application for certain prefixes (e.g., [[sub] [lunar]]). This move is not inherently implausible, but without independent motivation—which Hualde does not provide—it has the status of a deus ex machina. Given metrical integrity, which does have independent motivation, the correct results follow directly from the normal morphology of prefixation illustrated in (14). No ad hoc move is justified.

References

Bonet, E. 1990. X-bar structures in the PF component. Ms., MIT.

Bonet, E. 1991. Morphology after syntax: Pronominal clitics in Romance languages. Doctoral dissertation, MIT.

García de Diego, V. 1959. *Manual de dialectología española*. Madrid: Ediciones Cultura Hispánica.

Goldsmith, J. 1981. Subsegmentals in Spanish phonology. In *Linguistic Symposium on Romance Languages: 9*, ed. W. Cressey and D. J. Napoli. Washington, D.C.: Georgetown University Press.

Halle, M. 1990. Respecting metrical structure. *Natural Language & Linguistic Theory* 8:149–76.

Halle, M., J. Harris, and J.-R. Vergnaud. 1991. A reexamination of the Stress Erasure Convention and Spanish stress. *Linguistic Inquiry* 22:141–59.

Halle, M., and M. Kenstowicz. 1991. The Free Element Condition and cyclic versus noncyclic stress. *Linguistic Inquiry* 22:457–501.

Halle, M., and J.-R. Vergnaud. 1987. *An essay on stress*. Cambridge, Mass.: MIT Press.

Harris, J. 1991. With respect to accentual constituents in Spanish. In *Current studies in Spanish linguistics*, ed. H. Campos and F. Martínez-Gil. Washington, D.C.: Georgetown University Press.

Harris, J. In preparation. The representation of underlying glides in Spanish. Ms., MIT.

Hayes, B. 1989. Compensatory lengthening in moraic phonology. *Linguistic Inquiry* 20:253–306.

Hualde, J. I. 1991. On Spanish syllabification. In *Current studies in Spanish linguistics*, ed. H. Campos and F. Martínez-Gil. Washington, D.C.: Georgetown University Press.

Itô, J. 1986. Syllable theory in prosodic phonology. Doctoral dissertation, University of Massachusetts, Amherst.

Itô, J. 1989. A prosodic theory of epenthesis. *Natural Language & Linguistic Theory* 7:217–59.

Levin, J. 1985. A metrical theory of syllabicity. Doctoral dissertation, MIT.

Mascaró, J. 1983. *La fonologia catalana i el cicle fonològic*. Department de Filologia Hispànica, Universitat Autònoma de Barcelona.

Mascaró, J. 1984. Continuant spreading in Basque, Catalan, and Spanish. In *Language sound structure: Studies presented to Morris Halle by his teacher and students*, ed. M. Aronoff and R. Oehrle. Cambridge, Mass.: MIT Press.

Mascaró, J. 1987. A reduction and spreading theory of voicing and other sound effects. Ms., Universitat Autònoma de Barcelona.

Myers, S. 1991. Structure preservation and the Strong Domain Hypothesis. *Linguistic Inquiry* 22:379–85.

Poser, W. 1989. The metrical foot in Diyari. *Phonology* 6:117–46.

Prince, A. 1985. Improving tree theory. In *Proceedings of the 11th Annual Meeting of the Berkeley Linguistics Society*. Berkeley Linguistics Society, University of California, Berkeley.

Sloan, K. 1991. Syllables and templates: Evidence from Southern Sierra Miwok. Doctoral dissertation, MIT.

Steriade, D. 1988. Greek accent: A case for preserving structure. *Linguistic Inquiry* 19:271–314.

Trigo, R. 1988. On the phonological derivation and behavior of nasal glides. Doctoral dissertation, MIT.

Watanabe, A. 1991. Some problems in Tokyo Japanese accentuation: A study of the notions of "stem" and "affix." Ms., MIT.

Zamora, J., and J. Guitart. 1982. *Dialectología hispanoamericana: Teoría, descripción, historia.* Salamanca: Ediciones Almar.

Chapter 5

Interrogatives

James Higginbotham

1 Introduction

It is a pleasure to be able to present this paper as part of a volume to honor Sylvain Bromberger. My subject, interrogative sentences and the questions that they express, is one on which he has thought and written deeply and at length. I am specifically indebted to Sylvain for discussion in our seminar from some time back, and for many conversations over the years. Above all, however, I am grateful to him for his support early on of my hybrid research into language and philosophy, and I hope he may think that this work justifies it at least in part.

In this paper I advance some parts of a view of interrogative sentences and their interpretations, with reference to English examples. The details of this view depend upon assumptions about the semantics of embedded indicative sentences that I use but do not defend here. I therefore distinguish at the beginning the major theses I advance about interrogatives, which I would urge even apart from these assumptions, from others that will show up in the details of execution. The major theses are these:

1. The semantics of interrogative sentences is given by associating with them certain objects, which I will call *abstract questions*; I will say that the interrogative *expresses* an abstract question. To utter the interrogative is to ask the abstract question that it expresses.

2. Pairs of *direct* questions, as in (1), and their corresponding *indirect* questions, as in the italicized complement of (2), are related in this way: the direct question expresses what the indirect question refers to.

(1) Is it raining?

(2) John knows *whether it is raining*.

3. Indirect questions are singular terms, and they occupy quantifiable places of objectual reference. Thus, for example, the argument (3) is valid.

(3) John is certain (about) whether it is raining;
    Whether it is raining is Mary's favorite question; therefore,
    John is certain about (the answer to) Mary's favorite question.

4. *Elementary* abstract questions (what is expressed by simple interrogatives, or referred to by simple indirect questions) are partitions of the possible states of nature into families of mutually exclusive (and possibly jointly exhaustive) alternatives. *Complex* abstract questions (the result of quantifying into interrogatives, or conjoining them, as explained below) are constructed out of elementary ones. These form a hierarchy of orders, with abstract questions of order n being sets of sets of abstract questions of order $n - 1$.

5. Abstract questions can be constructed by generalizing along any of several different semantic dimensions, and can be referred to by appropriate syntactic means even when their dimensions of generality are not domains of quantification in the indicative fragment of a language; such categories include those of predicates, quantifiers, and even parts of words. However, most abstract questions are not the reference of any interrogative sentence at all.

In sections 2–5 I present informally a number of definitions and illustrations of the point of view I advance. In section 6 I turn to a defense of theses 1 and 2. In the final section, which I have labeled an appendix because it involves more material from logic and linguistics than the others, I argue that an explanation of the licensing of negative polarity items in interrogatives can be seen to follow from the proposal I develop here and in other work.

2 Preliminary Definitions and Illustrations

An *abstract question*, what is expressed by an interrogative form, is not itself a linguistic form (although it is in a sense constructed from linguistic forms, in a way explained more fully below), but on the present view a nonempty *partition* Π of the possible states of nature into *cells* P_i for $i \in I$, having the property that no more than one cell corresponds to the true state of nature (i.e., the cells are mutually exclusive). If in addition at least one cell must correspond to the true state of nature, then Π is a *proper* partition (i.e., the cells are jointly exhaustive). The elements of a cell P_i can be thought of as statements, so that P_i corresponds to the true state of nature if and only if all the statements that it contains are true.

Partitions are used in probability theory, and I will freely adapt terminology from there. If Π is a partition, and S is a set of statements, let

$\Pi + S$ be the result of adjoining S to each P_i. Thus, if

$$\Pi = \{P_i\}_{i \in I}$$

then

$$\Pi + S = \{P_i'\}_{i \in I}$$

where, for each i,

$$P_i' = P_i \cup S$$

Since Π is a partition, so is $\Pi + S$; but Π may be proper while $\Pi + S$ is improper.

A cell of a partition may be *satisfiable* or *unsatisfiable*. Let F be some designated unsatisfiable set, fixed throughout the discussion, for example, $F = \{p \& \neg p\}$. F is the *degenerate* set, and the improper partition $\{F\}$ is the degenerate partition. If Π is a partition, let Π^- be the result of deleting the unsatisfiable cells from Π (or $\{F\}$ if all are unsatisfiable). If S is a set of sentences, let Π/S, or the *conditionalization* of Π on S, be $(\Pi + S)^-$. Then Π/S is a partition. Also, we evidently have

$$(\Pi/S_1)/S_2 = (\Pi/S_2)/S_1 = \Pi/(S_1 \cup S_2)$$

An *answer* to a question Π is a set S of sentences that is inconsistent with one or more cells in Π. If Π is the degenerate partition $\{F\}$, then S answers Π for every S. S is a *proper* answer if it is an answer and Π/S is not $\{F\}$.

The notions introduced by the above definitions may be illustrated through a fabricated example. Let Π be a partition whose cells are statements about the possible outcomes of rolling two dice A and B, where the outcomes are distinguished according to the total shown by the dice. There are eleven cells, which will be represented by the numbers 2 through 12, each of which stands for a complex disjunctive statement giving the outcomes that would add up to those totals; thus, cell 6 is

(Die A: 1 & Die B: 5) or (Die A: 2 & Die B: 4) or ...

... or (Die A: 5 & Die B: 1)

Then Π is a partition, since the outcomes are regarded as functions of A and B, and it is proper given the background information that the values of these functions are integers between 1 and 6.

The above proper partition Π is one way of construing the question expressed by (4),

(4) What was the total of the dice?

incorporating further information about how totals in a throw of two dice may be obtained. A person who asks (4) will be said, following Belnap (1963), to have *put* the question Π.

Consider now the statements in (5) as responses to (4).

(5) a. (The dice totaled) 12.
    b. (I don't know but) one came up 4.
    c. The sun is shining.
    d. The dice were never thrown.

In much of the literature on interrogatives, it is answers like (5a) that have been chiefly considered. Their relation to the interrogative sentence is particularly intimate: they provide *instances* of the matrix

the total of the dice was (the number) _____

instances that are also in a sense *canonical* to the type of question asked; that is, they are *numerical* instances, rather than nonnumerical instances like

the total of the dice was the number of the apostles

Objects themselves, rather than their standard names, can also be taken as filling the blank in the matrix above. Following this course, I regard the instances arising from substitution of names as *presentations* of the instances arising from assignment of the objects themselves.

In discussions including Karttunen 1977 and Hamblin 1973 the question expressed by an interrogative was simply the totality of its instances (Hamblin), or alternatively the totality of its true instances (Karttunen). The totality of instances for (4), which might be indicated by abstracting over the empty matrix position as in (6),

(6) λx (the total of the dice was x)

is a natural candidate for the abstract question expressed by (4), and the question arises whether the further step to partitions does not create a needless complexity.

My belief is that the definition of answerhood requires the more complex structure. Besides canonical and noncanonical instances, there are answers that give only partial information, as illustrated by (5b). Partial answers give information by being inconsistent with some, but not with all but one, of the possibilities enumerated in the partition. Obviously, they must be distinguished from irrelevant remarks like (5c).

Not that (5c) is necessarily irrelevant. If it is known that the dice are crooked, loaded somehow to show double-six when the sun shines on them, it may be just as informative as (5a). Such knowledge, and background information more generally, is appealed to in seeing that Π really is a partition (thus, the more general notion is that of a partition *relative to* background B). An answer that contravenes background conditions violates the *presuppositions* of a question, in an appropriate sense of this term.[1] Technically, if X is a presupposition of Π, then every cell of Π implies X, and so if S is inconsistent with X, then S is inconsistent with every cell of Π, so that $\Pi/S = \{F\}$. The response (5d) thus violates the presupposition of (4) that the dice were thrown.

Summing up, I have suggested that simple interrogatives express partitions (relative to background assumptions), and that complete and partial answers, nonanswers, and responses that violate presuppositions can all be appropriately characterized on that assumption.

Consider now some examples of interrogatives. The partitions corresponding to yes-no questions are the simplest possible. They have two cells, one representing the affirmative, the other the negative. The elements of these cells need not be contents, in any sense over and above that of the sentences themselves, as interpreted in the indicative part of the language. Thus, for the question *Did John see Mary?* we have the partition (7).

(7) $\{\{John\ saw\ Mary\} \mid \{John\ did\ not\ see\ Mary\}\}$

(I use bars rather than commas to separate the cells of a partition.)

For a simple *wh*-question, as in (8),

(8) Who did John see?

I assume the logical form (9).

(9) $[WH\alpha: person(\alpha)]$? John saw α

The cells of the partition expressed by (8) run through all the possibilities for John's seeing of persons. If in contexts there are just two persons in question—say, Fred and Mary—then a typical cell is

$\{John\ saw\ Fred,\ \neg(John\ saw\ Mary)\}$

representing the possibility that John saw Fred but not Mary.

The question (8) with its quantification restricted to persons must be distinguished from the question (10), involving unrestricted quantification.

(10) Which things are such that John saw them and they are persons?

This can be seen by noting that (11) is a (partial) answer to (10), but is in response to (8) simply an irrelevant remark.

(11) Fido is not a person.

It is also seen, rather more vividly, in pairs like (12)–(13).

(12) Which men are bachelors?

(13) Which bachelors are men?

The unrestricted question corresponding to both of these examples is (14).

(14) Which things are both bachelors and men?

But of course (12) and (13) are very different.

The generalization that the quantifications *which N* must be understood as restricted, with the variable ranging over things that in fact satisfy *N*, is supported by examples like (15),

(15) Which philosophers would you be annoyed if we invited?

where we never have an interpretation that would "reconstruct" the noun within the scope of the modal, giving a meaning like that of (16).

(16) For which things x would you be annoyed if x was a philosopher and we invited x?

See Reinhart 1992 for similar examples.

Higginbotham and May (1981) showed how to characterize presuppositions of singularity, as in (17).

(17) Which person did John see?

An utterance of (17) in virtue of its form carries the presupposition that John saw one and only one of Fred and Mary. Its partition will carry the presupposition in question by having only two cells, one affirming that John saw Mary and not Fred, and the other that John saw Fred and not Mary. The cells for affirming that John saw both and that he saw neither will not be represented. Similar remarks hold for presuppositions that are expressed by words rather than morphologically, as in (18).

(18) Which two articles did Mary read?

Nothing prevents our asking *wh*-questions ranging over infinite domains, or domains for which we could not possibly have a singular term for every object in the range. Thus, the question expressed by (19) is perfectly in order, although we shall be powerless to give it a complete answer.

(19) Which real numbers are transcendental?

The partition expressed by this interrogative will have cells on the order of the set of all subsets of the real numbers.

Multiple questions call for more refined partitions, as in (20).

(20) Which people read which books?

The elements of the cells of these partitions will be sentences like

John read *War and Peace.*

and their negations.[2] The account of single and multiple *wh*-questions extends to the case where the position interrogated is not in the main clause, but in one or another embedded position or positions, as in (21).

(21)   Which people did he say like to read which books?

Finally, it should be noted that many *wh*-forms incorporate prepositions or subordinating conjunctions, as *where* incorporates *at*, and is effectively equivalent to *at which place*, and *why* incorporates either *because* or *in order to*. The latter gives a simple example of interrogatives that generalize over predicate positions, so that (22), in one of its interpretations, should be taken up as in (23).

(22)   Why did John go to the refrigerator?

(23)   [WHF] ? John went to the refrigerator in order to F

Questions like (24) have long been noted ambiguous.

(24)   What did everybody say?

Intuitively, (24) asks, for each person in the range of the quantifier *everybody*, what that person said. There are some syntactic limitations on expressing questions of this form.[3] Our interest here, however, is quite general: what is the question expressed by an interrogative as in (25), where Q is a restricted quantifier, ϕ is the restriction on Q, and θ is another interrogative?

(25) [Qv: ϕ] θ

The answer is that the question should be composed of sets of questions, one set for each way in which the quantifier, construed as a function from pairs of extensions to truth values, gives the value *true*.[4] A simple example like (26) will generate the basic idea.

(26) Where can I find two screwdrivers?

A person who asks (26) may mean to inquire what place is an x such that there are two screwdrivers at x. But she may also mean just to get hold of information that will enable her to locate two screwdrivers, and in this sense of the question it arises from the interrogative (27).

(27) [Two x: screwdriver(x)] [What α: place(α)] x at α

The partition for the embedded interrogative

[What α: place(α)] x at α

is given by our previous semantics: 'x' is simply a free variable here. Now, the numeral *two*, construed as a restricted quantifier, is such that

Two ϕ are θ

is true if and only if at least two things satisfy both ϕ and θ. So the question expressed by (27) will be the class of all classes of partitions each of which, for at least two screwdrivers a and b as values of x (and for no other objects than screwdrivers as values of x), contains the partition for the interrogatives

[What α: place(α)] a at α

[What α: place(α)] b at α

The classes of partitions I call *blocs*, and classes of them *questions of order 1*. To *answer* a question of order 1 is to answer every question in one of its blocs. It follows that to answer (26) is to answer both the question where a is and the question where b is, for at least two screwdrivers a and b.

The above method of quantifying into questions extends to all quantifiers, since it is completely determined by their extensional meanings. A scrutiny of actual cases shows that any quantifier that is not monotone-decreasing (in the sense of Barwise and Cooper (1981); see the discussion in section 5 below) can in principle get wide scope in an interrogative, including even the existential quantifier, as in one interpretation of (28).

(28) What does somebody here think?

Intuition suggests that a speaker of (28) would expect from whoever elects to be his respondent the answer "*I* think so-and-so"; and that any such answer would be sufficient for the question. The theory accords with this intuition, since the abstract question expressed by the interpretation of (28) shown in (29) consists of all nonempty sets of sets of abstract questions of the form in (30), where a is a person in the domain of quantification.

(29) [$\exists x$] [WHα] ? x thinks α

(30) [WHα] ? a thinks α

Truth-functional *and* and *or* are recruited for conjunction and disjunction of interrogatives, as in (31) and (32).

(31) Will it be nice tomorrow, and will you go on a picnic if it is?

(32) Is Mary happy or is John happy?

Their role is clarified by the analogy between connectives and quantifiers. Conjunctive interrogatives, as in (31), are obviously answered only by statements that answer both conjuncts. In the present terminology, (31) expresses a question of order 1, whose sole bloc consists of the partitions expressed by the conjuncts. Disjunctive interrogatives, as in one interpretation of (32), will have the meaning, "Choose your question, and answer it." They express questions of order 1 whose blocs consist of one or both of the partitions expressed by the disjuncts.

The more common type of disjunctive question is the *free-choice* type, exemplified by (33) in an airline setting.

(33) Would you like coffee, tea, or milk?

My view of the role of disjunction in these cases, as explained in Higginbotham 1991a, is that they represent universal quantification into a yes-no question, as in (34).

(34) $[\forall x: x = \text{coffee} \lor x = \text{tea} \lor x = \text{milk}]$?   you would like x

Thus, the steward who asks (33) is asking for each of coffee, tea, and milk whether you would like it (subject to the understood condition that you will have at most one of these).

Finally, multiple quantification into questions is possible, and will generalize so as to produce questions of arbitrary finite order. Such questions include (35),

(35) What did everybody say to everybody?

with both quantifiers taking wide scope.

Thus far I have considered partitions and abstract questions of higher orders with respect to domains of quantification that have not been incorporated into the abstract questions themselves. Consider (8), repeated here.

(8) Who did John see?

The proper representation of the abstract question that it expresses must include the information that the property of having been seen by John is under consideration only for persons as values. Let K be the class of persons, and let $\Pi = \pi(\textit{John saw } \alpha[K])$ be the partition obtained by assigning just the objects in K as values of α. If the abstract question expressed by (8) is to be distinguished from the extensionally equivalent one expressed by *Which rational animals did John see?*, then information about how the class of values is determined must be incorporated somehow.

We have already seen that domain restrictions cannot be represented by conjuncts within a question—for example, that (8) must be distinguished from *Which things are persons such that John saw them?* However, we could include in each cell of the abstract question expressed by (8) the information, about each thing in K, that it is a person. If $[person(\alpha)[K]]$ is the class of atomic sentences

person(a)

for $a \in K$, we can propose the partition $\Pi' = \Pi + [person(\alpha)[K]]$ as answering to (8), thus distinguishing it from extensional equivalents.

However, Π' still fails to contain the information that the class K comprises *all* persons. This further information can be added where feasible, but is not finitely representable when the restriction is to an infinite class, for instance as in (36).

(36) Which natural numbers are prime numbers?

Similarly, a set of instances constituting a complete true answer cannot always be replaced by a finite list L, together with the information that all the positive (negative) instances are to be found on L. Such is already the case for (36) since the set of prime numbers is neither finite nor cofinite.[5]

3   Indirect Questions

An *indirect question* is an interrogative sentential form used as an argument. In general, I believe no distinction except a syntactic one should be made between the sentential argument S and the nominal argument *the question S*: both are singular terms. Thus, we have both (37) and (38).

(37) I asked whether it was raining.

(38) I asked the question whether it was raining.

Now, certain verbs that take interrogative complements cannot take nominal complements; thus, (39) is ungrammatical.

(39) *I wondered the question whether it was raining.

Pesetsky (1982) observes, however, that this fact may be reduced to an issue of abstract Case (the verb *wonder* does not assign Case to its complement, which therefore cannot be nominal); and that the introduction of morphemes, normally prepositions, for the purpose of assigning Case gives grammatical sentences whose meaning is just that of the corresponding sentence with a sentential complement. Thus, we have both (40) and (41).

(40) I wondered whether it was raining.

(41) I wondered about the question whether it was raining.[6]

Inversely, the verbs that take both nominal and sentential complements can appear with Noun Phrase complements whose interpretation is that of interrogatives. These are the so-called concealed questions, exemplified by (42).

(42) I asked the time (what the time was).

In all the above cases, in the view developed here, the complements refer to the abstract questions that they would refer to if used in isolation (with the necessary superficial syntactic adjustments). Thus, to ask whether p is to ask

$$\{p ; \neg p\}^7$$

With the epistemic verbs, and indeed with all verbs whose arguments are naturally taken to refer to propositions or to facts, interrogative complements are mediated by relations to answers to the abstract questions that they refer to. Thus, I assume that (43) is interpreted as in (44).

(43) Mary knows who John saw.

(44) Mary knows the (or an) answer to the question who John saw.

Berman (1989) has called attention to sentences with indirect questions in conjunction with quantificational adverbs, as in (45) and (46).

(45) Mary mostly knows who John saw.

(46) With some exceptions, Mary knows who John saw.

Examples are not limited to epistemic verbs, as (47), modeled after examples in Lahiri 1990, 1992, attests.

(47) John and Mary mostly agree on who to invite.

I look upon these adverbs (differently from Berman) as qualifying the nature of the answers said to be known, or as in the case of (47), agreed upon; for example, (47) will be true if, out of a potential guest list of 20,

John and Mary have agreed for (say) 15 on whether to invite them or not. See Lahiri 1992 for further discussion.

Finally, there are interrogative arguments to verbs that have nothing to do with acts of speech or mental states. Karttunen (1977) noted indirect questions in contexts such as (48).

(48) What will happen depends on who is elected.

Predicates like *depend on* express relations between abstract questions, and the notion of dependence at stake, applied to (48), comes to something like: Answers to the question who is elected, together with other facts, imply answers to the question what will happen. There are many other similar locutions, such as *is influenced by, is relevant to*, and of course their negations.

It is worth observing that (48) leaves open the exact nature of the dependency, or the ways in which who is elected will influence what happens. In the parallel and simpler example (49), it may be that rising temperature causes rain, or prevents it; and you may know (49) without knowing which it is.

(49) Whether it will rain depends on whether the temperature will rise.

4   Extensions to Higher Types

The basic apparatus developed here can be applied to construct abstract questions with respect to expressions of any syntactic category, independently of whether they occupy quantifiable places in the indicative fragment of a language. The sense in which the variables bound by *wh*-expressions have a range then dwindles toward the substitutional. For instance, interrogatives like (50) are likely to be put forth only where a fairly narrow range of linguistic alternatives is envisaged.

(50) What (profession) is John?

Even questions expressed with *which* are often best answered simply by filling in appropriate material in the site of syntactic movement. So for (19), repeated here, an answer might be as in (51).

(19) Which real numbers are transcendental?

(51) Those real numbers that are not solutions to any equation are transcendental.

Engdahl (1986) has called attention to interrogatives like (52),

(52) Which of his poems does no poet want to read?

where, understanding the pronoun as a variable bound to *no poet*, the answer might be as in (53).

(53) His earliest poems.

I accept Engdahl's view that these interrogatives likewise involve quantification over nonarguments, in this case over functions. Thus, their logical forms might be represented as in (54).

(54) [Which f: $(\forall x) f(x)$ is a poem by x] [For no poet y]
y wants to read $f(y)$

The need for functional interpretations of this kind is not confined to questions, since it occurs also with relative clauses, and even with definite NPs, as in (55).

(55) John made a list of the dates no man should forget.

John's list might read as follows:

children's birthdays
own wedding anniversary
Independence Day

. . . .

The list is a list of those f whose domain is the class of men and whose range is included in the class of dates $f(x)$ such that no man x should forget $f(x)$.[8]

The recent discussion by Chierchia (1991) shows that for many purposes quantification into interrogatives can be replaced by the functional interpretation. I illustrate using the example (24), repeated here.

(24) What did everybody say?

Suppose we understand *what* as having a functional interpretation, as in Engdahl 1986, and incorporate an appropriate description of the functions over which it ranges, as in (56).

(56) [WHf: $(\forall x)$ x says $f(x)$] ? $(\forall y)$ y said $f(y)$

(56) must be allowed as possible anyway, because of possible answers to (24) such as (57).

(57) The speech she had memorized.

But now we might regard the listiform answer (58) as simply one way of specifying a desired function f.

(58) Mary said this, and Susan that, and Margaret the other.

The representation of (24) as (59) appears then to become redundant.

(59) $(\forall y)$ [WHα] ? y said α

There are several points that would have to be clarified before (56) and (59) could be declared equivalent. As I have defined the interpretation of (59), true and complete answers to it must exhaustively specify for each person y what y said and also what y did not say. If this view is carried over to (56), then exhaustive information about the functions f would be required to answer it, and not merely the specification of some f. On the other hand, in any context in which (58) is a complete and true answer to (59), it is a complete and true answer to (56) as well.

The logical limitations of functional interpretation surface when the exported quantifier binds a variable within a larger *wh*, as in (60).

(60) Which picture of each student should we put in the yearbook?

A complete answer to (60) might be listiform, as in (61), or involve pronouns as bound variables, as in (62).

(61) (We should put) this picture of Jones, and that picture of Smith, and ..., and that picture of Robinson.

(62) The picture in which he is wearing a hat.

From (60) we have the representation (63).

(63) $[\forall x: \text{student}(x)]$ [WHα: α a picture of x] ? we should put α in the yearbook

For a functional interpretation of (60) we can no longer apply the routine exemplified in (56), but would instead have to posit something like (64).

(64) WHf: $domain(f)$ = the students & $(\forall x) f(x)$ is a picture of x]
    ? $(\forall y)(\forall z)$ [y is a picture of $z \to$ (we should put y in the
    yearbook $\leftrightarrow y = f(z)$)]

There are also a number of cases where listiform answers are unavailable, which nevertheless admit functional interpretation. Among these are (65) and (66).

(65) Who did President Vest shake hands with after each student introduced him to?

(66) Which of his relatives does every student really love?

Only functional answers like

His or her mother.

are appropriate for (65) and (66).[9] On the assumption that listiform answers are salient only where there is quantification into questions, these data follow from known conditions on scope of quantifiers and pronominal binding. Thus, in (65) we do not expect to be able to assign *each student* wide scope, since it is not interpretable with wide scope in (67).

(67) President Vest shook hands with his mother after each student introduced him to her.

Taken all together, then, these problems indicate that, besides functional interpretations of *wh*, genuine quantification into questions is possible in rather basic sentences of English. And in any case there is no difficulty in constructing sentences with *explicit* quantification into questions, as in (68).

(68) I want to know for each person what that person said.

I return now to some final points about higher types for *wh*. One can sweep out positions for whole clauses (with *why*) or adverbs (with *how*) and even quantifiers, with *how many*, as in (69).

(69) How many books have you decided to read?

Note that (69) is ambiguous, having either the interpretation indicated in (70) or that in (71).

(70) [WHQ] ? You have decided to read [Q books]

(71) [WHQ] ? [Qx: book(x)] you have decided to read x

All of the cases just discussed seem to fall under the theory presented here.[10]

5   The Presentation of Questions

The semantics of questions, as I have presented it above, abstracts completely from the ways in which the objects, or the things in ranges of higher types that are values of the interrogative variables, are given to us, or may be given to a questioner or respondent. It furthermore abstracts from the questioner's motives, if any, and other pragmatic matters. It seems to me that semantic theory, and especially the theory of truth for sentences with interrogative complements, requires this abstraction. We can raise questions that we do not know how to answer, and for which, as Bromberger (1966 and elsewhere) has pointed out, we do not even know what an answer would look like. There is, thus, no requirement in the general case that we have an effective procedure for determining whether a statement is a complete answer to a question, or indeed whether it is an answer at all.

The distinction between abstract questions and the ways they are presented to us is clearest when the questions are about objects, which may be given from many different perspectives. Thus, to the question *Who did John see?*, the response

John saw Bill.

is, technically, not even a partial answer, since we are not given which object as value of the interrogative variable α is the reference of *Bill*.

In context, however, matters are not so bleak. We can conceive that the values of the variable are referred to by antecedently given singular terms, and thus regard the response as a partial answer after all. More generally, given an abstract question $\Pi = \pi(\theta(\alpha)[K]) + [\phi(\alpha)[K]]$, where ϕ is the restriction on the values of α, K is the class of objects satisfying it, and $\theta(\alpha)$ is the matrix predicate over which the partition is constructed, and given a class C of closed singular terms in 1-1 correspondence with the members of K, if $[\phi(\alpha)[C]]$ is $\{\phi(c/\alpha): c \in C\}$ and $\pi(\theta(\alpha)[C])$ is the partition obtained from $\pi(\theta(\alpha)[K])$ by replacing the objects in K by the respective terms in C that refer to them, we may define

$$\Pi_C = \pi(\theta(\alpha)[C]) + [\phi(\alpha)[C]]$$

as the *presentation* Π_C *of* Π *with respect to the substitution class* C.

A presentation of an abstract question is an abstract question in its own right. In practice we are interested in presentations. If Jones asks me who is playing which position in the outfield, and I respond that the left fielder is playing left field, the right fielder is playing right field, and the center fielder is playing center field, I have understood his question all right, and feign not to understand his presentation. It should not be inferred, however, that we can take the presentations and let the questions of which they are presentations go. We can, for example, ask questions whose presentations we know we would not recognize, or for which we have no particular presentations in mind. Furthermore, by relating abstract questions to their presentations, we clarify for instance the sense in which we say two persons may ask the same question, perhaps without realizing it.

Special attention must still be paid to questions [WHα: $\phi(\alpha)$] ? $\theta(\alpha)$ where in fact nothing satisfies ϕ at all. Their abstract questions will be $\{F\}$, and so not distinct from any number of other questions expressing

$\{F\}$. Going intensional does not ameliorate the situation, since there are also restrictions $\phi(\alpha)$ that are not even possibly satisfied by anything. These cases underscore the fact that in practice the presentations are more nearly what matters to us than the questions they represent. I do not see this consequence as a difficulty of principle; but it does show that a full pragmatic theory must consider the case where a person for instance thinks she is asking a nondegenerate question, but fails to do so.

A further pragmatic and computational issue that is clarified by the conception of abstract questions as partitions, and of partial answers as statements or sets of statements that eliminate certain of the possibilities that the cells of the partitions represent, is that of interpreting what Hintikka (1976) has called the *desideratum* of a question, or the quantity of information that is wanted by the person asking it. A simple *wh*-question such as example (8), repeated here, may be associated with different desiderata.

(8) Who did John see?

On the view that I have defended, (8) has the logical form (9),

(9) [WHα: person(α)] ? John saw α

and the partition it expresses runs through all the possibilities for John's seeing of persons in the domain of quantification, or at least all that are left open by the background theory.

The desideratum of (8) is, therefore, not represented in the question expressed. But desiderata can be so expressed, and among these (as Belnap and Hintikka have pointed out) the *existential*, represented by (72), and the *universal*, represented in Southern American English by (73), are quite common.

(72) Who for example did John see?

(73) Who-all did John see?

(72) asks for an example, and (73) for an exhaustive list, of persons John saw. But intermediate desiderata are possible, as in (74).

(74) Who are two or three people John saw?

The desideratum of an abstract question may be regarded as a set of statements, namely, those that are "sufficiently informative" (even if possibly false) with respect to that abstract question. Each abstract question comes with its own *minimal desideratum*, namely, those statements that are partial answers to it. But not all partial answers meet even the existential desideratum; thus, (75) is a partial answer to (9), but would not meet the desideratum that at least one value of α be supplied that is a person John saw.

(75) John saw Mary or Bill.

This desideratum, signaled explicitly in (72), is the class of those S implying, for some person a, *John saw* c_a. Similarly, the desideratum of (73) is

$\{S$: For all persons a, S implies *John saw* c_a *or* $\neg$ *(John saw* $c_a)\}$

Note that (74) has a desideratum in between the universal and the existential. Desiderata may also involve substantive conditions not limited to quantity, as in (76).

(76) What is a surprising/routine example of popular novel?

In general, a partial answer to an abstract question $\mathcal{Q}$ with desideratum D is a statement in D that is a partial answer to $\mathcal{Q}$; and the ordering of desiderata by stringency corresponds to an ordering of partial answers by informativeness.

I return now to some points about quantifying into questions. First of all, with which natural-language quantifiers can one quantify in? Certainly, I think, with all of those that are not monotone-decreasing in the sense of Barwise and Cooper (1981), where a quantifier Q, interpreted via a map f_Q from ordered pairs of subsets of the domain A of quantification into truth values, is monotone-decreasing if $f_Q(X, Y) = $ truth and $X' \subseteq X$ then $f_Q(X', Y) = $ truth. Examples of quantifiers not monotone-decreasing have been used in the illustrations above. Monotone-decreasing quantifiers, such as *at most two people* (77) or (at an extreme) *no one* (78), can never take wide scope.

(77) What do at most two people have to say?

(78) Is no one at home?

The reason is intuitively clear: it is that, when a question [WHα: $\phi(\alpha)$] ? $\theta(x, \alpha)$ is to be answered for at most two values of x, as in (77), or for none of them, as in (78), then it may be answered by answering for none—that is, by saying anything at all. This intuition corresponds to the feature of our construction that since there is a bloc for each set of persons consisting of at most two of them (for (77)) or none of them (for (78)), there is in each case a bloc for each set of persons consisting of none of them—that is, a bloc $\{\{F\}\}$. Answerhood then becomes degenerate. From the definition, S answers either of the questions expressed by (77) or (78) with the quantifier taking wide scope if S answers $\{F\}$, the sole question in the bloc $\{\{F\}\}$, and it answers $\{F\}$ if inconsistent with F, an unsatisfiable sentence. Then S answers F, and so answers the question, no matter what S may be.

6 Mood and Reference

My discussion thus far has gone forward on the assumption that theses 1 and 2 of my introduction are correct: namely, that interrogative sentences express abstract questions, and embedded interrogatives refer to the questions that would be expressed by their direct counterparts. There are three major alternatives to these assumptions.

The first, which has been taken up in various forms, is that the interrogative, like the imperative, optative, and perhaps other moods, is constructed by attaching an indicator of mood to an indicative (moodless) core. The meaning of the mood indicator then becomes an issue, and the issue of the reference of indirect questions is left up in the air. However, the idea that the difference between

It is raining.

and

Is it raining?

semantically speaking is only in their mood and not in their content is one that has enjoyed wide appeal, and I will therefore consider it in some detail.

The second alternative, elaborated especially by Jaakko Hintikka. is that all questions, whether direct or indirect, dissolve upon analysis into the more ordinary apparatus of propositional attitudes and ordinary quantifiers. On this view, not only are there no moods but there are also ultimately no quantifications like *wh* distinctive of questions. This view faces serious difficulties once we move outside direct questions and the complements to epistemic verbs and propositional attitudes, as noted by Karttunen (1977); I will therefore say no more about it here.

The third alternative, which has been prominent from time to time and is defended elegantly if briefly by Lewis (1972), is that all questions are really indirect, and apparently direct questions amount to indirect questions as complements of an unexpressed performative prefix, with the meaning of "I ask," or "I ask you." To the obvious objection that it seems absurd to call interrogatives true or false, it may be responded that we do not call performatives true or false either. However, on the view I will defend, this alternative is not so much mistaken as it is redundant: of course it is true that whoever utters an interrogative asks a question; but we do not need the higher-performative analysis to explain this.

A theory of meaning must explain why uttering an indicative sentence is saying something (not necessarily asserting it), and it must explain why uttering a *that*-clause is not saying anything, but simply referring to a proposition. The explanation in truth-conditional semantics is that only sentences, or utterances of sentences, admit of truth and falsehood. That is why, in uttering a sentence, one may, in Wittgenstein's words, "make a move in the language game," and inversely why in uttering a *that*-clause in isolation no move is made at all.

This explanatory charge carries over to nonindicatives. In uttering *the question whether it is raining* one merely refers to a question, but in uttering *Is it raining?* that question is necessarily asked. But since direct questions do not appear to have truth values, the sense in which utterances of them must ask things is not apparent.

The higher-performative analysis reduces the problem of direct questions to the previous case of indicatives. Utterances of *Is it raining?* are regarded as notational variants of utterances of *I ask (you) (the question) whether it is raining*. Since the latter are indicatives, and say things, so do the former. The type of saying is asking, since that concept was built into the analysis.

But in fact all of this is unnecessary. Just as the semantic value of an indicative is a truth value, so the semantic value of a direct yes-no question is an unordered pair of truth values, one for each cell of its partition. Just as the semantic value of a *that*-clause is a proposition, so the semantic value of an indirect yes-no question is an unordered pair of propositions, and just as the proposition that it is raining is expressed by *It is raining*, so the pair {the proposition that it is raining, the proposition that it is not raining} is expressed by *Is it raining?*. It follows immediately: first, that interrogatives cannot be called true or false; and second, if we assume that *ask* is nothing but that variant of *say* whose proper objects are questions, that whoever utters an interrogative asks a question.

Care must be taken in not freighting up the notion of asking here with any of the motives for raising a question. English has *say* and *assert*, where to assert is to say with assertive force. The verb *ask*, however, is ambiguous. In one sense it amounts to *say*, but its objects must be questions. In another sense it involves what we might call interrogative force (and is so understood in the higher-performative analysis). One can raise questions to which one perfectly well knows the answer, or doesn't care what the answer may be, and one can also raise questions nonseriously. An actor on a stage says things without asserting them, and utters questions without interrogative force. I take it: that the verb *ask* may be so understood that an utterance by *a* of (79) justifies the subsequent assertion by anyone of (80).

(79) Is dinner ready?

(80) *a* asked whether dinner was ready.

The position I have outlined may be clarified by being expressed in an extension of the language IL of intensional logic. In that language there are sentences of the syntactic type t of truth values and expressions for propositions, of syntactic type (s, t), corresponding semantically to propositions—that is, sets of possible worlds. Interrogatives as I have interpreted them here would call for an extension of the type theory so that there would be a type $\{t, t\}$ of unordered pairs of type t, whose semantic interpretation would be unordered pairs of truth values, and a type $\{(s, t), (s, t)\}$ of unordered pairs of propositions. Verbs like *ask* and *wonder* would take arguments of this type. In this setting, the extension of an interrogative is a pair of truth values, and its intension a pair of propositions. Indeed, the account of interrogatives given here can be expressed in its entirety in the setting envisaged.

If we assume that the reference of indirect questions is as I have suggested, then the higher-performative analysis of direct questions becomes redundant. Whether that analysis is adopted or not, however, the semantics of interrogatives does not take us out of the truth-conditional arena. In particular, there are no moods in the semantics of questions, either because they are not represented at all, or because any work they might have done is taken up by the higher performative verb. However, there is a weighty tradition of thinking of moods as semantically independent items. and I wish to turn briefly to the difficulties in making out just what this tradition has in mind.

The question we were considering was, Why can saying an interrogative sentence such as (81) constitute asking a question, namely, the question whether (82)?

(81) Is it raining?

(82) It is raining.

An answer that suggests itself is that the syntactic element represented in English by inversion and a characteristic intonation pattern, and in other languages by other syntactic devices, is a sign that the speaker of the sentence is performing a speech act with interrogative force, whose content is given by the clause on which the syntactic element operated. Thus, the datum (83) is an application of a rule of English.

(83) If u is an utterance of (2), then the speaker of u asks (with interrogative force) the question whether (82).

As Davidson (1979) points out, however, the above and kindred conceptions of mood fail to make room for nonserious uses of language. Taken quite literally, this account of mood implies that when the minister at a wedding rehearsal says (84),

(84) Do you take this woman for your wife?

then he (or she) is asking with interrogative force whether the man addressed takes that woman for his wife. But he is not, in the desired sense, asking anything; it is only a rehearsal.

Note that the higher-performative analysis does not face counterexamples along these lines. Whether the minister is asking anything is determined by whether (85), which is what he in fact said, is true.

(85) I ask you whether you take this woman for your wife.

But since we are only at a rehearsal, it is not true. My own view, which does not recognize a higher performative, has it that the minister in a sense asks a question, but without interrogative force.

The theory of mood developed in Davidson 1979 is specifically designed to allow for nonserious uses of language. Davidson's suggestion is that yes-no questions are a kind of portmanteau, where the indicator of mood, or as he calls it the mood-setter, functions as a comment on the indicative core. Thus, *Is it raining?* is understood as in (86).

(86) It is raining. That was interrogative in force.

The minister at the wedding rehearsal says nothing with interrogative force, even though in a way he says he does.

It is obvious that Davidson's suggestion runs into difficulties with *wh*-interrogatives (as Davidson notes in 1979:115), although it might be suggested that the indicative core is in this case an open sentence or utterance. But does his view really explain why interrogatives cannot be assessed for their truth values? Hornsby (1986) suggests that the explanation offered—namely, that interrogatives are a portmanteau of two sentences—is rather weak; for the same problem in more detail, see Segal 1988. Hornsby herself proposes that the convention or rules of language governing interrogatives be expressed adverbially, as in (87).

(87) By saying *Is it raining?* a speaker says interrogatively that
     (or: asks-whether) it is raining.

To say no more than this about interrogatives is to leave indirect questions in the lurch, as Hornsby recognizes. But her aim is to formulate a view according to which the speaker in asking a question is not, in contrast to Davidson's view. tacitly describing with words what he is doing. Still, the expression *says interrogatively* is left as an unanalyzed term of art. If it were interpreted as *says with interrogative force*, then I do not see that we would have better than Davidson's theory back again.

Now, if I am right to say that yes-no questions express partitions, unordered pairs consisting of a proposition and its negation, then we have an explanation of why yes-no questions may but need not have interrogative force that is parallel to the explanation of why indicatives may but need not have assertive force. There is no need of mood indicators at all, for the semantic work done by syntactic inversion or the abstract question morpheme formalized above by the question mark is just to convert propositions into appropriate unordered pairs. Indeed, the view that I have advocated here is partly based on the following thought: any correct account of indirect questions must assign them a reference, and that reference will have the property that, when presented via a main clause, its presentation can, but need not, constitute asking about it. If so, then we needn't suppose that an interrogative does not wear its whole logical syntax on its face.

Appendix: Licensing Negative Polarity

The English negative polarity items *any* and *ever* are freely licensed in interrogative environments, as in (88) and (89).

(88) Did anybody speak?
         John wonders whether anybody spoke.
       *Anybody spoke.

(89) Have you ever been to France?
         Whether he has ever been to France is known to the police.
       *He has ever been to France.
       *That he has ever been to France is known to the police.

In this appendix I will offer an explanation of such licensing, drawing on the discussion above and on the fuller account of English choice questions developed in Higginbotham 1991a.

Following the latter paper, I will assume without argument that English disjunction *or* is always to be construed as in construction with a possibly tacit occurrence of *either*, and that the latter is a quantifier admitting a universal interpretation. The data that support this view are exemplified by the ambiguity of modal sentences such as (90).

(90) John will play chess or checkers.

Besides the obvious interpretation that John will play chess, or else he will play checkers, (90) also has an interpretation equivalent to

John will play chess and John will play checkers.

The second interpretation, I will assume, arises because (90) has in fact a syntactic structure as in (91),

(91) [either]ᵢ [John will play [chess or checkers]ᵢ]

and at LF a structure as in (92).

(92) [either chess or checkers]ᵢ [John will play t_i]

The prefix is a universal quantifier, so that we have in effect (93).

(93) [∀x: x = chess or x = checkers] John will play x

Proceeding now beyond my earlier discussion, I will assume that the syntax of (90) puts *either* in the Spec position of its clause, so that we have at LF (94).

(94) [CP [Spec either chess or checkers]ᵢ [C′ C [IP John will play t_i]]]

This assumption is more specific than I will actually require. What will be necessary is that there be an intervening position, here C, between the quantification and the sentence over which it quantifies, and that this position be interpreted as the '?' of the discussion above is interpreted— that is, as passing from the type of propositions to the type of partitions.

It is obvious that English *whether* is *wh + either*, as *when* is *wh + then*, *where* is *wh + there*, and so on. Suppose now that this etymological point has semantic significance, so that *whether* is interpreted as a universal quantification in [Spec, CP], hence outside the scope of '?' in C. Unlike *either*, and unlike other *wh*-words, *whether* is restricted to this syntactic position. Thus, we do not have (95), in contrast to (96) or (97).

(95) *Who saw whether Mary or Bill?

(96) Who saw either Mary or Bill?

(97) Who saw who?

We may assume further that just as every occurrence of *either* must go together with an occurrence of the disjunction *or*, so must every occurrence of *whether*, the sole exception being the case where the disjunction is tacit, and over the whole indicative IP. Thus, (98) will have a structure as in (99), and (100) a structure as in (101), prior to ellipsis.

(98) whether John played chess or checkers

(99) $[_{CP} [_{Spec}$ whether$]_i [_{C'} [_C$?$] [_{IP}$ John played [chess or checkers$]_i$]]]

(100) whether John left (or not)

(101) [[whether] [? [John left or John did not leave]]]

Consider now the LF representation and the accompanying semantics of (101) on the assumptions given. The representation will be (102), and its interpretation will be that of (103).

(102) [[whether John left or John did not leave$]_i$ [? t_i]]

(103) [$\forall p$: $p =$ that John left or $p =$ that John did not leave] ? p

Applying the semantics, the constituent '?p' expresses the partition

$\{p \mid \neg p\}$

with 'p' a free variable. Quantification into this position by the universal quantifier gives the question of order 1

$\{\{$John left $\mid$ John did not leave$\}, \{\neg$ (John left) $\mid \neg$ (John did not leave)$\}\}$

Manifestly, the latter is equivalent, in the sense of having all the same partial and complete answers, to

$\{$John left $\mid$ John did not leave$\}$

so that the quantification has accomplished nothing, semantically speaking.

On the assumptions stated, however, *whether*-questions in which the scope of *whether* is the whole clause all have the property at LF that the elements of the clause appear within the restriction of a universal quantification, and such appearance is known to license negative polarity items. For the licensing itself I will adopt the explanation proposed by Ladusaw (1983) and others, that negative polarity items may appear only within the scope of *downward-entailing* expressions (definitions and a theoretical discussion are provided below). It follows at once that negative polarity items are licensed within interrogatives, where the licenser is overt or tacit *whether*.

A crucial point for the above analysis of the licensing of negative polarity items in interrogatives is seen in minimal pairs such as (104)–(105) and (106)–(107).

(104) Mary knows whether John played chess or checkers.

(105) Mary knows whether anyone played chess or checkers.

(106) Did John play chess or checkers?

(107) Did anyone play chess or checkers?

(104) and (106) are of course ambiguous. On the view taken here, the ambiguity derives from the possibility of construing the disjunctive constituent *chess or checkers* either with *whether*, giving the interpretation of the embedded clause as a choice question, or else with its own tacit *either* within that constituent, giving the interpretation of that clause as a yes-no question. But (105) and (107) are not ambiguous: the complement cannot be interpreted as a choice question about chess versus checkers. The explanation in terms of the analysis above is that for the choice question we have the representation (108).

(108) [[whether chess or checkers]$_i$ [? [John/anyone played t_i]]]

But this representation fails to license the negative polarity item *anyone*. To license it, we require that the entire clause *anyone played chess or checkers* be within the scope of *whether*, as in (109).

(109) [[whether anyone played chess or checkers (or not)$_i$ [? t_i]]

But then the disjunction of *chess* or *checkers* is not construed with *whether*, so that the possibility of a choice question is precluded.

The interpretation of *whether* as universal quantification is not confined to the domain of interrogatives, but is corroborated by the use of *whether* analogous to a free relative pronoun, as in (110).

(110) You'll have a good time whether you go to London or Paris.

The sentence means that you'll have a good time if you go to London, and also if you go to Paris. This interpretation follows from the assignment of the LF representation (111), or, with variables explicit, (112).

(111) [whether London or Paris]$_i$ [you'll have a good time if you go
       to t_i]

(112) [∀x: x = London or x = Paris] [you'll have a good time if you
      go to x]

When negative polarity is licensed within the scope of some other *wh*-expression than *whether*, as in (113), we assume that a tacit *whether* is present anyway, giving the LF representation (114).

(113) Who had anything to say?

(114) [WHα] [∀p: p = that α had anything to say or p = that
      ¬(α had anything to say)] ? p

The equivalences noted above carry over to this case, so that the interpretation is not disrupted.

There are a number of further linguistic points relevant to the hypothesis presented here that I hope to expand upon in later work. To review, the hypothesis is that negative polarity items are licensed in interrogatives because the latter are governed by the disjunction-host *whether*. This word behaves like its counterpart *either* in admitting an interpretation as a universal quantification. When that quantification is over propositions, then the constituents of the interrogative clause will be within its scope, and the environment will satisfy known conditions on the licensing of negative polarity in English.

I turn now to some formal points that have been so far left in abeyance. Ladusaw's notion of downward-entailingness is defined in terms of implication, and thus applies in the first instance only to indicative sentences. A quantifier Q is downward-entailing (with respect to its restriction) if the schema in (115) is valid.

(115) [Qx: F(x)] G(x)
      [∀x: H(x)] F(x)
      ‾‾‾‾‾‾‾‾‾‾‾‾‾‾
      [Qx: H(x)] G(x)

By analogy with the indicative case, an expression of generality Q (which may be a quantifier, *wh*, or perhaps a "mix" of the two, such as *which two*) will be said to be *downward-entailing for interrogatives* if, where $\mathcal{Q}$ is the question expressed by the result of prefixing '[Qx: F(x)]' to '?G(x)', and $\mathcal{Q}'$ is the question expressed by the result of prefixing '[Qx: H(x)]' to '?G(x)', then we have (116).

(116) If [∀x: H(x)] F(x), then if S is a partial (complete) answer to $\mathcal{Q}$,
      then S is a partial (complete) answer to $\mathcal{Q}'$.

In other words, speaking derivatively in terms of answers to sentences rather than to the questions they express, the schema (117) is valid.

(117) S partially (completely) answers $[Qx: F(x)]$? $G(x)$

$\quad\quad [\forall x: H(x)]\ F(x)$

$\quad S$ partially (completely) answers $[Qx: H(x)]$? $G(x)$

We shall need the observation about quantifiers in natural language that they are all *intersective* in the sense of Higginbotham and May (1978, 1981). I construe quantifiers Q as model-theoretically interpreted by functions f_Q from ordered pairs (X, Y) of subsets of the domain of quantification A into truth values. Q is *intersective* if

$$f_Q(X, Y) = f_Q(X, X \cap Y)$$

From intersectivity it follows that a natural-language quantifier that is downward-entailing, or for purposes of this exposition *downward-entailing (DE) for indicatives*, is DE for interrogatives as well. For suppose that Q is DE for indicatives, and let S be a partial answer to (118).

(118) $[Qx: F(x)]$? $G(x)$

Each question $\mathcal{Q}_a$ expressed by '? $G(x)$' when a is assigned to x will be of some given order n, the same for all a. If $\overline{F}$ is the extension of 'F', then for every subset A' of $\overline{F}$ such that $f_Q(\overline{F})(A') = \text{truth}$, there is a bloc $B_{A'}$ in the question $\mathcal{Q}$ of order $n + 1$ expressed by (118), and $\mathcal{Q}$ consists entirely of such blocs. Since S answers $\mathcal{Q}$, there is a bloc B in $\mathcal{Q}$ and a subset A' of $\overline{F}$ such that S answers $\mathcal{Q}_a$ for every $a \in A'$. Consider the interrogative (119).

(119) $[Qx: H(x)]$? $G(x)$

If $\overline{H}$ is the extension of 'H', then since Q is DE for indicatives, if $\overline{H} \subseteq \overline{F}$ then $f_Q(\overline{H})(A') = \text{truth}$. Since Q is intersective, $f_Q(\overline{H})(\overline{H} \cap A') = \text{truth}$. Then S answers every $\mathcal{Q}_a$ for $a \in \overline{H} \cap A'$, and is therefore an answer to (119); and S is a complete answer if it was a complete answer to (118). So if Q is DE for indicatives and Q is intersective, then Q is DE for interrogatives. Since all natural-language Q are intersective, this completes the proof.

The converse inclusion, that if Q is DE for interrogatives it is also DE for indicatives, requires stronger assumptions than the intersectivity of Q. Following the customary terminology, say that Q is *monotone-increasing (-decreasing)* if $f_Q(X)(Y) = \text{truth}$ and $Y \subseteq Z$ ($Z \subseteq Y$) implies $f_Q(X)(Z) = \text{truth}$, and *indefinite* if $f_Q(X)(Y) = f_Q(Y)(X)$, for all X, Y, and Z. All natural-language quantifiers are monotone-increasing, monotone-decreasing, or indefinite (including combinations of these). If Q is monotone-decreasing, then Q does not quantify into interrogatives, and we have seen pragmatic reasons why. For those same pragmatic reasons, we may assume that $f_Q(\phi)(Y) =$ falsehood, and, if Q is indefinite, that $f_Q(X)(\phi) =$ falsehood as well.

Suppose then that Q is not DE for indicatives, and consider a model $\mathcal{M}$ where (120) and (121) are true and (122) is false.

(120) $[Qx: F(x)]\ G(x)$

(121) $[\forall x: H(x)]\ F(x)$

(122) $[Qx: H(x)]\ G(x)$

Then the extension $\overline{F}$ of 'F' is nonempty. Consider with respect to this model the interrogatives (123) and (124).

(123) $[Qx: F(x)]\ ?\ (G(x)\ \&\ H(x))$

(124) $[Qx: H(x)]\ ?\ (G(x)\ \&\ H(x)))$

We are going to show that there is a true partial answer to (123) that is not a partial answer to (124), so that Q is not DE for interrogatives either. Assume on the contrary that Q is DE for interrogatives.

Because (120) is true in $\mathcal{M}$, the question expressed by (123) in $\mathcal{M}$ will have a bloc for the nonempty subset $\overline{F} \cap \overline{G}$ of $\overline{F}$. Hence, if there is an object a in $\mathcal{M}$ that lies in $\overline{F}$ and $\overline{G}$ but not in $\overline{H}$, then (125) is a true partial answer to (123) that is not a partial answer to (124).

(125) $G(a)\ \&\ \neg H(a)$

Hence, $\overline{F} \cap \overline{G} \subseteq H$. Then Q cannot be indefinite; for if it were, then since it follows from the truth of (121) in $\mathcal{M}$ that $\overline{F} \cap \overline{G} = \overline{G} \cap \overline{H}$, and the truth values of (120) and (122) depend only on the respective cardinalities of $\overline{F} \cap \overline{G}$ and $\overline{G} \cap \overline{H}$, these formulas would have the same truth value in $\mathcal{M}$, contrary to hypothesis. The only remaining possibility is that Q is monotone increasing, but not indefinite. The blocs of the question expressed by (124) in $\mathcal{M}$ correspond to those subsets Σ of $\overline{H}$ for which $f_Q(\overline{H}, \Sigma) =$ truth. If we could choose $\Sigma \subseteq G \cap H$, then since Q is monotone-increasing, (122) would be true in $\mathcal{M}$. If there are no Σ for which $f_Q(\overline{H}, \Sigma) =$ truth, then the question expressed by (124) in $\mathcal{M}$ is degenerate, and so has no proper partial answers. But otherwise there are elements in $\overline{G}$ that are not in $\overline{H}$; and by the previous argument (125) is then a partial answer to (123) but not to (124).

The proof above can be strengthened to show that there are complete answers to (123) that are not complete answers to (124). I omit the details here.

Notes

Most of this paper is expanded from the less technical parts of one presented at a meeting of the Ockham Society, Oxford, March 1990, Roger Teichmann commenting; at the Workshop on Logical Form, University of California, Irvine, April 1990: and at the meeting of the Association for Symbolic Logic, Carnegie-Mellon University, Pittsburgh, January 1991. Other material is new, and some of it would not have been possible without class discussion in a seminar at MIT in the spring term of 1992 taught jointly with Irene Heim. For a technical supplement on direct questions, see Higginbotham 1991b: secs, 6 and 7. I have incorporated some remarks prompted by Teichmann's comments, and discussions with a number of persons, including especially Utpal Lahiri, Gabriel Segal, and Robert Stainton, have also been very helpful.

I note here the background to this paper. My first work on the topic of interrogatives was carried out jointly with Robert May, and some was published in Higginbotham and May 1978, 1981. I presented a more extended view at the CUNY Graduate Center, New York, October 1978, and at MIT, November 1979. This work was influenced particularly by Levi (1967); May (1989) has also carried out some of the further development. Further research was done at the University of Texas at Austin in 1980 under grant BNS 76-20307 A-01 from the National Science Foundation. I am grateful to Stanley Peters for this opportunity, and to him, Hans Kamp, and Lauri Karttunen for comments and discussion. The views that I then arrived at, and presented in a seminar at MIT in 1982 together with Sylvain Bromberger, I subsequently found to overlap in part with the research report Belnap 1963, some of the material from which was published as Belnap and Steel 1976. Discussion with Belnap at a conference sponsored by the Sloan Foundation at McGill University, 1982, confirmed that the method he and Michael Bennett envisaged for adding quantification over questions was similar to mine as well. (I have noted below where I follow Belnap's terminology, but have not in general cited specific parallels to his work.) Finally, Groenendijk and Stokhof (1984, 1989) have independently arrived at a view of what simple interrogatives express that is similar to what I advance here in section 1.

1. Belnap (1969) observes that interrogatives may be expected to have presuppositions even for a language whose indicatives do not.

2. The presuppositions of multiple singular *wh*-questions are examined in Barss 1990.

3. See May 1985.

4. For a different implementation of the same basic idea, see Belnap 1982, following work by Michael Bennett.

5. If the background theory is ω-incomplete, even finiteness (or emptiness) of the set of positive instances is not enough to guarantee that an answer is attainable. For example, let the background theory be Peano arithmetic, where $\mathscr{P}$ represents provability and $g+$ is the numeral for the Gödel number of a sentence g provably equivalent to its own unprovability, and consider (i), representing the question *What is a proof of* g?

(i) [WHα] ? $\mathscr{P}(\alpha, g+)$

In the standard model, only the cell containing '$\neg\mathscr{P}(a+, g+)$' for each numeral $a+$ is consistent with the background theory, but the true and complete answer '$(\forall x)\ \neg\mathscr{P}(x, g+)$' is not provable.

6. There is another, irrelevant interpretation of (41), parallel to the natural interpretation of *I wondered about school*.

7. In the interest of readability I omit extra curly brackets when no ambiguity threatens. Thus, what is displayed in the text would be fully articulated as $\{\{p\}\,\{\neg p\}\}$; similarly for a number of later examples.

8. I believe that the functional interpretation also provides the proper mechanism for the examples in Geach 1969 such as (i) (p. 121).

(i) The one woman whom every true Englishman honors above all other women is his mother.

9. Examples like (66) are due to Engdahl (1986); (65) is modeled after an example in Collins 1992.

10. See Kroch 1989, Cinque 1990, and Szabolcsi and Zwarts 1990 for a discussion of ambiguities of this type.

References

Barss, A. 1990. Optional movement, absorption, and the interpretation of WH-in-situ. Paper presented at NELS 21, Université du Québec à Montréal. Ms., University of Arizona.

Barwise, J., and R. Cooper. 1981. Generalized quantifiers and natural language. *Linguistics and Philosophy* 4.2: 159–219.

Belnap, N. 1963. *An analysis of questions: Preliminary report.* Technical Memorandum 7 1287 1000/00, System Development Corporation, Santa Monica, Calif.

Belnap, N. 1969. Questions: Their presuppositions, and how they can fail to arise. In *The logical way of doing things*, ed. K. Lambert, 23–38. New Haven, Conn.: Yale University Press.

Belnap, N. 1982. Questions and answers in Montague Grammar. In *Processes, beliefs, and questions*, ed. S. Peters and E. Saarinen, 165–98. Dordrecht: Reidel.

Belnap, N., and T. Steel. 1976. *The logic of questions and answers.* New Haven, Conn.: Yale University Press.

Berman, S. 1989. The analysis of quantificational variability in indirect questions. Ms., University of Massachusetts, Amherst.

Bromberger, S. 1966. Questions. *The Journal of Philosophy* 63: 597–606.

Chierchia, G. 1991. Functional WH and weak crossover. In *Proceedings of the Tenth West Coast Conference on Formal Linguistics*, 75–91. Stanford Linguistics Association, Stanford University, Stanford, Calif.

Cinque, G. 1990. *Types of $\overline{A}$-dependencies.* Cambridge, Mass.: MIT Press.

Collins, C. 1992. A note on quantifying into questions and functional readings. Ms., MIT.

Davidson, D. 1979. Moods and performances. In *Meaning and use*, ed. A. Margalit, 9–20. Dordrecht: Reidel. Reprinted in D. Davidson, *Inquiries into truth and interpretation*, 109–21. Oxford: Oxford University Press (1984).

Engdahl, E. 1986. *Constituent questions*. Dordrecht: Reidel.

Geach, P. 1969. Quine's syntactical insights. *Synthese* 19.1/2. Reprinted in P. Geach, *Logic matters*, 115–27. Oxford: Basil Blackwell (1972).

Groenendijk, J., and M. Stokhof. 1984. Studies on the semantics of questions and the pragmatics of answers. Doctoral dissertation, University of Amsterdam.

Groenendijk, J., and M. Stokhof. 1989. Type-shifting rules and the semantics of interrogatives. In *Properties, types, and meaning*. Vol. II: *Semantic issues*, ed. G. Chierchia et al., 21–68. Dordrecht: Kluwer.

Hamblin, C. 1973. Questions in Montague English. *Foundations of Language* 10:41–53. Reprinted in *Montague Grammar*, ed. B. Partee, 247–59. New York: Academic Press (1976).

Higginbotham, J., and R. May. 1978. A general theory of crossing coreference. *CUNYForum: Proceedings of NELS IX*, 328–36. Graduate Center of the City University, New York.

Higginbotham, J., and R. May. 1981. Questions, quantifiers, and crossing. *The Linguistic Review* 1:41–80.

Higginbotham, J. 1991a. Either/or. Forthcoming in *Proceedings of NELS 21*.

Higginbotham, J. 1991b. Interrogatives I. In *MIT working papers in linguistics* 15, 47–76. Department of Linguistics and Philosophy, MIT.

Hintikka, J. 1976. *The semantics of questions and the questions of semantics*. Acta Philosophica Fennica 28, 4. Amsterdam: North-Holland.

Hornsby, J. 1986. A note on non-indicatives. *Mind* 95:92–99.

Karttunen, L. 1977. The syntax and semantics of questions. *Linguistics and Philosophy* 1:3–44.

Kroch, A. 1989. "Long" WH-movement and referentiality. Ms., University of Pennsylvania.

Ladusaw, W. 1983. Logical Form and conditions on grammaticality. *Linguistics and Philosophy* 6:373–92.

Lahiri, U. 1990. Questions, answers, annd selection. Ms., MIT.

Lahiri, U. 1992. Embedded interrogatives and the predicates that embed them. Doctoral dissertation, MIT.

Levi, I. 1967. *Gambling with truth*. New York: Alfred E. Knopf.

Lewis, D. 1972. General semantics. In *Semantics of natural language*, ed. D. Davidson and G. Harman, 169–218. Dordrecht: Reidel.

May, R. 1985. *Logical Form: Its structure and derivation.* Cambridge, Mass.: MIT Press.

May, R. 1989. Interpreting Logical Form. *Linguistics and Philosophy* 12:387–435.

Pesetsky, D. 1982. Paths and categories. Doctoral dissertation, MIT.

Reinhart, T. 1992. Interpreting WH-in-situ. Ms., Tel Aviv University.

Segal, G. 1988. In the mood for a semantic theory. Ms., King's College, London.

Szabolcsi, A., and F. Zwarts. 1990. Semantic properties of composed functions and the distribution of WH-phrases. In *Proceedings of the Seventh Amsterdam Colloquium*, ed. M. Stokhof and L. Torenvliet, 529–54. Institute for Language, Logic, and Information, University of Amsterdam.

Chapter 6

Triggering Science-Forming Capacity through Linguistic Inquiry	Maya Honda and Wayne O'Neil

In this paper we discuss curriculum development in science education that we have been doing for the past several years in two somewhat different educational settings. The goal of our work is to activate the science-forming capacity available to us all by virtue of our very nature (see section 3), or as Sylvain Bromberger (1992:1–2) has so elegantly written:

> We start out with little prior information about [the] world, but we are endowed with the ability to come to know that there are things about it that we don't know, that is, with the ability to formulate and to entertain questions whose answers we know we do not know. It is an enormously complex ability derived from many auxiliary abilities. And it induces the wish to know the answer to some of these questions. Scientific research represents our most reasonable and responsible way of trying to satisfy that wish.

For reasons given in some detail below, we believe that the questions that arise in linguistic inquiry represent a reasonable way to induce in students the wish to know the answers to some of their questions, and thus to introduce them to scientific research.

1 Background

Over a four-year period (1984–1988), we wrote, piloted, and tested a set of linguistics lessons, part of a four-week unit on the nature of scientific inquiry meant to replace the standard unit introducing junior high school students to general notions of scientific method. The unit—in various forms, but always with a linguistics component—was developed during this period by a team of secondary school science teachers and university people. The linguistics component was widely tried out and continually revised in after-school sessions with small groups of students and finally put to the test in regular science classes at the seventh- through twelfth-grade levels in Cambridge, Newton, and Watertown, Massachusetts, with the emphasis being on its use in the seventh grade, where formal science education normally begins in the school curriculum in the United States. We (together with Carol Chomsky and Risa Evans of the Harvard Graduate School of Education, in the earlier and later stages of the work, respectively) were responsible for the linguistics part of the unit; for choosing and piloting linguistics problems in after-school sessions; for formulating and writing lesson plans and trying them out in real time; for working with teachers in their classrooms as they used the lessons; and for assessing the effects of the lessons (see Carey et al. 1986, 1989, Chomsky et al. 1985).

This linguistic work was done in a corner of the Harvard Graduate School of Education's Educational Technology Center, the U.S. Office of Educational Research and Improvement–supported center in which questions about the appropriate school uses of technology were to be answered and in which questions about improving math and science education were partially addressed. "In a corner" of the Educational Technology Center, because our work was not—strictly speaking—what the Center was about; for we ran, and continue to run, a decidedly low-tech enterprise, one requiring only paper, pencil, chalk, blackboard, and minds (both the teachers' and the students').

This project was different from other such linguistics programs that we have been involved in, or that we know about, because we were working with secondary school science teachers and in the science curriculum, and not with teachers of English or language arts, the place in the school curriculum that linguistics had tried to move into beginning in the 1950s— with only limited success. See, for example, the linguistics component of the Oregon Curriculum Study Project materials that O'Neil initiated, developed, and contributed to in the mid-1960s (Kitzhaber 1968).

In addition to Kitzhaber 1968, English-based curricular materials in which linguistic inquiry for the primary and secondary school curriculum has been proposed and/or developed have appeared at several times during the past three decades (see, for example, O'Neil 1969, Keyser 1970, and Fabb 1985).

Analogous, non-English-based school materials have been tried out among desert aboriginal communities in central Australia and among American Indian communities in the southwestern and midwestern United States (see, for example, Hale 1975, White Eagle 1983). This work exploited the low-cost benefits of linguistics-based science curriculums in third-world and marginalized communities, where the expense of equipping and maintaining laboratories is a significant constraint on science education—a matter not to be overlooked at less well endowed, first-world schools and colleges during this time of extreme academic recession.

In these two radically different settings, results of the preliminary studies were highly encouraging. As discussed below and in Chomsky et al. 1985, the classroom trials were quite successful. Classroom observations showed that students generally grasped the problems, had no trouble generating the relevant data, and were able to make the necessary linguistic judgments easily. They formulated relevant questions, came up with tentative answers, and looked for counterexamples, revising their hypotheses as needed. With help and through discussion, they worked out principles that amounted to serious explanations of the data.

The aboriginal and native American Indian experiments were likewise very encouraging, although measures are not yet available to document success in these projects.

Although we have not used these linguistics materials in the schools since 1988, our interest in the issues that they raise and the problems that they are aimed at continues, but our work has been redirected in the following way: If one understands that the way teachers are educated is central to advancing science education, why not try to affect teacher preparation? In a small way we are now doing that at Wheelock College in Boston, a major regional center for preparing early childhood and elementary school teachers. There, in a class we teach on bilingualism and language acquisition, we use lesson plans similar to those described here in the linguistic education of our students. Although the central goal of this instruction is to teach the students something about the knowledge that is acquired in both first and second language acquisition through an examination of their tacit knowledge of their own languages, another goal is to overcome their ignorance and fear of the scientific style. In the next year or so we hope to be able to present a linguistics course at Wheelock College that will satisfy in part the undergraduate science distribution requirement at that institution.[1]

Thus, beginning in 1990, our new work became directed toward the undergraduate college curriculum, in particular toward students who are being educated to work as teachers in primary schools. In this setting we plan to incorporate a certain amount of basic mathematical logic into the work as well. In what follows we discuss our work, drawing primarily from our experience in the schools (the most controlled setting in which we have worked), as well as from our more recent experience at Wheelock College.

2   The Problem(s)

Our work is meant to address a general and well-documented problem in the scientific education of the greater part of the school-age population of the United States: after years of sitting in science and mathematics classrooms or avoiding these experiences as much as possible, students have little or no conceptual grasp or appreciation of the science and mathematics enterprises. Moreover, as presently constructed, the introductory science and mathematics courses available to first- and second-year college undergraduates generally do little to change their narrow, school-bred notion that science is simply a fixed body of knowledge given by authority and that mathematics is a set of algorithms for cranking out the right answers.

This problem is further compounded at colleges like Wheelock whose student populations are often overwhelmingly female and consequently both underprepared in science and mathematics and fearful of these subjects, and thus lacking in intellectual confidence. Women's loss of interest in mathematics and science and their loss of confidence in their ability to do mathematics or science are largely shaped by negative early school experience (American Association of University Women (AAUW) 1991, 1992). The undergraduate education of prospective teachers of young children—the majority of whom are women—must find ways to foster positive attitudes toward science and mathematics and must develop students' ability to work in these areas, for they will inevitably in turn influence their own students' early school impressions of and attitudes toward these subjects, especially as role models for their female students (see AAUW 1991 : 10–12).

The "crisis" in science and mathematics education, especially in the education of women, is well documented in studies and reports from numerous sources, including the AAUW, the National Science Foundation, the National Council of Teachers of Mathematics, the Mathematical Sciences Education Board (MSEB), the National Research Council, the American Association for the Advancement of Science, and the Massachusetts Institute of Technology (Latanision et al. 1991, 1992).

Comment on the crisis is ubiquitous; In a recent issue of *Science*, for example, the guest editorial is entitled "Science Education: Who Needs It"—the answer being that we all benefit/suffer from good/bad science education (Hackerman 1992 : 157). This view can easily be extended to mathematics education, for we all benefit/suffer from good/bad mathematics education as well.

However, little is done in schools or in teaching (as opposed to research) colleges and universities to actively engage students in scientific inquiry, to bring together in a serious way their study of the various sciences and branches of mathematics, or to build students' confidence in their ability to do science and mathematics.

Moving beyond these general and specific descriptions of the crisis, a number of proposals have been made for change in both mathematics and science teaching that emphasize intellectual challenge (e.g., MSEB 1990, National Science Teachers Association (NSTA) 1992).

Given its present direction and form, our work now aims to achieve the following educational goals:

• To develop in students, and in particular in future teachers of young children, an understanding of the scientific achievements in linguistics (as well as their limits) and of linguistically relevant branches of mathematics (logic and set theory).
• More importantly, to establish an intellectual climate in the classroom in which students can develop in themselves a scientific style of argumentation, or a deep appreciation of it at least, in linguistics, in related branches of mathematics, and in the connections among these fields.
• By meeting the first two goals, to help students build confidence in their ability to deal with unfamiliar problems in science, separating these from questions or mysteries that are not—at least for the moment—subject to rational inquiry.

3 Rationale

The novelty of our work is that it takes linguistics—the best understood of the cognitive sciences—as its domain of scientific inquiry, linking it in its currently developing form with the independently motivated study of mathematical logic so as to reveal the relationships between subjects in a way that is rare, but desirable, in the science curriculum. For connecting subjects up in a serious way will better lead students to a deep understanding and appreciation of scientific ideas and argumentation (see Eisner 1992, citing NSTA 1992).

This novelty derives from our belief—also novel—that a science education can only fruitfully and fairly build on the mind's science-forming capacity, taking that expression to refer to the idea that in making science, humans are natively endowed to do science as well as tightly constrained in their options and perhaps even in what they can make science about.[2]

We believe that these constraints are also at work in the core areas of what we refer to as "natural" mathematics: "the simplest mathematical ideas [that] are implied in the customary lines of thought of everyday life and [that] all sciences make use of" (Newman 1956:1747).

This view of the mind guides our curriculum development toward phenomena that are conceptually accessible to students, that is, those that not only challenge their already existing ideas, but for which possible explanations are also within their grasp. This view of the mind has also guided our pedagogy toward the Socratic, and toward cooperative teaching and learning.

As a matter of definition, all students speak at least one language natively and thus have tacit knowledge of a language. Their tacit knowledge of other languages ranges from native or near-native fluency in a second language to knowledge at various levels of second, third, *n*-th languages. Our linguistic work builds on this largely tacit knowledge in the belief that depth of scientific understanding of knowledge of language can begin to be reached through Socratic introspection and cooperative inquiry.

By virtue of their mathematics education and miseducation, however, students end up with more than a tacit knowledge of number, another faculty of human cognitive capacity (see Gelman 1978)—one that, on Chomsky's view, lay largely unused for most of the course of human evolution. Human beings have number because of what we are and where we are. It was "[Bertrand] Russell [who] once wrote that we would not have developed the concept of number had we lived on the sun. Perhaps [then] the opportunity to employ those faculties of mind that present us with a world of individual objects provides a triggering effect for the growth of the 'number faculty,' but beyond that it seems reasonable to suppose that this faculty is an intrinsic component of the human mind" (Chomsky 1980:38–39).

Thus, it is our view that like the linguistics curriculum, the related mathematics part of our curriculum will build on the tacit knowledge that students bring to these studies simply by virtue of their cognitive maturity. On this view, Aristotelian logic is then understood to be a representation of the way human beings ideally think; sets and numbers are the central concepts of intuitive mathematics; and "scientific method is simply," in the words of Randolph Bourne, "a sublimely well-ordered copy of our own best and most fruitful habits of thought" (cited in Fox 1985). In the same way, Euclidean geometry—a subject that would naturally parallel the course of study proposed here—makes sense of the three-dimensional space that our visual system presents us with, rather than the n-dimensional space (invisible to the mind's eye) that physicists argue for.

"Why linguistics in the science curriculum?" is, then, a question raised over and over again by the school and college people (teachers and students) that we work with.[3]

Since it is insufficient to answer this question simply by indicating the novel aspects of our work, we provide the following detailed and lengthy response.

First of all, linguistic inquiry meets the basic pedagogical principle of the proposed lessons: that the material be in some sense conceptually and readily accessible, and that the students (as well as the instructors) have a rich prior experience that will guide their inquiry more or less straight in an interesting fashion. From this perspective, linguistic inquiry appears to be a fairer way to appeal to the science-forming capacity than what usually goes on in the science classroom.[4]

In general, students are introduced to science in areas where their experience is impoverished and/or where their commonsense understanding is strikingly at odds with things in nature. Thus, very little inquiry is possible in class or laboratory encounters in which many of the problems of science seem—from a commonsense point of view—quite unproblematic to the students. Much of cosmology, for example, deals in questions that simply do not arise in the world of common sense: whether the sun rises and sets, or whether our sense that it does is artifactual; whether the earth is spherical or not; whether it is revolving and orbiting through space at tremendous speeds or not; whether the universe is expanding or contracting; whether the visible objects of the universe account for merely 1 percent of its mass or not; whether black holes exist or not, and if they do, whether they are best understood as two-dimensional or as four-dimensional objects; and so on. Or consider something more commonplace: "the so-called *Taylor instability*, whereby if you turn over a glass of water, the water will spill although the air pressure should be sufficient to hold it in the glass—as, in fact, it does if, to prevent the instability, you place a sheet of paper over the glass" (Rossi 1990:81). In our commonsense physics water does what it is supposed to do, and the fact that the water does *not* spill when the glass is covered with a sheet of paper is completely counterintuitive, having nothing to do with the porosity of water or atmospheric pressure, which are themselves not notions readily available to common sense.[5]

An examination of one's language, on the other hand, can immediately provide a set of problems and an area of inquiry that has certain advantages for students. For example, why is it not possible to contract *want to* to *wanna* in fast speech whenever—so to speak—you "wanna"? Simply consider the grammaticality contrast between the contracted forms in sentences (1a) and (1b), and the ambiguity of (1c) with respect to contraction, where "*" indicates grammatical deviance of some sort.

(1) a. Where do you *wanna* go?   ←   Where do you want to go?
    b. *Who do you *wanna* go?   ←   Who do you want to go?
    c. Who do you *wanna* visit?   ←?-   Who do you want to visit?

Apparent mysteries of this sort—in which the null hypothesis fails—are readily turned into questions, which can then yield answers of general interest and considerable depth. For further development of this and other examples, see section 4 and appendixes 1 and 2.

We have learned from our curriculum work at both the secondary and college levels that in linguistic inquiry, where there are few solid answers to offer them, students can come up with quite interesting hypotheses and come up with them rather quickly (see Chomsky et al. 1985).

Moreover, since scientific investigation is generally attempted in areas of experience where explanation is in conflict with students' commonsense notions or intuitive science (see, e.g., McCloskey 1983, Carey 1986), linguistics has a distinct advantage—for as far as we are able to understand it, there is no commonsense linguistics of any depth for linguistic theory to be in tension with, nothing like the commonsense mechanics, say, that undercuts a student's coming to terms with Newtonian mechanics.

On the other hand, although there does not appear to be a commonsense linguistics more complicated than the notion that a language is a list of words, any attempt to look at language in a scientific way is in tension with school grammar and other such sorts of language mythologizing not subject to scientific explanation: prescriptive notions about language use; the conviction that the real object of the study of grammar is writing, thus equating knowledge of language with writing and reading skills; the view that certain varieties of a language or certain languages are esthetically, logically, or in some way superior to others; and so on.

Second—another part of our rationale—students should come to know that science is not exhausted by the topics covered in their standard high school science textbooks or by the list of names of departments in a college's faculty of science. Science is a way of forming questions about the world we occupy and seeking their answers, though it is not simply that; nor is science problem solving—except derivatively. For it is only insofar as a measure of progress (in the way of depth of understanding as opposed to breadth of description) is made in accounting for some naturally bounded thing-in-nature that the rational pursuit of answers to coherent questions becomes science.

Third, linguistic inquiry ensures equal access to all students, for inquiry in this domain presents few barriers to people with physical handicaps, lends itself to cooperative inquiry by an entire classroom of students and/or by smaller subgroups, and is not on its surface gender-biased—of particular importance at overwhelmingly female institutions where prospective early childhood teachers are educated.

Also, in our experience, students who speak English as a second language are able to participate fully, relying on their native English-speaking classmates simply for grammaticality judgments, but not for scientific insights into the nature of language. For on the basis of very restricted triggering experiences, the science-forming capacity kicks in to do much of the work—often allowing quite interesting generalizations to be reached. Of course, linguistic inquiry need not be restricted either to English or to spoken language (as opposed to signed language), as it is in this initial stage of our work; in fact, the ideal situation would be to be able to take advantage of the linguistic diversity of a class of students to examine cross-linguistic, cross-dialectal, and cross-modular phenomena (see O'Neil 1991 for some discussion).

Since mathematics is not "concerned with the things we wish to discuss but rather with the way we wish to discuss them" (Newman 1956:1591–92), less demand is made on us to justify including set theory and logic in a linguistics course directly focused on scientific argumentation and its appreciation. However, our recent decision to include these branches of mathematics in the linguistics course has prompted some science educators to ask, "Why mathematics in a linguistics course?"

Our rationale for including mathematics is threefold.

First, together with number theory and the mathematics of three-dimensional visual space, we understand logic and sets to be the core of "natural," more-or-less accessible mathematics—accessible for many of the same reasons given above for linguistics.

Second, there are cognitive and evolutionary relationships between language and numbers to motivate this inclusion, namely, the fact that "human language has the extremely unusual, possibly unique, property of discrete infinity [the concept of adding one, indefinitely], and the same is true of the human number faculty..., [it being] essentially an 'abstraction' from human language, preserving the mechanism of discrete infinity and eliminating the other special features of language" (Chomsky 1988: 169).

Third—and most important—beyond this conceptual relationship between language and numbers, basic principles of set theory and logic can naturally be developed and directly linked to the linguistics course where relevant. For example, some aspects of the relationship between the structure of sentences and their meaning are naturally captured in set-theoretic terms. Consider the sentences in (2), in which only the definiteness of the subject noun phrases and their plurality vary. A natural and apparently sufficient way of expressing just the difference in meaning between universal and existential quantification (a function of whether a noun phrase is definite or indefinite), between plural and singular (cardinality of set intersection), as well as some of the constant aspects of the meaning of these sentences (predication as set inclusion and noun modification of a particular sort as set intersection), is shown in (2) (examples taken from Chomsky 1977:48–51).

(2) a. *The books we ordered arrived.* The intersection of the class of books B and the class of things we ordered O is included in the class of things that arrived A, taking the cardinality of the intersection B, O to be ≥ 2.

    b. *The book we ordered arrived.* The intersection of the class of books B and the class of things we ordered O is included in the class of things that arrived A, taking the cardinality of the intersection B, O to be $= 1$.

    c. *Some books we ordered arrived.* There exists a class of books K included in the intersection of the class of books B and the class of things we ordered O, which is itself included in the class of things that arrived A, taking the cardinality of K to be ≥ 2.

    d. *A book we ordered arrived.* There exists a class of books K included in the intersection of the class of books B and the class of things we ordered O, which is itself included in the class of things that arrived A, taking the cardinality of K to be $= 1$.

Complex relationships of this sort, between the syntactic structure of sentences and their meaning expressed in basic mathematical terms (through symbolic logic, numbers, and sets), can thus be one focus of a linguistic inquiry course and can also form one way of assessing the students' depth of understanding of one or another aspect of the material.

We turn next to a description and discussion of some of the materials that we have developed and their effect, the latter being largely based on our work in the schools.

4 Curriculum Construction

The linguistics lessons that we have developed, and that we continue to develop in our Wheelock College course, take a very simple form: we ask students to attend closely to apparently uncomplicated facts about the language they speak, in this case English (although, as suggested above, there is no doubt that similar lessons could be developed for any language). In our preliminary, after-school sessions, we tried a number of phenomena out to see if they "worked," by which we mean that the phenomena brought students to understand that there were questions about their linguistic world whose answers they thought they knew but then realized that they did not know, which realization "induce[d in them] the wish to know the answer to some of these questions" (Bromberger 1992: 1–2, once again). And we also mean that a certain depth of explanation of the phenomenon seemed possible as opposed to a merely descriptive organization of the data.

Thus, we rejected potentially interesting problems either because their solutions could not possibly reach beyond simple description in principle, or simply because of the limited classroom time available to us. For example, the problems that are raised by tag questions and yes-no questions (with their related *do*-support complication) led us to drop questions about these and related phenomena for the latter reason, and also because they appeared to be too dependent on traditional grammatical terminology that students did not know or did not want to learn and that can be—as mentioned above—in tension with linguistic inquiry (Chomsky et al. 1985: 57–62).

When finished, the linguistics materials will consist of sets of intricately related problems and some proposed solutions aimed toward building overt understanding of a general theory of linguistic knowledge, knowledge that is held tacitly by speakers of a language. The solutions to the problem sets will, and some presently do, go far beyond a simple discussion and evaluation of proposed solutions, covering as well topics in the acquisition of language (both first and second languages) and language use. With this in mind, we give a couple of brief examples of linguistics problems, one from syntax and another from phonology. The latter is now well worked out—both the problem and its solutions; the former is under development.

For example, a set of syntactic problems on reflexives could take off from data like those in (3). Examples (3a) and (3b) illustrate that reflexive pronouns in English cannot occur independently, but must have an antecedent from which they derive their reference; (3c) and (3d) show that this antecedent must stand in a certain structural relation to and must occur within a certain distance of the reflexive.

(3) a. *Herself left.
　　b. Emma likes herself.
　　c. *Herself likes Emma.
　　d. *Emma said that John likes herself.

In the problems, the students' task is to come up with the notion of a dependent item and to make some approach to the constraints on where reflexives must occur vis-à-vis their antecedents. This entails construction of a scientific theory of reflexive distribution (part of what is referred to in linguistics as the binding theory), including recognition of the phenomenon to be explained, data collection, data classification, and hypothesis formation. Students then test their hypotheses by looking for counterexamples, and revise the hypotheses until they account for the data in as parsimonious a way as possible and in a way that makes accurate predictions.

Another set of problems is organized around the phonology of the plural forms of regular nouns in English: the distribution of the sounds /s/, /z/, and /iz/ with respect to the phonological characteristics of the final segment of the singular noun (e.g., dog/z/ : cat/s/ : dish/iz/). See the immediately following discussion, the problem set in appendix 1 (in its present form intended to be the first problem that students deal with prior to beginning the linguistics course), and the problem set in appendix 2 (which can be used either to assess the students' ability to generalize from an account of plurals to one of past tense forms in English or to deepen their understanding of the connections among the phenomena involved).

Problems of the sort described here are meant to build tightly on one another, an approach that contrasts quite sharply with the disconnected presentation of material in the usual science or mathematics course at this level.

Thus, asking students to generalize hypotheses to account for related linguistic phenomena offers a way of evaluating their understanding of linguistic inquiry. For example, from their hypothesis about the syntax of reflexives, students can be asked to begin to make sense of the somewhat parallel data from the distribution of reciprocal pronouns, as in (4).

(4) a. *Each other* left.
   b. *Emma and Alex* like *each other*.
   c. *Each other* likes *Emma and Alex*.
   d. *Emma and Alex* said that John likes *each other*.

And—looking forward to successfully having incorporated logic and set theory into our lessons—in evaluating the mathematics of the course, we will wish to know if the students can, for example, use their understanding of set theory and symbolic logic to capture certain essential aspects of the meaning of sentences as well as to formalize their linguistic hypotheses.

Initially then, and as a result of our after-school work at the secondary level, we settled on two phenomena that were themselves unrelated but each of which was itself interestingly related to other phenomena. On the basis of these two, we aimed to formulate coherent questions and to move toward tentative answers. These are the phenomena:

• The morphophonology of the plural forms of regular nouns: the distribution of /s/, /z/, and /iz/ with respect to the phonological characteristics of the final segment of the singular noun (e.g., *dog*/z/ : *cat*/s/ : *dish*/iz/).
• Certain constraints on contraction: the failure of *wanna*-contraction over a *wh*-trace and the blocking of *is*-contraction before a gap or trace (e.g., the ungrammaticality of **Who do you wanna go?* and **I wonder where Emma's today*, **Emma's tall and Peter's too*, etc., vs. *Where do you wanna go?* and *I wonder when Emma's at home, Emma's tall and so's Peter*, etc.).

Answering the questions that arose once the students dug into the data enough to uncover the apparent mysteries involved meant *their* inventing a certain amount of terminology as needed, though in the lesson plans that were finally codified, more-or-less standard terminology (e.g., "voiced") was fastened on—one of the results of reducing freewheeling ideas to lesson plans to be used by real teachers with real students in real schools, in recognition of the constraints of a standard educational system (Honda and O'Neil 1988).

As suggested above, simple and natural extensions of the tentative answers to related questions offer a way of evaluating the students' understanding of the material. For example, once having collectively worked through to a solution of the morphophonology of plural forms of regular nouns, we want to know whether students individually can figure out how the regular past tense morphophonology of verbs works. And having come up with an explanation for the constraints on *wanna*-contraction and *is*-contraction, can students generalize their knowledge of the phenomena to account for the constraint on *hafta*-contraction (see section 5)?

So starting with apparent mysteries (e.g., the fact that you really can't say *wanna* whenever you wanna), turning them into questions, and proceeding to offer tentative answers for these questions, we hoped to show that students working together can build a theory as they go—a theory that will undergo constant revision in the course of study as its empirical consequences become more detailed. Moreover, it is only by staying with a problem and pushing it through to some sort of resolution—a way of proceeding that is quite different from if not directly opposed to the helter-skelter pace of typical science lessons—that work of this sort can be done.

5   Curriculum Trial: E/Affect

In our pilot studies in the schools, we worked after hours with small groups (generally four or five students). Following a relaxed Socratic method, we worked through problems at whatever pace seemed appropriate: moving quickly when answers came easily, spending more time when phenomena demanded more of the students' attention. For example, in one hour-long session, a group of seventh graders worked through the plural formation problem from start to finish, beginning with a spelling rule ("Add -*s, -es, -ies*"), moving to an interim phonological account ("Add an /s/ or /z/ or /iz/ depending on how the word ends"), and eventually arriving at a set of ordered rules in which "how the [singular] word ends" was precisely specified. Along the way, they constructed the notion "sibilant," calling such sounds "sorta-like-*s*," and they discovered "voice-box vibration," or the contrast between what one student called "sharp, less vibrant" sounds and voiced sounds.

With a group of ninth graders, however, the discussion of plural formation extended into two sessions as students—on their own initiative—pursued the most parsimonious rule. They revised an interim hypothesis to refer to the voicing of the appropriate plural ending, as well as to the voicing of the final sound of the singular noun. Much to our surprise, one of the students reinvented what used to be called alpha rules in phonology (α a variable ranging over the values " $+$ " and " $-$ ") by collapsing two statements about when to add /s/ and /z/ into a simpler statement, "Keep

[the] end sound going," or as the group later rephrased it, "Continue the voicebox vibration of the last sound." An argument over whether to label the rule an "*s*-sound rule" or an "end-sound rule" was resolved in favor of the latter during a third session when these ninth graders worked through regular past tense formation and noted the similarity of their solution to the one they had constructed for the plural. One of the students visualized a diagram that abstracted the phenomenon of voicing assimilation from the two accounts for the past tense and the plural, and made the proposal in (5).

(5) Put this hypothesis in a diagram. You could have a bigger circle being "continue the voicebox vibration of the last sound," and then off of it you could have the S-ending, D-ending, etc., etc., etc.

Our pilot studies indicated the farthest reaches of "success" in engaging students in scientific inquiry into their own language. "Freewheeling" and "open-ended" accurately describe the nature of the pilot study sessions. In part, this is one sort of success: pursuing data and students' ideas about data in a variety of ways in order to construct an explanation of a phenomenon.

Another sort of success that came out of these pilot sessions involved the students' teaching us better ways of presenting the material as they worked it out among themselves. For example, when one student was having difficulty distinguishing word-final /s/ and /z/, as in *rock* and *bugs*, another student suggested that she put the words in a phrase with a vowel following (e.g., *rocks on the floor* vs. *bugs on the floor*) in order to bring out the voicing contrast to its fullest, intuitively recognizing that in citation form the /z/ of *bugs* does shade off into /s/ as the voice shuts down. This was a lesson for us on how to better help the students deal with their observations, one that we later built into the lesson plans.

Unconstrained by long-term curriculum demands, by large classes, or by the daily demands of a forty-five minute class period, with time taken for attendance and by intermittent announcements over the loudspeaker system—the real conditions of the school day—we were free in these after-school sessions to engage students in framing problems on the basis of puzzling over observations, gathering relevant data, organizing and abstracting from the data, learning, naming, and using linguistic concepts to account for data, formulating hypotheses, testing them by first imagining what a counterexample would look like and then searching for disconfirming evidence, and—if necessary—reformulating or rejecting hypotheses.

And the questions did indeed engage students. In both our pilot studies and regular classroom sessions, the teachers we worked with were impressed by the eagerness with which their students pursued solutions to the problems. One seventh-grade science teacher who observed a pilot session noted with some surprise the active participation of two students neither of whom did well in school. When asked to evaluate the linguistics sessions, one of these students said, "It's not really hard, but it makes you think."

Another measure of success was the new intellectual confidence that the students showed as they moved from the linguistics lessons to other subjects in the science curriculum. For example, after completing the linguistics lessons in regular seventh-grade science classes, students began a new unit on weight and density. The science teacher noted that the seventh graders used the methods of inquiry and the relevant terminology of the linguistics lessons. When asked to record their observations of things that sink and things that float, several students noticed there was no space available on their worksheets for their hypotheses. Students spontaneously suggested the need to make a hypothesis, test it, and then try to "find something that doesn't follow our hypothesis"—that is, a counterexample.

The transition to working with whole classes of students required us to consider the demands of and on classroom teachers as well as students. For us, an important question was whether this transition could be made while preserving the intellectual focus of the pilot-study sessions. The answer to this question is a qualified yes, largely because of the difficulties of fully involving the regular classroom teachers, who felt burdened by teaching yet another subject about which they knew very little and by being asked to adopt an unorthodox and thus—for them—uncomfortable teaching style. And so—at the risk of undercutting the more open classroom style that we wanted to cultivate—the need arose for us to provide carefully worked out lesson plans with standardized terminology, a set of likely hypotheses, worksheets to be done in class and for homework, and a written test to evaluate students.

Even in the regular classes, however, students were easily engaged in puzzling over linguistic phenomena, phenomena so familiar that they seemed initially unproblematic. For example, students were introduced to plural formation via the fiction of a Martian scientist who is learning English and who wants to make plurals so that she sounds like an ordinary English-speaking person (see appendix 1). In response to the question of what the Martian scientist must discover about how plurals are formed in speech, most students usually stated a standard spelling rule. And when *wanna-* and *is*-contraction were first introduced, students agreed that "everyone slurs words 'cause it's easier." Just as students shared the same schooled "answer" to questions about plural noun formation, so they also shared a certain schooled confusion about contraction (Is it correct? If so, when is it correct? etc.) as well as the naive belief that, as one student said, "You can say *wanna* whenever you wanna."

Nor were the teachers initially any more at ease with the material. For example, one teacher denied ever being so sloppy as to say *wanna*, thus setting herself up for her *wanna*'s to be successfully hunted down by her students. Others rejected sentences like (6)

(6) Who do you wanna see?

because of its violation of the *who* ~ *whom* distinction.

It requires little effort to reveal the shortcomings of these initial normative notions or naive conceptions of the phenomena under consideration, and thus to motivate the real questions and the pursuit of their answers. And given arrays of data, students were generally able to give clear judgments about the acceptability of forms. Here we found that the seventh graders were quicker and surer of their judgments, with entire classes booing or shouting out, "No way!" in response to an unacceptable form. On the other hand, the eleventh- and twelfth-grade students were very hesitant when faced with the linguist's query, "Does this sound okay? What's your gut reaction?" This is likely due to schooling—that is, to their having learned prescriptive rules that call into question ordinary patterns of language use. As one twelfth grader said, "If you're in a business atmosphere, you're not gonna use the word *wanna*."

But there is another effect of schooling that might explain the older students' hesitancy: their judgments are rarely sought or valued, and are certainly never an input to inquiry. And so they were afraid and unsure in the face of our questions, as if they were being set up for a trick or potential embarrassment. For example, when we interviewed the older students after completing the unit, one student complained that we knew all along what the answer was, and rather than giving it to them in the way they were used to, we had made them work for it. Another student believed that we were using the class to get answers to problems that we couldn't solve ourselves in order to become rich and famous, a standard suspicion that dogs anthropologists in the field. In these respects, the college students we have worked with differ not at all from the high school students, for the former are the descendants of the latter, the difference being that they have suffered even longer in the standard educational system.

Although discussion was more constrained by the fact of the lesson plans, working with regular classes of students had certain advantages. For one, more people are likely to come up with more ideas. Under certain conditions, this can be a difficulty as well. For example, on the way to an explanation of the constraint on *wanna*-contraction in terms of its being blocked by a *wh*-trace falling between *want* and *to*, two seventh-grade students came up with the beginnings of a simple equi-NP solution (7).

(7) When someone is talking to you about yourself, it is OK
     [to contract]. When someone is talking to you about someone else,
     it is not OK [to contract].

For they had noticed that the question (8),

(8) Where do you wanna go? (← Where do you want to go?)

for example, can be answered with something like (9),

(9) I wanna go to Club Med.

in which the "wanter" and the "goer" are the same, but that the ungrammatical (10)

(10) Who do you *wanna go? (← Who do you want to go?)

can only be answered with something like (11),

(11) I want Jim to go.

in which the "wanter" is different from the "goer." Since the lesson plans had not foreseen their entirely reasonable hypothesis—one that did not use the notion "*wh*-trace," but at this early stage of discussion was perfectly equivalent in its coverage of the data to an account based on traces —the science teacher dismissed it, declaring that it was "overly complicated." And by not running the students' hypothesis through, the teacher clearly had not gotten the point of the enterprise: that to teach inquiry is to engage in inquiry. Thus, a perfect opportunity for trying to decide between two seemingly equivalent explanations was lost. We had hoped that providing a set of options would increase the teacher's confidence in dealing with unfamiliar material, but instead, the lesson plans led the teacher to think that there was in fact a closed set of possible answers for quite open-ended questions. By our creating lesson plans that met the teacher's needs, the teacher was led to not meeting the students' needs.

There is the potential for a similar sort of problem to arise in the evaluation of individual students. For example, we developed the test item in (12) to assess students' understanding of the contraction phenomena.[6]

(12) The Martian scientist hears two students having the following conversation:

Student A: Where do you *have to* go tonight?
Student B: What?
Student A: I said, Where do you *hafta* go tonight?
Student B: Oh, I *hafta* go to the mall tonight.

The Martian scientist discovers *hafta*-contraction. It seems to her that you can always contract *have to* to *hafta*. The next day she goes into a sub shop and she asks the following question:

*What kinds of subs do you *hafta* go?

The person at the counter says, "You must be a Martian because an ordinary speaker of English wouldn't say that! That sounds really weird. You should say,

What kinds of subs do you *have to* go?"

Write a hypothesis that explains why the Martian scientist cannot contract *have to* to *hafta* in sentences like this one. Give examples that show how your hypothesis works.

Since the lessons focused on the role of *wh*-traces in accounting for *wanna*-contraction and *is*-contraction, we expected the students to make use of this notion to account for *hafta*-contraction. And indeed, many students did. For example, one seventh grader wrote the answer shown in (13).

(13) She can't contract *have* and *to* if there is a word or reference point [i.e., a *wh*-trace, represented as ·] in between *have* and *to*. Otherwise it's OK.

Ex. 1—Where do you have to go · tonight?
Ex. 2—What kinds of subs do you have · to go?

Given the thrust of the lessons, this answer was the "correct" one. However, other students gave semantically based accounts. For example, an eleventh-grade student wrote the answer in (14).

(14) When *have* means possession, you can't contract it in these sentences.

As with the equi-NP solution offered for *wanna*-contraction, this student's semantically based account is equivalent to the syntactic one, given the data presented.

Another seventh grader gave an answer almost identical to (13), but with the examples in (15).

(15) Do you have *a person* to go to the store? Do you have *dogs* to sell?

And when asked in an interview to explain these examples, the student said,

(16) Both of them have a word in between them so you can't contract them 'cause it wouldn't sound right. If I could it would sound like, Do you hafta a person to go to the store? Do you hafta dogs to sell? And it wouldn't sound right to an ordinary person.

The student also showed the interviewer how the *wh*-trace blocked contraction in the question, *What kinds of subs do you have to go?* However, when asked to explain when contraction *is* possible, this same student gave the semantically based account in (17).

(17) You *can* contract it ... when you're talking about what you do, what you hafta do—what you *must* do. And it's OK to say it if you're saying something like, I hafta go to the store. I hafta get that book. I hafta get that dress. ... What kinds of subs do you hafta go! Well, you can't say it there because you're talking about ... what somebody *has*. And—yeah, what somebody has.

This student apparently had two explanations of *hafta*-contraction in mind. What should have been done—a step not taken in the context of the posttest interview—was to push the student to try to choose between the two by thinking through what counterexamples to the hypotheses would look like and by then trying to expand the set of data to include such counterexamples as those given in (18), say, in which *have to* has the meaning 'must', but where contraction is not always possible.

(18) a. I have only to ask and I get what I want.
     b. He hadda go home yesterday, and he hasta go home today, but yet I don't mind his/him having to go home all the time.

As with the lesson plans, it is difficult to anticipate all answers consistent with the data, nor, as we found, is it desirable—even on a test. For this closes off opportunities to fully develop inquiry.

6 Conclusion

There are two ways to deal with problems of the sort raised immediately above. The classic way is to try to build teacher-proof materials that provide detailed roadmaps covering every possible contingency. This apparently simple solution is demeaning of teachers and unrealistic; for when the material is easily "accessible" and its explanations relatively open, there is the strong possibility of a student's coming up with a reasonable alternative hypothesis at any time.

The right thing to do, and the hard thing, is to educate teachers to the scientific style. The problems that we encountered in the science classroom had little to do with linguistics or with the students, and very much to do with the fact that the science teachers were not themselves comfortable pursuing rational inquiry and taking the classroom risks that this involves: participating *with* students in the scientific enterprise, respecting the students' ideas, questioning their own, and admitting the limits of their own understanding, a matter to which we have now begun to turn our attention. But that brings us to the other, unfinished part of our story, one that we will not be able to tell until our work at Wheelock College has developed beyond its present, formative stages.

Appendix 1: Plural Formation

A scientist from Mars has just arrived in the Boston area. The Martian scientist is learning to speak English, and she wants very much to sound like an ordinary speaker of English. Right now, the Martian scientist is having problems making plurals. *Plurals* are used when we talk about more than one of something. For example, the plural of cat is cats, and the plural of day is days. The Martian scientist does not know how to pronounce plurals correctly.

1. The Martian scientist listened carefully to English speakers' pronunciation of some plurals. She noticed that the plural endings sounded like the last sound in the word buzz. For example, say the following sentences aloud. Concentrate on the sound of the plural endings of the underlined words.

There are bugs on this plant.
The pears are rotten.
There are two birds in the sky.

On the basis of such data, the Martian scientist made up a simple hypothesis: *Add a Z sound to a word to make it plural.* If the Martian scientist follows this hypothesis to make plurals for the words below (and similar words), will she sound like us? Why or why not?

pig   rat   judge   rock
lunch   cloud   shape   star

2. The Martian scientist heard someone say the sentences shown below, and noticed differences in the way the plural endings of the underlined words sound. Say the sentences aloud. Concentrate on how the plural endings of the underlined words sound.

All of the spoons and cups and dishes are on the table.
There are goats and horses and cows on the farm.

Some of the plural endings sound the same. Which of the underlined words have plural endings that sound the same?
3. Say the plurals for the following words aloud. Listen to how the plural endings sound.

graph   myth   wish   lunch   rock   shape
rib   room   snake   star   tree   dove
cloud   law   kiss   watch   lie   breeze
box   bus   rat   bell   judge   pig
toe   bush   hen   fuse   day   crew

Put the words into groups according to how their plural endings sound.
4. Look at your answers to problems #2 and #3. Think about what your work shows about how we make plurals. Formulate a simple hypothesis that will help the Martian scientist say plurals so that she sounds like any ordinary speaker of English. (Hint: Say the words in each group without adding their plural endings. Listen to the final sound of each word.)
5. If the Martian scientist follows your hypothesis, will she be able to make plurals that sound "right"? Why or why not?

Appendix 2:   Past Tense Formation

The Martian scientist has come to understand many things about the English language. But now she is having problems making the simple past tense for words. The *simple past tense* is used when we talk about something that has already happened. For example, the simple past tense of kick is kicked, and the simple past tense of smile is smiled. The Martian scientist does not know how to form the simple past tense.

1. The Martian scientist listened carefully to English speakers' pronunciation of past tense forms, and heard the sentences shown below. She noticed differences in the way the past tense endings of the words sound. Say the sentences to yourself. Concentrate on the sound of the past tense endings of the words.

He cried and stomped his feet, and sounded awfully upset.
She jumped up, climbed a tree, and waited at the top.

First put the underlined words into groups according to the sound of their past tense endings. Then think of a way to write the *sound* of the past tense endings, and label the groups.

2. Say the simple past tense of the following words to yourself. Listen to how the past tense endings sound.

walk   rob   kiss   knead
shout   flip   treat   laugh
play   raid   buzz   hug

Put these words into groups according to how their past tense endings sound.

3. Look at your answers to #1 and #2. Think about what the data show about how we make the simple past tense. Formulate a hypothesis that will help the Martian scientist say the past tense of words so that she sounds like a native speaker of English. (Hint: Think of how the words in each group sound without their past tense endings.)

4. If the Martian scientist uses your hypothesis, will she be able to pronounce the past tense of words so that she sounds just like a native speaker of English? Why or why not?

Notes

This paper began as our presentation to the January 1991 Linguistic Society of America Meeting workshop entitled "Linguistics in the School Curriculum," the workshop itself leading to the Society's establishing a Committee on Linguistics in the School Curriculum. Then in April 1991, at a New York Academy of Sciences workshop on historical linguistics, O'Neil's remark that a lot of traditional beliefs and current foolishness about language are a result of a general low level of linguistic literacy resulted in our 23 September 1991 colloquium at the Academy: "Constructing and Evaluating Theories Using Linguistics in the School Science Curriculum," an expanded version of which (Honda and O'Neil, to appear) will be published in Otero, in press. The present paper is a much expanded and somewhat differently revised version of the Academy presentation, the result of our working with, adapting, and expanding these same materials and ideas for a course on bilingualism and language acquisition at Wheelock College (Boston).

Some of the material in this paper is taken from "Triggering Scientific Thinking through Linguistic Inquiry" (M. Kamii and W. O'Neil, proposed Co-Directors), a proposal recently submitted to the Undergraduate Curriculum and Course Development unit of the National Science Foundation. For their comments and help in preparing the proposal and thus this paper as well (at least in part), we wish to thank S. Glick, M. Kamii, and P. Willott, all of Wheelock College. They are, of course, not responsible for the material in its present setting.

1. Another reason for trying to trigger the Wheelock students' science-forming capacity through linguistic inquiry follows from the fact that at the College, human development majors account for approximately 80 percent of the undergraduate liberal arts majors; thus, some understanding of linguistics as well as of first and second language acquisition is necessary to their proper education and preparation for teaching young children, in particular for the large Life Span Development subset of these majors.

We have also used the general approach developed in these lessons in our ongoing work (1985–) with Nicaraguan-English-speaking teachers in that country's bilingual-bicultural education program, mainly as a way of having teachers understand and appreciate the integrity of the variety of English they speak (see O'Neil 1991).

2. For discussion of the notion "science-forming capacity" (Peirce's "abduction," more or less), see Peirce 1957, Chomsky 1968:78–79, 1980:139–40, 1988:156–59, O'Neil 1990. For the possible relevance of this notion to science education, see Preece 1984 and Sebastià 1989; for an opposing, Piagetian view, see Gil-Perez and Carrascosa 1990.

3. We do not address the prior question of "Why science education?" since its answers are many and various. Note, however, that we do not subscribe to the notion that a science education is necessary in the late 20th century so that a citizenry can vote in an informed way on issues that are increasingly scientific in nature; that more and more the demands of the jobs available in this country are also scientific in nature; and so on. For in a democracy of the type that prevails in the United States and increasingly in the rest of the world, a citizenry is not offered the opportunity of making any decisions of significance and certainly not decisions of a scientific or technical nature. And the cant that a good science education is going to lead to a good job is simply a way to cover up the extreme social and economic disarray that the United States finds itself in.

If anything, a science education conducted in the way we envision it would undercut the scientism that exists in the society by bringing students to an understanding of the nature of scientific explanations: their limits and tentativeness, and not simply their elegance and beauty.

For a discussion of "why" questions, of some of the linguistic and interpretive problems they raise, and of questions in the philosophy of science central to our work, see Bromberger 1987, reprinted in Bromberger 1992 along with other essays relevant to our work.

4. Another aspect of the physical world that somewhat parallels linguistics in this respect is the explanation of why some things float and others sink. Together with other workers at Harvard's Educational Technology Center, we also developed a

low-tech floating-sinking part for the unit, lessons that played off of students' beliefs in the importance of weight to the phenomenon and subsequently pushed this along to a weight-for-size formulation of the notion "density."

5. For some discussion of the sorts of questions about water that continue to baffle scientists, see Amato 1992.

6. About the nature of the testing that we did: the high school students easily recognized that the multiple choice format that they were used to was not relevant. For example, we noted the interchange in (i).

(i) Student A: Is this a multiple choice test?
Student B: It couldn't be—that wouldn't make sense for the stuff we've been doing.

References

Amato, I. 1992. A new blueprint for water's architecture. *Science* 246 (26 June): 1764.

American Association of University Women. 1991. *The executive summary: Short-changing girls, shortchanging America.* Washington, D.C.: AAUW.

American Association of University Women. 1992. *The AAUW report: How schools shortchange girls.* Washington, D.C.: AAUW.

Bromberger, S. 1987. What we don't know when we don't know why. In *Scientific inquiry in philosophical perspective*, ed. N. Rescher. Lanham, Md.: The University Press of America. (Reprinted in Bromberger 1992.)

Bromberger, S. 1992. *On what we know we don't know: Explanation, theory, linguistics, and how questions shape them.* Chicago: University of Chicago Press, and Stanford, Calif.: Center for Study of Language and Information.

Carey, S. 1986. Cognitive science and science education. *American Psychologist* 41.10:1123–30.

Carey, S., R. Evans, M. Honda, E. Jay, and C. Unger. 1989. "An experiment is when you try it and see if it works": A study of grade 7 students' understanding of the construction of scientific knowledge. *International Journal of Science Education* 11:514–29.

Carey, S., M. Honda, E. Jay, W. O'Neil, and C. Unger. 1986. *What junior high school students do, can, and should know about the nature of science.* Educational Technology Center Technical Report 86-11, Harvard Graduate School of Education.

Chomsky, C., M. Honda, W. O'Neil, and C. Unger. 1985. *Doing science: Constructing scientific theories as an introduction to scientific method.* Educational Technology Center Technical Report 85-23, Harvard Graduate School of Education.

Chomsky, N. 1968. *Language and mind.* New York: Harcourt, Brace, and World.

Chomsky, N. 1977. *Essays on form and interpretation.* New York: Elsevier North-Holland.

Chomsky, N. 1980. *Rules and representations.* New York: Columbia University Press.

Chomsky, N. 1988. *Language and problems of knowledge: The Managua lectures.* Cambridge, Mass.: MIT Press.

Eisner, R. 1992. Science education: Science teachers offer a plan. (News and Comments.) *Science* 256 (10 April): 171.

Fabb, N. 1985. Linguistics for ten-year-olds. In *MIT working papers in linguistics* 6, 45–61. Department of Linguistics and Philosophy, MIT.

Fox, R. W. 1985. Review of B. Clayton, *Forgotten prophet: The life of Randolph Bourne. New York Times Book Review* (13 January): 12.

Gelman, R. 1978. *The child's understanding of number.* Cambridge, Mass.: Harvard University Press.

Gil-Perez, D., and J. Carrascosa. 1990. What to do about science "misconceptions." *Science Education* 74.5:531–40.

Hackerman, N. 1992. Science education: Who needs it? (Guest Editorial.) *Science* 256 (10 April): 157.

Hale, K. 1975. *Navaho linguistics.* Unpublished ms., MIT.

Honda, M., and W. O'Neil. 1988. Linguistics lesson plans. In *Nature of science lesson plans.* Educational Technology Center, Harvard Graduate School of Education.

Honda, M., and W. O'Neil. To appear. Constructing and evaluating theories using linguistics in the school science curriculum. In Otero, in press.

Keyser, S. J. 1970. The role of linguistics in the elementary school curriculum. *Elementary English* 47.1:39–45.

Kitzhaber, A., ed. 1968. *The Oregon curriculum: A sequential program in English, language/rhetoric.* 2 vols. New York: Holt, Rinehart and Winston.

Latanision, R.M. et al. 1991. *Education: To move a nation.* Report of the MIT Committee on K–12 Education, MIT.

Latanision, R. M. et al. 1992. *Education: To move a nation.* Strategic Plan of the MIT Council on Primary and Secondary Education, MIT.

Mathematical Sciences Education Board. 1990. *Reshaping school mathematics: A philosophy and framework for curriculum.* Washington, D.C.: MSEB.

McCloskey, M. 1983. Intuitive physics. *Scientific American* 248.4:122–30.

National Science Teachers Association. 1992. *The core content: A guide for curriculum designers.* Washington, D.C.: NSTA.

Newman, J. R., ed. 1956. *The world of mathematics.* Vol. 3: *The mathematical way of thinking.* New York: Simon and Schuster.

O'Neil, W. 1969. Foreword to N. R. Cattell, *The new English grammar: A descriptive introduction*. Cambridge, Mass.: MIT Press.

O'Neil, W. 1990. Dealing with bad ideas: Twice is less. *English Journal* 79.4:80–88.

O'Neil, W. 1991. El inglés nicaragüense II. *Wani: Revista del Caribe Nicaragüense* 10:18–35.

Otero, C., ed. In press. *Noam Chomsky: Critical essays*. London: Routledge.

Peirce, C. S. 1957. The logic of abduction. In *Charles S. Peirce: Essays in the philosophy of science*, ed. V. Tomas. New York: Liberal Arts Press.

Preece, P. F. W. 1984. Intuitive science: Learned or triggered. *International Journal of Science Education* 6.1:7–10.

Rossi, B. 1990. *Moments in the life of a scientist*. Cambridge: Cambridge University Press.

Sebastià, J. M. 1989. Cognitive constraints and spontaneous interpretations in physics. *International Journal of Science Education* 11.4:363–69.

White Eagle, J. 1983. Teaching scientific inquiry and the Winnebago language. Doctoral dissertation, Harvard Graduate School of Education.

Chapter 7
Evidence for Metrical Constituency

Michael Kenstowicz

The study of stress has always occupied a central position in generative grammar. It was the focus of one of the first generative publications (Chomsky, Halle, and Lukoff 1956). A good half of Chomsky and Halle's (1968) landmark book *The Sound Pattern of English (SPE)* was devoted to working out the stress contours of English. In the ensuing twenty years the study of stress has engendered some of the most fruitful and influential concepts in phonological theory. One of the reasons stress has proved so challenging is that unlike other phonological properties, it has no fixed or uniform phonetic interpretation. Rather, it is an abstract phonological category that is phonetically manifested through genuine features—principally the prosodic features of pitch and length and sometimes more subtle aspects of vowel and consonantal quality. This fact as well as others suggested to researchers in the early 1970s that the *SPE* treatment of stress as a feature [±stress], parallel to other distinctive features such as [±nasal] or [±voice], was misguided. In their work on the topic, Liberman and Prince inaugurated a new approach that has become known as Metrical Phonology (Liberman 1975, Prince 1975, Liberman and Prince 1977). They introduced two ideas upon which all later research has built: the metrical grid and metrical constituency. Liberman and Prince's leading idea was that stress reflects a grouping or chunking of the phonemic string at various levels such that one element of each group is singled out as more salient than the others. The hierarchical grouping was represented by a tree structure and the scaling of the salient positions was represented in the metrical grid. Liberman and Prince demonstrated that many of the generalizations discovered in *SPE* are more insightfully interpreted when viewed in metrical terms. Hayes (1981) applied and extended the metrical model beyond English. He resolved the myriad stress patterns reported in the descriptive literature into a small number of parameters for building up the metrical trees. A central topic of Hayes's study were alternating stress contours. In his survey of the literature, he identified four major types, schematized in (1).

(1) a. 'V V 'V V   'V V 'V V 'V   (e.g., Maranungku)
    b. V 'V V 'V   'V V 'V V 'V   (e.g., Weri)
    c. 'V V 'V V   V 'V V 'V V   (e.g., Warao)
    d. V 'V V 'V   V 'V V 'V V   (e.g., Araucanian)

Hayes showed that these stress contours could be generated from a parsing procedure whose principal parameters are direction of iteration (left to right or right to left) and whether the resultant groupings are metrically strong-weak (SW, left-headed) or weak-strong (WS, right-headed) constituents.

Prince (1983) streamlined the emerging metrical theory. He was able to describe the central data in Hayes's study without appeal to grouping. The basic idea was that alternating stress patterns instantiate a primitive rhythmic structure of alternating strong and weak positions (2a).

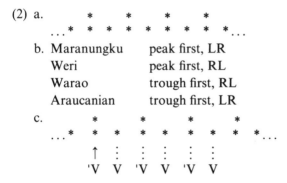

(2) a.   *   *   *   *
       ...*   *   *   *   *   *   *   *   *...

    b. Maranungku   peak first, LR
       Weri   peak first, RL
       Warao   trough first, RL
       Araucanian   trough first, LR

    c.   *   *   *   *
       ...*   *   *   *   *   *   *   *   *...
                ↑   :   :   :   :   :
               'V   V 'V   V 'V   V

The stress patterns of (1) can be generated by fixing two binary parameters: whether the mapping starts (i) with a rhythmic peak or trough (ii) at the left or right edge of the word (see (2b)). Once this determination has been made, the rest of the stress contour derives from simply matching the remaining syllables of the word one-to-one with positions on the bottom line of the grid. A six-syllable word from Maranungku receives the analysis in (2c).

While Prince's (1983) "grid-only" thesis simplified the model, it nullified one of the original tenets of the metrical approach. Much of the research in the ensuing period has been devoted to shoring up the original intuition that stress reflects a metrical grouping. In this paper I survey the kinds of evidence that has emerged to support this hypothesis.

1 Deletion of Stressed Vowel

Halle and Vergnaud (1987) report a number of cases in which the deletion of a vowel occasions a shift of stress. The position to which the stress shifts systematically correlates with the metrical grouping required to establish the original nondisturbed stress contours. The metrical structure of an Arawakan language of the Amazon discussed by Payne (1990) provides another example of this phenomenon. Like many of the indigenous languages of the Americas, Asheninca parses the word into binary right-headed constituents from left to right. The final syllable is systematically unstressed, an extrametricality effect that we will ignore. An Asheninca word such as *nok'owaw'etaka* 'I wanted it in vain' receives the analysis in (3a) under the grouping theory.

(3) a. nokowawetaka

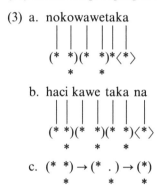

   b. haci kawe taka na

   c. (* *) → (* .) → (*)
         *   *   *

Payne describes a process that deletes [i] after [s, c] before a voiceless consonant. When [i] occupies a metrically strong position, the stress retracts to the preceding syllable. Underlying [hacikawetakana] (3b) 'he almost bit me' is realized as *h'ackaw'etak'ana* with initial stress. Payne stipulates a rule to retract the stress one syllable backward from such deletion sites. No such rule is needed, however, if a principle of Constituent Conservation is accepted. In the Halle-Vergnaud theory, stress (a line 1 asterisk in the grid) marks the head of a constituent. Since every constituent has a head, when this position is removed headship is transferred to the remaining position in the foot; the line 1 asterisk marking the head then shifts to the newly designated head (3c). In the theory of Hayes (1991), deletion of the line 0 asterisk violates the Continuous Column Constraint, according to which each asterisk in the grid must be supported by an asterisk on the immediately lower line. In order to maintain the stress, the stranded line 1 asterisk shifts to the closest available position: the adjacent position in the foot. Under either interpretation, metrical grouping is fundamental to determining the direction in which the stress shifts. But in a "grid-only" analysis of Asheninca there is no particular reason to expect the stress to shift to the left or to the right—precisely because any position is equally related to its neighbor on either side.

When presented with the case from Asheninca, the skeptic might argue that stress shifts towards the edge of the word in order to avoid a clash with the interior stress and thus does not reveal anything about the postulated grouping. While this explanation would suffice for Asheninca, there are other examples on record where it fails. For instance, stress in Yupik Eskimo has the same gross properties as stress in Asheninca: left-to-right, right-headed (iambic) grouping, as in *aŋyáXlaXláŋyuxtúq* 'he wants to make a big boat'. The Central Alaskan dialect has a rule that syncopates syllables whose nucleus is schwa. When the schwa is located in a strong metrical position, the stress shifts to the preceding syllable—just as in Asheninca. In his discussion of the phenomenon Hayes (1991), following Jacobson (1985), cites underlying [qanRutəkaxka] 'I talk about them'. Like a number of other dialects, Central Alaskan counts underlying closed syllables as heavy when they begin the word. Consequently, the schwa occupies a metrically strong position: [qánRutə́kaxka]. Upon schwa deletion, stress steps leftward to abut the initial stress: *qánRútkaxka*.

It is clear that avoidance of clash is not sufficient to determine the direction of stress shift in Yupik. But preservation of constituency explains both the Yupik and Asheninca cases. In sum, as more examples of stress shift under deletion are identified and continue to behave as predicted, the postulated metrical grouping is strongly supported.

2   Initial Strengthening, Medial Weakening

Another line of evidence for metrical grouping proceeds from the premise that certain types of sound change typically arise in initial versus medial positions in the constituent. For example, it is well known that English implements its consonant phonemes differently depending on the location of the stressed vowel. Prestress is a "strong" position characterized by aspiration, while $\acute{V}$__V is a "weak" position marked by voicing, sonorization, and deletion: compare *á*[D]*om*, *a*[t^h]*ómic*; *vé*[ ]*icle*, *ve*[h]*icular*. Forms such as *Àpalàchicóla*, *Wìnnipesáukee*, and more generally the reflexes of the Latin stress rule in the core vocabulary argue that English groups syllables into left-headed (trochaic) metrical constituents. The aspiration of *a*[t^h]*ómic* and the flapping of *á*[D]*om* are thus assigned in foot-initial versus foot-medial position: *a*(tómic) versus (átom). In an iambic-parsing language that groups unstressed-stressed, weak and strong positions are inverted: the consonant preceding the stressed vowel is foot-medial and the one following a stressed vowel occupies a strong position. Certain sound changes in Yupik furnish evidence that this is the correct grouping. A process found in a number of dialects is fortition of foot-initial consonants (Leer 1985). Word-initial consonants are systematically fortis. So are some word-medial consonants. For example, in *akútamék* 'a dessert (abl.sg.)' [t] is fortis while [k] is not. The difference follows as a function of the metrical grouping, shown in (4): [t] onsets the first syllable of the foot while [k] is buried inside the foot.

(4) aku tamek

(* *) (* *)
       *   *

Leer also describes a number of processes that weaken foot-internal consonants. In the Alutiq dialect, for example, [r] and [g] drop from syllable codas: [kégturyáq] 'mosquito' is realized as *kégtuyáq* or *kegtu'aq*. Since Alutiq counts closed syllables as heavy only in word-initial position, this word parses as (keg)(turyaq), with [ry] in the middle of the foot.

The hypothesis that fortition and lenition discriminate foot-initial from foot-medial position requires further testing. If it continues to hold up, then inputs to these sound changes cannot be determined merely by the location of the stressed syllable. Reference to the metrical grouping is required, as depicted in (5).

(5)   ...C V C 'V C V C 'V ...
     iambic   w   s   w   w = "weak"   s = "strong"
     trochaic   s   w   s

3 Iambic versus Trochaic Asymmetries

A third argument for metrical constituency derives from Hayes's (1985) discovery of a statistical skewing in the distribution of SW (trochaic) versus WS (iambic) feet with respect to quantity sensitivity. In quantity-sensitive languages, a heavy syllable attracts a stress independent of its odd/even position in the string. In his survey of over 100 languages, Hayes found that quantity-insensitive systems tend to group trochaically: in the original typology of (1), Maranungku and Warao thus exhibit common patterns while Weri and Araucanian do not. Furthermore, while both SW and WS grouping are found among languages that distinguish long and short vowels, there is still a difference. A number of systems that group SW (e.g., Finnish) allow a long CVV syllable to occupy the weak position (in effect defining a quantity-insensitive system even though they have long vowels). But Hayes finds no case of iambic (WS) grouping that allows a heavy CVV syllable in the W position. In other words, while trochaic systems can ignore quantity, iambic systems cannot. They must place a heavy syllable in a strong position.

Hayes explains the affinity of quantity and iambism for each other as reflecting a general law of rhythmic perception, brought out in experiments like the following (Bell 1977). Imagine a series of evenly spaced auditory pulses, as at the beginning of (6a) and (6b). A modulation is then introduced by enhancing every other pulse. Subjects impose a different grouping on the pulses depending on the nature of the enhancement.

(6) a. . . . . . ⇒ . . . -.-.-. . . ⇒ . . . (. -)(. -)(. -). . . .

    b. . . . . . ⇒ . . . o.o.o. . . ⇒ . . . .(o .)(o .)(o .). . .

If a pulse is enhanced by increasing its duration (6a), it groups with a preceding unenhanced element. But if the pulse is enhanced by increasing its intensity (6b), it groups with a following unenhanced element. In other words, contrasts in duration (quantity) favor iambic grouping while contrasts in intensity favor trochaic grouping.

If this law truly underlies the statistical asymmetries, it strongly supports the thesis of metrical constituency. Rhythmic theorists have argued that the iambic-trochaic asymmetry plays an active role in the phonology, encouraging quantitative changes that enhance the system's stress rhythm. For example, in many iambic languages such as Yupik, a light syllable is made heavy when it occupies the head of a binary foot: underlying [qayani] 'in his kayak' is realized as [qayá:ni]. The lengthening reinforces the (WS) stress contrast. Since trochaic systems shun contrasts based on length, we expect (SW) grouping to minimize quantitative differences within the foot. At least a few cases are reported where a (heavy-light) grouping becomes (light-light). However, their interpretation is less straightforward and so quantitative optimization of trochaism is more controversial (see Kenstowicz 1991 for discussion).

While more study and documentation are required, the iambic-trochaic law promises the most powerful evidence for metrical constituency—a kind of "interface constraint" between the linguistic and perceptual systems.

4   Bidirectional Parsing

Languages that parse the string of phonemes from both edges furnish another argument for metrical grouping (Levin 1988, Hayes 1991). Pike (1964) was the first to detect this phenomenon in his analysis of the "stress trains" in the Ecuadorian language Auca. In Auca stems group (SW) from left to right while suffixal material groups (SW) from right to left. The parses must be separate, as shown by words of odd length: *g'o # t'amõn'apa* 'we two went', *y'iwæm'õ # ŋ'ãmba* 'he carves, writes'. These systems yield to a straightforward trochaic analysis on the assumption that the metrification process is distributed over two strata in the sense of Lexical Phonology (see discussion in Halle and Kenstowicz 1991, Hayes 1991). As illustrated in (7), in the first (cyclic) stratum the stem parses left to right; suffixes then metrify right to left as a block in the second (noncyclic) stratum.

(7)

Halle and Kenstowicz (1991) propose a constraint that blocks the parse from jumping across previously established structure. The Crossover Constraint thus forces the metrification in the second stratum to proceed from the opposite direction. In any case, the point to be made here is that the grouping type (SW) is the same in both parses—the unmarked state of affairs, to judge by the number of cases in which bidirectionality has been identified. This makes sense if stress is assigned by metrical grouping: just a single parameter must be switched, namely, directionality (which in turn follows from the Crossover Constraint). But if stress is assigned by fixing a peak or a trough at one of the edges, then exactly the opposite prediction ensues: left-to-right (SW) parsing should combine with right-to-left (WS) parsing. The resultant mixed footing is contradicted by virtually every example in which bidirectionality has been detected. Finally, antepenultimate-stressing Latin and penultimate-stressing Polish furnish a diachronic variant of this argument. Each is commonly assumed to derive from an earlier stage with initial stress. With trochaic grouping, the diachronic change is simply enhancement of the final foot instead of the initial one: *('V V)...V V V > V V...V('V V). These cases suggest that iambic/trochaic grouping has more the character of a pervasive, system-wide parameter than simply a rule defining one step in the derivation.

5 Prosodic Minimality

Many languages require free-standing (nonclitic) words to be of a minimal prosodic size (typically disyllabic or bimoraic). Subminimal items are either barred from the lexicon entirely or brought up to code through various augmentation processes. For example, in the Australian language Yidin[y] all roots conform to a $CVCV(CV)_0$ template (Dixon 1977a) and hence are minimally disyllabic. Yidin[y] stress, as well as several other aspects of the phonology, crucially depends on a binary grouping of syllables (see Dixon 1977b, Hayes 1982 for discussion). McCarthy and Prince (1990) have interpreted minimality in terms of a prosodic hierarchy. The idea is that a phonological word (PWd) is composed of metrical Feet (which in turn are composed of Syllables built from Moras). By this prosodic syntax, expansion of the category PWd entails at least one metrical foot. Assuming that the metrical foot in this sense diagnoses the same structure as that required in the analysis of stress, it becomes clear why minimality requires two positions: it reflects the metrical foot as the composition of a strong element with a weak one.

6 Opacity

In a number of languages clitics occasion a shift of stress on their hosts, reflecting a (re)metrification of the host # clitic string. In their study of the phenomenon, Halle and Kenstowicz (1991) identify an opacity in which the poststress syllable of the base is inaccessible to remetrification. For example, Latin (Steriade 1988) *úbi* 'where' but *ubi # libet* 'wherever' suggests that the host # clitic structure undergoes the antepenultimate stress rule. But in trisyllabic bases such as *li:mina* 'thresholds' the poststress syllable is inaccessible, and enclitic stress must lodge on the base's final syllable: *li:miná # que*. Given that final syllables are extrametrical in Latin, the bases contrast as (ú)⟨bi⟩ versus (lí:mi)⟨na⟩. The stress contrast on the host # clitic string follows if the antepenultimate stress rule applies twice—once to the base and again to the base # clitic combination—and also respects Prince's (1985) Free Element Condition that only unparsed positions are accessible to the metrification rules: (u)⟨bi⟩ → (u)*bi # libet* → (u)(bí # li)⟨bet⟩ versus (li:mi)⟨na⟩ → (li:mi)*na # que* → (li:mi)(ná) # ⟨que⟩. This explanation is premised on the idea that the assignment of antepenultimate stress involves grouping the antepenult and the penult into a (SW) metrical constituent.

7 Speech Perception

Finally, there is suggestive but incomplete evidence that metrical grouping can be detected experimentally. Cutler and Norris (1988) report experiments in which subjects are presented aurally with strings of nonsense syllables containing hidden words. For example, [mintesh] and [mintayve] contain the word *mint*. Subjects are tested for the amount of time required to recover the hidden word. In a carefully controlled experiment Cutler and Norris found a significant difference in recovery time depending on whether or not the substring was interrupted by a metrical bracket. Specifically, recognition of *mint* took longer in SS [mintayve] than in SW [mintesh]. This makes sense if a stressed syllable starts a new constituent and if metrical grouping provides a preliminary analysis of the speech signal. Given that feet are composed of syllables, recovery of [mint] will take more processing time in [mintayve] since [t] belongs to a separate metrical constituent, as shown in (8).

(8)

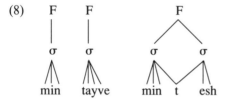

Unfortunately, since consonants in the context V̂_V are ambisyllabic in English, subjects may simply be responding with the first syllable, in which case the experiment would show nothing directly about metrical as opposed to syllabic constituency. Depoux and Hammond (1991) report a longer monitoring latency for the substring [clim] in SS *climax* than in SW *climate*. They conclude from this result that the syllable functions as a perceptual unit in English.

Assuming that the issue of syllabic versus metrical constituency can be resolved, an equally important question is how iambic systems might be expected to work in similar experiments. If parsing respects metrical structure, then we expect a difference in the processing of a WSW string such as [tom'ato]. [tom'a] should be easier to recover than [m'ato] in an iambic system while the inverse relation should hold in a trochaic system. If this result were not obtained and the iambic system showed no difference between [tom'a] and [m'ato] or ranked [m'ato] faster than [tom'a], it would imply that the perceptual parsing strategy is not completely determined by the grammar and operates as an independent module. I know of no evidence bearing on this question. It is true that Bell (1977) tested speakers of different languages on nonlinguistic stimuli such as those in (6). He found no differences and concluded that linguistic rhythm has no influence on the perception of other auditory stimuli. The crucial question is whether grouping plays a role in the perception of one's own language. If it does, then we might envision experiments that could help resolve controversial questions of metrical grouping for which the system-internal evidence is inconclusive or contradictory.

8 Bracket Matching

Earlier I cited fortition and lenition as targeting the initial versus medial positions in the metrical constituent. The evolution of tone in certain Eastern Bantu languages marks both the beginning and the end of the constituent; it graphically illustrates the chunking of the phonemic string. Downing (1988) documents in great detail a rule that shifts high tone one syllable to the right of its etymological source in the Tanzanian Lacustrine language Jita (E-20). Tone shift applies both within the word and between words at the phrasal level. The paradigms of trisyllabic nouns in (9) illustrate. Nouns with a final high (H) in the isolation form like *i:ndará* 'leopard' transpose their tone to the initial syllable of the following word. Nouns with a high on the penult break down into two subclasses: a constant one such as *tu:ngúru* 'onions' and an alternating one such as *nanáji* 'pineapple' where the high tone shifts to the ultima when the word is embedded in a phrase.

(9) omu-lamusi 'judge'

    i:ndará 'leopard'

    ya:Bilima 'ran'
    i:ndara yá:Bilima 'the leopard ran'

    eBi-tu:ngúru 'onions'
    mucikápo 'in the basket'
    eBitu:ngúru mucikápo 'onions in the basket'

    li-nanáji 'pineapple'
    lya:malí:Bwa 'was eaten'
    linanají lya:malí:Bwa 'the pineapple was eaten'

Downing resolves the paradigm into underlying representations in which a high tone freely appears on any syllable (10a), accompanied by a tone-shifting process (10b) that autosegmentally spreads high tone to the following syllable, simultaneously delinking it from its source.

(10) a. lamusi   i:ndara   nanaji   tu:nguru

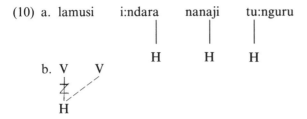

b. V   V

H

The rule does not target phrase-final syllables (possibly reflecting extratonality). An alternating stem such as *nanáji* thus shows its underlying form in pause and shifts its high in a phrasal context.

Spreading of high tone to the following syllable is of course a paradigm case of assimilation of a marked feature. What is odd from an autosegmental perspective is the second step, in which the spreading feature detaches from its source. Other cases of feature spread typically do not display such delinking: for example, *CãCa → CãCã (→ CaCã?)*. Recent advances in metrical theory allow an alternative accentual interpretation of Jita tone shift that is not subject to this objection. Working within the Halle-Vergnaud framework, Idsardi (1991) proposes two revisions of the model that bear on Jita. First, he suggests that unpredictable lexical accent in languages such as Russian be represented not by marking of line 1 asterisks but instead by metrical brackets, extending the device introduced by Halle (1990) to do the work of line 1 asterisks in the original Halle-Vergnaud (1987) model. The metrical parse constructs constituents that respect these lexically assigned brackets. Second, Idsardi drops the assumption that metrification always sweeps from one end of the word or phrase to the other, exhaustively assigning every position to some constituent. Specifically, he allows for systems in which metrical constituents arise only from the lexically assigned brackets. Furthermore, in contrast to the original model in which line 1 asterisks necessarily imply heads, these brackets need not mark the head of the constituent. Headship is determined separately, once the constituents have been formed by assigning a matching closing bracket. This proposal accommodates the representation of pre- and postaccenting morphemes in a maximally simple fashion.

Accepting Idsardi's proposals, Jita tone shift may now be analyzed in metrical terms. I suggest that the system has been reinterpreted in such a way that syllables that bore the etymological high tone are now regarded as marking the beginning of binary, right-headed metrical constituents. High tone now enters the system only at the phonetic level to mark the head of the metrical constituent. On this interpretation, the derivations in (11) ensue.

(11)

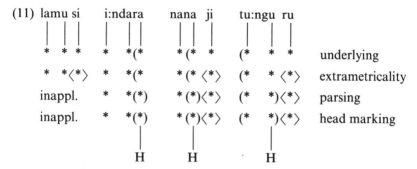

lamu si	i:ndara	nana ji	tu:ngu ru	
* * *	* *(*	* (* *	(* * *	underlying
* *⟨*⟩	* *(*	* (* ⟨*⟩	(* * ⟨*⟩	extrametricality
inappl.	* *(*)	* (*)⟨*⟩	(* *)⟨*⟩	parsing
inappl.	* *(*)	* (*)⟨*⟩	(* *)⟨*⟩	head marking
	H	H	H	

Tone is not shifted in the course of the derivation. Rather, a binary metrical constituent is constructed in stages: one side is erected in the lexicon and the other is attached later in the phonology by the metrical parse. No autosegmental delinking is required. In sum, tone shift in Jita is an epiphenomenon arising from a particular selection among the parameters provided by Universal Grammar metrical theory.

Our discussion of metrical constituency has so far focused on binary constituents—metrical feet. In the Halle-Vergnaud model all instances of stress reflect a metrical grouping. Consequently, initial- and final-stress languages such as Latvian and French are regarded as constructing unbounded left-/right-headed constituents that encompass the entire word, as in (12).

(12) a. Latvija   b. originalité

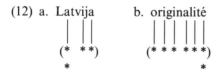

Is there any independent evidence that such grouping takes in the entire word? Couldn't we simply say that stress is assigned to the initial/final syllable? Some light is shed on this question by a phenomenon that parallels the Jita tone shift but operates over an unbounded distance. It is found in Shingazidja, a dialect of Swahili spoken on the Comorian Islands off the Tanzanian-Mozambique coast. The discussion closely follows the analysis of Cassimjee and Kisseberth (1989). Paradigms such as (13) exhibit the following peculiar generalization. When a pair of words are combined into a phrase, two high tones are replaced by a single high on the syllable immediately preceding the one that bears the high tone of the second word in its isolation form.

(13) nyumbá   'house'
     djuú   'on'
     nyumba djúu   'on a house'

     ma-sohá   'axes'
     -(b)ilí   'two'
     ma-soha ma-íli   'two axes'

Cassimjee and Kisseberth suggest a metrical analysis having the following ingredients: syllables bearing etymological high tones count as "heavy"; unbounded, left-headed constituents are constructed from heads dominating heavy syllables; phrase-final syllables are extrametrical; a special rule realizes the high tone on the final syllable of the foot, in effect shifting it from the left to the right edge. Finally, the ubiquitous Bantu process dissimilating adjacent high tones (Meeussen's Rule) deletes the second of two abutting highs. On this analysis, *ma-soha ma-ili* receives the derivation sketched in (14).

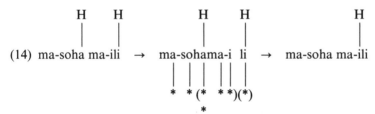

We may simplify Cassimjee and Kisseberth's analysis if we say that syllables bearing the etymological high tones have been reinterpreted as initiating unbounded, right-headed constituents. Once again high tone is a phonetic reflex of the metrical head. Finally, Meeussen's Rule can be expressed metrically as deletion of an accent clash. On this analysis, *ma-soha ma-íli* receives the derivation in (15).

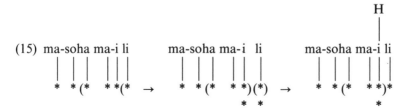

The analysis is corroborated by particles such as *nde* 'it is' that cause a high tone to appear on the following noun—one syllable before the noun's underlying high tone. The derivation in (16b) illustrates.

(16) a. mezá   'table'
         nde méza   'it is the table'
         godoró   'mattress'
         nde le godóro   'it is the mattress'

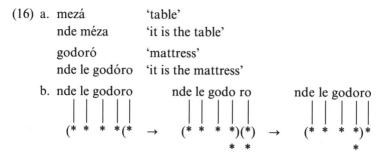

   b.

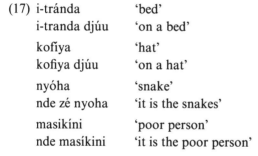

Shingazidja nominals with high tone on the penult in the isolation form break down into two tonal classes in a phrasal context. The paradigms in (17) illustrate the first class.

(17) i-tránda   'bed'
     i-tranda djúu   'on a bed'

     kofíya   'hat'
     kofiya djúu   'on a hat'

     nyóha   'snake'
     nde zé nyoha   'it is the snakes'

     masikíni   'poor person'
     nde masíkini   'it is the poor person'

Nouns such as *tránda* 'bed' and *masikíni* 'poor person' shown in (18) behave as if their penultimate syllable initiates a metrical constituent. This constituent extends up to the start of the next constituent contributed by the following word: *i-tranda djúu*. When they are phrase-final, a preceding constituent stretches to the antepenult. Given that phrase-final syllables are extrametrical, the foot opens and closes on the penult. The resultant degenerate constituent then deletes under clashing accents: *nde masíkini*.

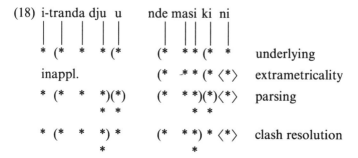

Nouns in the second class behave differently in a phrasal context, as shown in (19). They allow high tone to surface on the final syllable of *djuú* and *-(b)ilí*; and when preceded by the focalizer particle *nde*, high tone appears on the penult—not the antepenult.

(19) u-pándo   'wall'
     u-pando djuú   'on the wall'
     nde u-pándo   'it is the wall'

     ŋ-góma   'drum'
     ŋ-goma m-bilí   'two drums'
     nde ze ŋ-góma   'it is the drums'

Cassimjee and Kisseberth suggest that these nouns lack an underlying high tone. They derive from Proto-Bantu disyllabic low-toned stems and thus lack the etymological high tone that developed into an opening metrical bracket. As a result, as shown in (20), they fail to initiate a metrical parse and thus allow the degenerate constituent of *djuú* to surface. For the very same reason, they do not block construction of the unbounded constituent started by *nde*.

(20) u-pando dju u   nde ze ŋ-goma

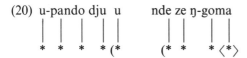

To account for the isolation form with a high on the penult, let us suppose that Shingazidja follows Indo-European and Slavic in invoking Halle and Vergnaud's (1987) Basic Accentuation Principle, according to which if a word lacks an accent, then the entire word is wrapped in metrical brackets. Modulo extrametricality, this delivers representations of the form (12b): $VV \ldots VVVV \rightarrow (VV \ldots VV'V)\langle V \rangle$.[1]

To summarize, the evidence from Jita and Shingazidja indicates that both edges of a metrical constituent are singled out by the phonology: the left edges are marked lexically while the right edges are computed by binary or unbounded metrical parses. These languages strongly confirm the basic intuition that motivated the metrical approach to accent some fifteen years ago: that metrical structure reflects a chunking of the string of phonemes.

Notes

I am pleased to dedicate this paper to Sylvain Bromberger, especially in view of his long-standing interest in phonology.

1. See Cassimjee and Kisseberth 1992 for much additional data and analysis supporting the metrical reinterpretation of the Shingazidja tone shift.

References

Bell, A. 1977. Accent placement and perception of prominence in rhythmic structures. In *Studies in stress and accent* (Southern California Occasional Papers in Linguistics 4), ed. L. Hyman, 1–14. University of Southern California.

Cassimjee, F., and C. Kisseberth. 1989. Shingazidja nominal accent. *Studies in the Linguistic Sciences* 19.1:33–62.

Cassimjee, F., and C. Kisseberth. 1992. Metrical structure in Shingazidja. Paper read at Chicago Linguistic Society.

Chomsky, N., and M. Halle. 1968. *The sound pattern of English*. New York: Harper & Row.

Chomsky, N., M. Halle, and F. Lukoff. 1956. On accent and juncture in English. In *For Roman Jakobson*, ed. M. Halle, 65–80. The Hague: Mouton.

Cutler, A., and D. Norris. 1988. The role of strong syllables in segmentation for lexical access. *Journal of Experimental Psychology: Human Perception and Performance* 14.1:113–21.

Depoux, E., and M. Hammond. 1991. More on language-specific comprehension strategies: The case of English. Ms., University of Arizona.

Dixon, R. 1977a. *A grammar of Yidin^y*. Cambridge: Cambridge University Press.

Dixon, R. 1977b. Some phonological rules in Yidin^y. *Linguistic Inquiry* 8:1–34.

Downing, L. 1988. Tonology of noun-modifier phrases in Jita. *Studies in the Linguistic Sciences* 18.1:25–60.

Halle, M. 1990. Respecting metrical structure. *Natural Language & Linguistic Theory* 8:149–76.

Halle, M., and M. Kenstowicz. 1991. The Free Element Condition and cyclic versus noncyclic stress. *Linguistic Inquiry* 22:457–501.

Halle, M., and J.-R. Vergnaud. 1987. *An essay on stress*. Cambridge, Mass.: MIT Press.

Hayes, B. 1981. A metrical theory of stress rules. Bloomington, Ind.: Indiana University Linguistics Club.

Hayes, B. 1982. Metrical structure as the organizing principle of Yidin^y phonology. In *The structure of phonological representations (part 1)*, ed. H. van der Hulst and N. Smith, 97–110. Dordrecht: Foris.

Hayes, B. 1985. Iambic and trochaic rhythm in stress rules. In *Proceedings of the 13th Annual Meeting of the Berkeley Linguistics Society*, 429–46. Berkeley Linguistics Society, University of California, Berkeley.

Hayes, B. 1991. Metrical stress theory: Principles and case studies. Ms., UCLA.

Idsardi, W. 1991. Stress in Interior Salish. In *Papers from the Twenty-seventh Regional Meeting, Chicago Linguistic Society*. Chicago Linguistic Society, University of Chicago.

Jacobson, S. 1985. Siberian Yupik and Central Yupik prosody. In *Yupik Eskimo prosodic systems: Descriptive and comparative studies* (Research Papers No. 7), ed. M. Krauss, 24–46. Fairbanks, Alaska: Alaska Native Language Center.

Kenstowicz, M. 1991. On metrical constituents: Unbalanced trochees and degenerate feet. Paper presented at the Conference on the Organization of Phonology: Features and Domains, University of Illinois, Urbana.

Leer, J. 1985. Evolution of prosody in the Yupik languages. In *Yupik Eskimo prosodic systems: Descriptive and comparative studies* (Research Papers No. 7), ed. M. Krauss, 135–58. Fairbanks, Alaska: Alaska Native Language Center.

Levin, J. 1988. Bidirectional foot construction as a window on level ordering. In *Theoretical morphology: Approaches in modern linguistics*, ed. M. Hammond and M. Noonan, 339–52. New York: Academic Press.

Liberman, M. 1975. The intonational system of English. Doctoral dissertation, MIT.

Liberman, M., and A. Prince. 1977. On stress and linguistic rhythm. *Linguistic Inquiry* 8:249–336.

McCarthy, J., and A. Prince. 1990. Foot and word in prosodic morphology: The Arabic broken plural. *Natural Language & Linguistic Theory* 8:209–84.

Payne, J. 1990. Asheninca stress patterns. In *Amazonian linguistics: Studies in lowland South American languages*, ed. D. Payne, 185–212. Austin, Tex.: University of Texas Press.

Pike, K. 1964. Stress trains in Auca. In *In honour of Daniel Jones*, ed. D. Abercrombie, 425–31. London: Longmans.

Prince, A. 1975. The phonology and morphology of Tiberian Hebrew. Doctoral dissertation, MIT.

Prince, A. 1983. Relating to the grid. *Linguistic Inquiry* 14:19–100.

Prince, A. 1985. Improving tree theory. In *Proceedings of the Eleventh Annual Meeting of the Berkeley Linguistics Society*, 471–90. Berkeley Linguistics Society, University of California, Berkeley.

Steriade, D. 1988. Greek accent: A case for preserving structure. *Linguistic Inquiry* 19:271–314.